DATE DUE

PHILOSOPHY AND ECONOMICS

PHILOSOPHY AND ECONOMICS

The Origins and Development of Economic Theory

Piero V. Mini

A University of Florida Book

The University Presses of Florida
Gainesville
1974

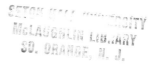

Library of Congress Cataloging in Publication Data

Mini, Piero V.   1936–
    Philosophy and economics; the origins and development
of economic theory.

    "A University of Florida book."
    Bibliography: p.
    1. Economics—History. 2. Economics—Methodology.
3. Philosophy—History. I. Title.
HB72.M5   330.1   74–7122
ISBN 0–8130–0318–4

PRINTED BY STORTER PRINTING COMPANY
GAINESVILLE, FLORIDA

Preface

IT MAY be appropriate to introduce a work dealing with the origins and development of economic theories with a few words about the origins and development of that very work. In retrospect, it seems to me that the psychological and intellectual roots from which this book sprang stretch back to the beginning of my studies in economics. I was struck at that time by certain peculiarities, especially by the wide gulf that seemed to separate economics as theory and economics as policy. Theoretical economics appeared to me to be oversubtle, formidable, and awesome. But the policies fathered by such theory struck me as ordinary, common, and ingenuous.

Nothing would have come out of this "discovery"—which, as I later realized, innumerable other economists have also made—if somewhat later I had not begun to pursue, first lazily, then with greater and greater interest, some readings in philosophy. These readings eventually provided me with an insight into the cultural forces that gave birth to and shaped the development of economic theories. Briefly, my readings in philosophy convinced me that the theories of classical economists and those of Marx and of Keynes stem from different philosophical doctrines which alternated themselves in the Western world from the seventeenth century to the present. From the framers of recondite philosophical theories, both orthodox and nonorthodox economists absorbed a way of looking at (or, as in the case of one of the three types of theory herein reviewed, of *not* looking at) the social world. This thinking cap shaped both the form and the content of economic analysis, and also the relationship of form to content. At length I had to conclude that, to paraphrase Keynes, economists have usually been the slaves of some defunct philosopher. This dependence, I hasten to add, takes nothing away from the creativeness of the individual econo- mist. It is merely caused by the fact that great economists have always been men of culture and have thus been particularly open to the intellectual currents of their days. Indeed, many economists have themselves been philosophers in a strictly technical sense, while others have been the pupils of philosophers.

It follows that large portions of this book deal with philosophi- cal matters. I make no apology for these forays into a discipline in which I cannot boast any formal training. Any interpreter of ideas must be willing to let the objects of his curiosity shape his interests. Smith, Marx, and Keynes, among others, were eclectic men, and anyone who tries to do somewhat more than summarize their ideas must dare to ignore our comfortable academic boundaries.

This book is a contribution toward the understanding of the economic mind, whose creations have always attracted criticism and which are now being attacked even by eminent orthodox theorists (see chapter 1). I myself have tried to stay clear of criticism; my goal is explication. Unfortunately, the flow of time, like that of glaciers, creates some debris. Since we can interpret past ideas only from the standpoint of present ones, the present perforce gives the impression of sitting in judgment of the past. Not many historians have found a way of overcoming these bounds which living in time imposes upon us. We can only warn the reader that to this human condition is due whatever semblance of criticism he may detect in these pages.

This essay took form during the self-congratulatory years that followed the Kennedy tax cut, which supposedly proved the supe- riority of the New Economics. Since then, regrettably, events have shown our rejoicing to have been premature. Inflation has become endemic and seems to be unresponsive to the customary policy tools. The "peace dividend" melted away. The energy and food shortages caught economists by surprise, as also did the urban crisis and every international humiliation of the dollar. "Positive economics" seemed to have lost its prognostic ability. It was natural that this atmosphere bred and renewed criticism of received doc- trine. To this new critical literature my essay makes no contribution.

It makes only an indirect contribution to the probable future reconstruction in economics by investigating the cultural factors which shaped economic thought during the past two centuries.

I wish to emphasize that this is not a methodological work, but rather an essay in intellectual history. It does not reflect my ideas as to what the method of economics should be. The method and substance of classical economics, and of Marx' and Keynes' writings, are the *explananda*, the objects of this essay. My task is to show that the different qualities of these economic writings are due to their having emanated from three different theories of truth.

I have tried to concentrate on the core of each economic theory studied in this work. Thus, classical economics is solely value theory and its macroeconomic corollary. By Marx, I mean his theory of the evolution of history and of ideas, and by Keynes I mean *The General Theory*. Nothing is said about the most recondite or peripheral branches of economics (capital theory, development studies, etc.), although I hope that this essay will shed more light on their nature as well. In harmony with the conclusions to which this study led me, I made up a slightly new classificatory scheme. I coined the term hyperclassical economics and I distinguished sharply between Keynes and Keynesian economics, as well as between Marx and Marxists. In dealing with the philosophers, I preferred as far as possible to let them speak for themselves. Hence the many quotations which, while causing perhaps some unevenness of style, allow the reader to draw his own conclusions.

I am happy to acknowledge the critical reading of large sections of my manuscript by Professors John S. Gambs of Hamilton College, Allan G. Gruchy of the University of Maryland, and Charles Morris of the Philosophy Department of the University of Florida. Professor William Woodruff, also at the University of Florida, has helped me in so many ways that without his kind interest this book might have never appeared. None of these scholars is, of course, responsible for anything in this book which may be justly criticized.

My wife has furthered my work in many ways. I am especially grateful to her for making me realize that clarity of expression deserves as much attention as any other aspect of book-writing.

Publication of this book was assisted by the American Council of Learned Societies under a grant from the Andrew W. Mellon Foundation.

Contents

A logical system is possible; an existential system is impossible.

SØREN KIERKEGAARD

The truth is that no thinking can be done without fictions. Not even the law, where exactness is so imperative, can get on without the notorious "legal fictions." Yet there is nothing more dangerous than to mistake these unavoidable verbalisms, these verbal myths, for entities of experience. Unless we keep well in mind that they are mere aids, mere nets for seizing and retaining the little of chaos that we can grasp and fix, unless we are constantly aware that they are no more than tools, no more than makeshifts in the struggle for expression, they will turn into those principles and dogmas philosophical, theological, ethical, political, which are the chief source, except for "acts of God," of most of the disasters that mankind has to endure.

BERNARD BERENSON

1

Some Observations on Methodological Studies

> *The philosophy of the sciences cannot be properly studied apart from their history.*
>
> *Comte*

THE GOAL of scientific thought is to bring wider and wider aspects of reality under its formulae. As it proceeds toward this goal, science becomes an aspect of human history. It is natural, then, that men ask themselves about science the questions that they ask about history in general: "How much do we really know?" and "What is the meaning of it all?" When thought thus turns inward, studies in the philosophy and method of science are born.

Ideally, such studies should be an integral part of the science to which they refer. Their goal should be to clarify the foundations of scientific thinking, to describe its mode of attaining truth, and to unearth those latent presuppositions and convictions that scientists *qua* scientists held but which they did not feel compelled to make explicit when their thoughts were turned outward toward reality. Methodological studies are to a science what self-knowledge is to a man.

However, just as men find it easier to act than to attain an understanding of why they act as they do, so are scientists more adept at discovering theorems about the physical and social worlds than at agreeing on the deeper whys and hows of their science. Not a few outstanding thinkers have succumbed to the despair of

1

asserting that "science is what science does." They obviously do not mean what they say; otherwise they would involve themselves in self-contradiction. Science originates in an attempt to understand reality. But is not science itself—the work and thought of, say, Galileo to Einstein—part of reality? If so, *it* demands to be explained just as much as planets, atoms, and electrons do.

Interpreted literally, the last sentence is an absurdity. The physical world makes no demand whatever on our intelligence. It had existed happily for eons before man even appeared on earth. It is man alone who makes demands on his intellect. And he demands an understanding of both types of reality: outer reality and the reality and meaning of his own work. There is no way to get around this need except by killing the intellect altogether.

These remarks would not be necessary if it had not become customary for economists introducing a work, like this one, on the method and nature of economics to be apologetic and self-conscious about their own undertakings. Menger, von Mises, and Robbins, among others, all stress the inanity of methodological studies while writing some themselves. They remind the reader that science is the work of Galileo, Newton, and Lavoisier, not of Bacon, Kant, and Locke. This is as true as it is irrelevant: Galileo is only a fraction of the human intellect; he labored in his own vineyard. Bacon labored in his. Each group addressed itself to different objects, the first to the physical world, the second to *man* in one of his highest callings.

The object of this book is to study the nature and progress of the economic mind during the past two centuries, with an attempt to answer the questions to which we made reference in the opening paragraph. Naturally, other men—and these not only economists— have concerned themselves with the same questions. Economic theory, dealing with an inherently important aspect of man's activity, pregnant with behavioral and political implications, has not enjoyed the benign neglect with which non-philologists, say, honor philology. A collection of judgments and opinions about economics would probably show that economics is second only to religion in the animosity that it has generated. Carlyle's characterization of economics as "pig philosophy" is relatively mild by comparison with other epithets. On the other hand, economics has been assigned, by most economic theorists, attributes that can only be called divine, in the sense of pertaining to God. Suffice it to mention the quality of "timelessness" which nothing familiar to man—not celestial bodies, not even life as such—possesses. Thus, at the outset, we are faced with a riddle. Why should a science which prides itself on the compelling clarity of its hypotheses and theorems generate so much misunderstanding? This is a fact which calls for an explanation.

Those who have attempted to reach a philosophical understanding of economics, of its meaning and propelling forces, can be broadly classified into two groups, the absolutists and the relativists. The absolutists defend the intellectual autonomy of economic science, its independence from both political facts and intellectual currents. The relativists usually find the roots of economic theory in factors external to it, e.g., in the problems of economic life facing society at different times. The absolutists' view of the origins of economics is fully in harmony with the claim of "timelessness" which they make about economic theory. Strictly, they portray economics as a non-human endeavor, independent of space and time and of their qualities, independent, therefore, of the thinkers and their philosophies, world views, and convictions. They adhere to what might be called the Little Jack Horner theory of the genesis of economics. The relativists do look beyond economic science proper for its source and meaning but have often succumbed to what has been called the Archimedes fallacy: the belief that, if we plant our feet solidly in some outside values (e.g., Marxist or Freudian values), we shall be able to lift the whole body of economics with a dialectic crowbar.

A study of the development of economics is a study in intellectual history: the error of the absolutists consists of overemphasizing the intellectual elements of economics—its inner logic—at the expense of the historical humus from which it sprang. That of the relativists consists in laying excessive stress on the historical, on what is outside the economic mind, at the expense of the inner logic of economic thinking. But, since historical facts as such are dumb, the relativists are forced to lean on other intellectual creations and frameworks (Marxism, etc.) to explain economic science as a fact of history. Thus, they often land in a contradiction: they criticize economic theory for being axiomatic and for defying empirical verification, while they themselves look at economic theory with a mind which is under the sway of a prioris (e.g., that intellectual currents are explained by material factors) which cannot be proved.

The absolutists have no explanation for the origin of economic theory, and they have only a purely formal explanation for its propelling force. They view theory as moving continually from error to truth. Since they do not make clear what truth is, the statement becomes question-begging. The logic of their position forces them to say that "truth is concentrated in the marginal increment to economic knowledge,"[1] the increment embodied in today's journal article. But tomorrow's article will render today's truth false or incomplete. So, in the end, the absolutist is cornered into what he detests most: a relativist position forced by the dictatorship of that element of existence which theory does not recognize, viz., time.

The defect of absolutist explanations is caused by their bringing to an understanding of economic theory the same structure and habits of mind, the same implicit metaphysics, that served them well in advancing economic analysis proper. They look at economic theory from the inside with the same categories they used in erecting the theory. Just as economics is unhistorical, so absolutist methodological writings do not really analyze economics as it actually developed with its faux pas, detours, contradictions, and debates. They deal with an immanent phenomenon (economic theory) under the categories of pure reason. Just as theory treats all the important phenomena of life as "data" (not as *explananda*), so absolutist methodological works treat the intellectual and social milieu as given and hence irrelevant to an understanding of the origins and development of economic theory. The intellect, prevented by its very successes from looking outward at cultural and political factors for a clue to understanding economic theory, is forced back inward again. It then concludes that economic theory is the discovery of ever more "sophisticated tools of analysis." Valuable as this insight may be, it fails to explain the principles guiding this flight toward ever increasing sophistication. If the difference between a Ricardo and a Marshall is that the latter had "better tools to work with," it behooves the absolutist to give an account of the hammer and anvil on which these tools have been forged. This the absolutist has never attempted to do. Just as he is prevented from looking at the world outside the mind for an explanation of the nature and significance of economic theory, so he is prevented from looking at the real mind, the existential mind, as we may call it. He looks only at a

1. M. Blaug, *Economic Theory in Retrospect,* p. 4. Complete citations appear in the Bibliography.

Cartesian fiction called "consciousness" (about which, more later) which does not reflect the de facto modus operandi of the mind. To put it briefly, absolutist methodologies are cut of the same idealistic cloth of which economic theory is made. They do not advance understanding of the nature and evolution of economic theory.

The desire to understand the nature of economic thinking is not only natural, it is also demanded by expediency. Only if we understand the true nature of economic theorizing will we understand the "revolutions" that have occurred in the past and will we be prepared for those with which present-day economics is pregnant. "I remember [Keynes wrote not too long ago] Bonar Law's mingled rage and perplexity in face of the economists because they were denying what was obvious. He was deeply troubled for an explanation."[2] Keynes' own explanation is rather thin: "One recurs to the analogy between the sway of the classical school of economic theory and that of certain religions. For it is a far greater exercise of the potency of an idea to exorcise the obvious than to introduce into men's common notions the recondite and the remote." Did classical economic theory "exorcise the obvious"? And if so, how did this paradoxical result come about? These are the questions which a study on the method of economics should answer.

Bonar Law's bafflement still exists. Theorists in the orthodox tradition admit that most economic theory is tautological, its conclusions proving what is already in the premises. But nobody knows *why* this is so. Few writers have even detected the contradiction, running throughout economics, of regarding men as politically free (hence capable of doing what they please) while the theory portrays them as acting in a predetermined, rigidly circumscribed way —like "puppets," Machlup rightly says.[3] Leslie Stephen, in his study on the English Utilitarians, has observed that, although the followers of Bentham often used the phrase "experience shows," they had a very low opinion of historical studies. Why did they not see the contradiction? In macroeconomics, we have today advanced beyond classical thought, but a new schism between economic thinking and society is emerging similar to the one Keynes tried to bridge. Many textbooks still refer to America as "the wealthiest nation on

2. John Maynard Keynes, *The General Theory of Employment, Interest and Money,* p. 350.
3. Fritz Machlup, "Theories of the Firm: Marginalist, Behavioral, Managerial," p. 27.

earth," while the belief is prevalent in many quarters that America is poor even in those things that economics has traditionally called "free goods." "An uneasy feeling about the present state of our discipline" has recently been detected by W. Leontief in his 1970 presidential address to the American Economic Association.[4] It is "caused not by the *irrelevance* of the practical problems to which present day economists address their efforts, but rather by the palpable *inadequacy* of the scientific means with which they try to solve them. . . . Uncritical enthusiasm for mathematical formulation tends often to conceal the ephemeral substantive content of the argument behind the formidable front of algebraic signs. . . . In no other field of empirical inquiry has so massive and sophisticated a statistical machinery been used with such indifferent results. . . . Most of these [models] are relegated to the stockpile without any practical applications. . . ." F. H. Hahn, president of the Econometric Society in 1968, voiced a similar complaint: "It cannot be denied that there is something scandalous in the spectacle of so many people refining the analysis of economic states which they give no reason to suppose will ever, or have ever come about. . . . It is an unsatisfactory and slightly dishonest state of affairs."[5] Harry G. Johnson, in his Richard T. Ely Lecture, notes that the "testing of hypotheses" on which the empirical and econometric revolution insists "is frequently a mere euphemism for obtaining plausible numbers to provide ceremonial adequacy for a theory chosen and defended on *a priori* grounds."[6]

Self-criticism has, indeed, given rise to a respectable literature of its own. Some economists even expect salvation (i.e., "relevance") from such groups as the Union of Radical Political Economists whose existence, in more normal times, would hardly have attracted any notice.[7] To this situation of confusion, methodological studies should bring the solvent of understanding. F. H. Hahn's allegations of "dishonesty," Leontief's and Johnson's suspicions of make-believe and "irrelevance," and J. G. Gurley's accusations should give way to a simple appreciation of how the state of affairs that they decry has come to pass.

4. W. Leontief, "Theoretical Assumptions and Nonobserved Facts." The quotation runs together several unrelated sentences. Emphasis in the text.
5. F. H. Hahn, "Some Adjustment Problems," p. 1.
6. Harry G. Johnson, "The Keynesian Revolution and the Monetarist Counter-revolution," p. 2.
7. See John G. Gurley, "The State of Political Economics."

But the unfortunate situation is this: methodological studies devoted to *understanding* the peculiar mode of thinking of economic theory are not very common. Normally, the spirit behind studies on method is either polemical or apologetic, motivated by a desire either to detract from or to reaffirm the formal correctness of economic theory. Theory is never taken as a fact whose birth and development call for explanation. Economic theory rather is stretched or shrunk so as to fit it into the methodologist's own standpoints and beliefs. This is why the classical methodological works tell us more on how theory "should" be interpreted than on why it developed the way it did.

Absolutist writers on method labor under certain handicaps. Trained to deal with purely intellectual, eternal concepts and constructs (marginal utility, indifference curves, marginal efficiency of capital, etc.), they are ill equipped to come to grips with an immanent, transitory, historical fact—that economic theory is the product of real men living in a certain cultural environment from which they cannot be completely divorced. The same inability to deal with the facts of evolving capitalist markets and relations manifests itself in an inability to deal with the intellectual evolution of economic theory. The graduate course catalogues of the better economics departments provide sufficient evidence of this failure. Whatever courses "on method" they advertise merely camouflage just another course in the mathematical applications of economic theory: linear programing and economic theory, "simulations" and economic theory, etc. It is as if the mathematical mode of thinking, having long conquered economic content (the "how" of reasoning), is now in the process of abolishing the very question of "why" economics developed the way it did, which a true methodology should answer.

This inability to provide an analysis of the genesis and growth of economics is sometimes justified on the grounds that, after all, natural scientists themselves are not very inquisitive about their own thought-processes. There is consolation in common failure. Machlup, for instance, approvingly quotes a mythical physicist who, when asked "Does the Neutrino really exist?" laconically replies, "Who cares!"[8] This alleged parallel between economics and physical science, like so many others, is at most a half truth. *Great* scientists and practically all those who carried on scientific revolutions were

8. Machlup, "Theories of the Firm," pp. 9–10.

just as curious about the material universe as they were about the origins and propelling forces of scientific thought.

In any case, disclaimers of methodological interest on the part of economists are at odds with the whole mentality that gave rise to the science of economics in the first place. Since its inception, economics has gone beyond appearances, beyond the phenomenal forms of reality, and has consistently sought to attain an understanding of the *ultimate* principles of economic life. All of "real" economics is a search for ultimates. It is only when trying to explain its own work that the economic mind becomes superficial, perhaps because it senses that the customary logico-mathematical modes of thinking are inappropriate.

Friedman's and Machlup's "positivism" is a new development. If theories explain what they set out to explain, they argue, we need not trouble ourselves further. But anybody even moderately conversant with the methodological writings of the recent past (Mill, Menger, von Mises, Robbins) well recalls repeated warnings that economic theories cannot be tested against facts. How do we account for this discrepancy? Is it true in methodological studies, too, that truth is the possession of the present only? Or is there an evolution in our views of the meaning and nature of truth?

Rather paradoxically, one may conclude that all the absolutist conceptions, *taken together*, destroy most of what is known as economic theory. Some assert that the whole reasoning process up to testing may well be unrealistic, but that this is immaterial to the truth of a theory, others that testing is impossible. What is left? Robbins eliminates a concern with the ends of the analysis, Friedman, with the beginning (the assumptions). What is left? Theoretically, only the "tools" are left. But these tools are logically contained in the assumptions: diminishing marginal utility is an assumption and the negatively sloped demand function (the tool) is really the assumption itself in another language, a fact recognized by the characterization of economics as tautological. So disregard for the realism of the assumptions means disregard for the realism of tools also!

We have asserted that absolutists bring to an understanding of economics the same habits of mind, the same axiology that they used in building the theoretical structure. It has often been remarked that economic theory portrays the world as it should be, not as it is. Perhaps for this reason it is often impossible to tell whether so-called positive methodological works are describing how economic theory really proceeds and has proceeded historically, or whether they are dealing with how it should proceed. It is not clear whether Robbins (or Friedman) intends to say that economics is not and has never been concerned with ends (or with the realism of the assumptions) or whether it should not be so concerned. Absolutist writings, in one word, are not positive and explicatory; they are "idealistic," normative, and hortative. At bottom, the relation between absolutist methodologies and economic theory proper may be compared to that between the superego and the id. The absolutists regard themselves the guardians of the science—as its conscience. And they are vaguely aware that the science actually develops in disregard of the higher rules of logic and positivism— hence their exhortations.

The methodologists who can be associated with the relativist outlook also labor under certain handicaps peculiar to the problem of relating something to something else. The mind has an infinite capacity for forming analogies and for associating one idea to another idea. It is, therefore, relatively easy to relate economic theory to environmental or cultural factors (which at bottom are only ideas, our way of perceiving reality). This relativism, however, although it may explain the spirit of economics, its underlying philosophy, never succeeds in explaining its movement and development. Not even Marx, the originator and most profound user of this method, succeeded in getting out of this impasse. He treated capitalism as a unit and economic thought from Adam Smith to his own days also as a unit. Thus, while his considerations are valuable in explaining the difference between the economics of Aquinas and that of Adam Smith, they are powerless to explain the reasons for the difference between Smith's and Ricardo's economics. Marx was perhaps justified in treating both the fact of capitalism and its intellectual expression (economic theory) as units, since he wrote from the perspective of universal history for which a few decades are a mere instant. But today's relativist has a longer time span behind him, and he is concerned with post-Smithian economics only. Then it becomes his responsibility to show how the movement in the guiding principle he has chosen preceded and caused the movement of the economic genius.

This book starts from a basic presupposition. It considers economic theory a historical phenomenon—the product of man's intellect, a *set of ideas* designed to understand the nature of economic life. Classical definitions of economics ("the allocation of scarce resources to satisfy unlimited wants," and the like) focus on the objective world outside the mind and thus divert the attention from the only true and objective fact: that economics is the product of man's head. Recently even physical scientists have recognized that science is the creation of man. In a reversal of classical convictions, Sir James Jeans asserted that "the Universe begins to look more like a great thought than a great machine."[9] The recent revolution in science, we suspect, has caused such a movement from Cartesian mechanicism to Berkeley's idealism. Economics, too, has had its revolutions. It is time that it, too, be considered as systematic thought, not as relations among objective facts. Economic theory, then, is a psychic product, originating from man's attempt to discover truth. Truth is the offspring of the relation between thinking and being, subject and object.

It follows that if we know how a certain age conceived the nature of this relation, we should also know what it meant by truth and what rules it laid down to facilitate its search for truth. Accordingly, we should understand how investigators of various aspects of life (e.g., economic life) went about building their theories. The definition of the relation between thinking and matter, and hence the nature of truth, is the subject of a branch of philosophy called epistemology, the study of knowledge. The seventeenth century, having witnessed the destruction of scholastic certainties, was the epistemological century par excellence. Shaken by the collapse of so many traditional truths and ways of looking at things, Descartes and other epistemological writers were determined never to be deceived again. They laid down very clear and stringent rules for the intellect to follow in its search. The connection between these rules and classical economic thought is suggested, first, by the fact that economics arose exactly at a time when Descartes' epistemology gained nearly universal acceptance and assent and, second, by the fact that many of the early economists wrote extensively on the theory of knowledge and proved to be followers of Descartes.

Strictly speaking, then, an explanation of the de facto method of analysis followed by classical economists has always existed. It is embodied not in the methodological writings of economists but

9. Sir James Jeans, *The Mysterious Universe,* p. 158.

in the *Discourse on Method*. Marx might have recognized the Cartesian bases of Ricardian thinking, for he criticized the classical school in the same terms and on the same grounds that he criticized Hegel. Implicitly, Marx saw that both Hegel and classical economics were the offspring of the same ancestor, Descartes.

The fundamental characteristic of the Cartesian theory of knowledge is the clear separation it made between the intellectual and the sensible worlds, the world "in the mind" and that "outside" it. The French thinker went so far as to separate thinking-as-a-process (existential thinking, as we may call it, or thinking that is motivated and propelled forward by passions, biases, and even error and falsehood) from the thinking of a fictive entity that he called "consciousness" or the "ego," whose qualities he described with proverbial Gallic clarity. Truth was within the reach of that mind which accepted the guidance of the thinking ego. Social reality was accordingly viewed, and fashioned, through the categories of the thinking ego.

Certain well-known characteristics of economics—its tautological and non-evolutionary nature, its detachment from, and even scorn for, the world of experience, its inability to adapt itself to changes in economic realities, and its mixture of pessimism and optimism, of determinism and freedom, of materialism and idealism—all stem from its having unequivocally accepted the ego as its guide and compass through the previously uncharted land of economic reality.

It is an interesting fact that the reaction against Cartesianism began less than a century after its acceptance. Bentham and Kant, in particular, saw clearly where it was leading. The latter wrote, "The fundamental principle ruling all my idealism is this: All cognition of things from mere pure Understanding [Descartes' method] is nothing but mere illusion and only in experience is there truth."[10] This aspect of their writings was ignored, however, and it did not resurface until the nineteenth century when a number of philosophers (Schopenhauer, Nietzsche, Kierkegaard, Bergson, and the pragmatists) mixed, in various ratios, a negative criticism of rationalism with a sympathetic understanding and appreciation of its ways.

By the middle of the nineteenth century, the critique of Car-

10. Immanuel Kant, "Prolegomena," in *Kant's Critical Philosophy for English Readers,* 2:147.

tesian modes of conceiving and grasping reality was in full swing. Basically, those who attacked economics—Marx, the German historical school, and Veblen—were the expression of the new definition of truth and of the new way of conceiving the relation between thinking and being. Far from adapting itself to the new outlook, economic theory not only retained the basic quality it had in classical thought, but became even more extremist: Ricardo's "machinery question" disappeared, Mill's semihistorical interests and humane outlook atrophied, textbooks became diagrammatical, the analysis became altogether more stringently Cartesian and, paradoxically, more palpably inadequate both in understanding the world and solving its problems.

Why was economic theory unable to adapt itself to the new non-rationalistic, historical method? We found the answer in what H. Vaihinger calls the "tendency of means to overtake ends," a tendency whose operation can be seen both in practical and intellectual aspects of life. Rationalistic thought is especially prone to fall victim to this tendency, which eventually causes a total divorce of intellectualistic contrivances (means) from the ends, purposes, or goals they were originally intended to serve. Robbins' discovery (or exhortation) that economics is not (or should not be) concerned with ends is the sanctioning of this tendency: the recognition that economic theory is (or should be) tool-making for the sake of tool-making. Not until Keynes' *General Theory* did the antirationalistic outlook penetrate economic thinking. His revolution, however, was ephemeral, as atavistic modes of thought absorbed the Keynesian outlook.

Our underlying presupposition is well expressed by Kierkegaard's motto at the front of the book. It is a presupposition shared by such diverse thinkers as Bentham, Kant, Nietzsche, Bergson, and Dewey. And it implies that existence is beyond the grasp of logical analysis. Thus, since economics has as its presumed object real men engaged in certain pursuits, it would seem that the logical method is not adequate in comprehending economic interrelations. And, in fact, economic historians (whose subject matter is the same as that of economic theory) do not push their thought forward on the wings of mathematics or the syllogism.[11] Nevertheless, with a few magical strokes, it is possible to bring the relations of men to

11. Recently some economic historians have succumbed to the Cartesian method and turned economic history into an "econometric" science.

men within logical molds. The Cartesian ego aspired to do exactly this. It answered questions pertaining to the realm of existence with tools designed to answer questions pertaining to the relations among the purely psychic entities of geometry. It recast the world of men into the world of geometrical symbols.

This book is the history of this recasting. It is an explanation of the modus operandi of the tool (the thinking ego) that fashioned the tools of economic analysis in value- and macro-theory.

2

The Epistemological Background

*The great basic question of all philosophy . . .
is that concerning the relation of thinking and
being.*

F. Engels

THE QUEST for truth has always occupied a significant portion of
man's intellectual efforts. Normally, the quest proceeds without
backward glances as the men involved in it follow, more or less
consciously, the well-established methodology of their age. But
there are times when the conventional methodology is itself called
into question. Then the search for truth takes an introspective character; it veers away from "science"—the explanation of the world
without—and moves toward the study of the nature of thought
itself.

An all-pervasive reorientation of thought from the outer to the
inner occurred in the seventeenth century. The very success of
scientific speculation demanded a re-examination of the familiar
epistemological standpoints. For a major victim of the new science
was the realistic outlook of scholastic epistemology. The world appeared flat, but Magellan's travels proved it to be round. The earth
appeared motionless, but Copernicus revealed it to revolve around
the sun. The new mechanics was based upon that which is not—
motion in a vacuum—and effected a revolution in science. All this

14

and the dethronement of God from His position as the ultimate vouchsafer of truth demanded a re-examination of the very bases of knowledge.

Of all those who concerned themselves with the epistemological problem, none was more influential than René Descartes. It is widely recognized that he laid down the methodology of correct thinking for the modern era. Arthur O. Lovejoy quotes approvingly an anonymous writer in the *London Times Literary Supplement* who asserted that "The history of modern philosophy is the history of the development of Cartesianism in its dual aspect of idealism and mechanism."[1] Bertrand Russell repeatedly pays homage to the sway of Descartes' epistemological "bifurcation of nature and mind,"[2] while Alfred North Whitehead indicts this epistemology as the source of those "quite unbelievable" abstractions by which "modern philosophy has been ruined."[3] It is also well known that Descartes' influence extended beyond philosophy. Basil Willey detects strains of the *Discourse on Method* in the theology and poetry of the age.[4] Such pervasive effect is not surprising, for Cartesianism is a *standpoint*, a thinking cap which students of practically any problem in the seventeenth and eighteenth centuries donned, at times without knowing that they did so.

From France, Cartesianism spread to England via the works of Locke and Hume. And through them it spread to economics, determining its nature and character down to our own days.

Descartes' self-imposed task was to give a firm and eternal foundation to human knowledge. To this task he brought two qualities: first, a deeply sensitive (almost morbid) nature;[5] second, a superb mathematical imagination. The first quality enabled him not simply to rejoice but also to *suffer* at the new world view being created by science. He perceived that the reconstruction of man's concept of the universe effected by Copernicus, Kepler, and Galileo entailed the *destruction* of the traditional conception in which men of equal intellectual stature (Ptolemy, Aquinas, Dante) had believed. Fur-

1. *The Revolt Against Dualism*, p. 2.
2. *Analysis of Matter*, pp. 10, 156; *Analysis of Mind*, pp. 108, 137. See also his preface to Frederick Albert Lange, *The History of Materialism*, pp. ix–x.
3. *Science and the Modern World*, p. 82.
4. *The Seventeenth Century Background: Studies in the Thought of the Age in Relation to Poetry and Religion*, p. 86.
5. See chap. 7, where Descartes' autobiographical dream is reviewed.

thermore, Descartes saw that the scientific reconstruction affected more than science. It reached into morality, religion, and the very role of man in the cosmos. Above all, it created a new problem: the "problem of knowledge."

Knowledge was not a problem in medieval philosophy. It was a commonplace that the natural world existed to serve man, just as man existed "to know God and enjoy Him in afterlife." Accordingly, the world was interpreted teleologically and in terms of categories "developed in an attempt to throw into scientific form the *facts and relations observed in man's unaided sense-experience of the world*."[6] Observation was the main medieval method of gaining knowledge. A realistic outlook prevailed before Descartes. Things that appeared different (ice, water, steam) *were* different. Things that appeared to move (like the sun) *did* move, and things that appeared motionless *were* motionless. A body's natural state was assumed to be rest, motion being the result of a force acting on it, a conception diametrically opposed to the Galilean one and evidently derived from observing a cart pulled by an ox.

The new science "commit[ted] a rape on [man's] senses," as Galileo expressed it.[7] In the first of the modern centuries, Appearance and Being—which were one in medieval philosophy—parted company. Appearances were deceptive and reality was hidden. It seemed as if man would never again be able to trust "common sense." The famous Cartesian doubt (*de omnibus dubitandum est*) was born out of, and is the response to, this new reality: the deceptiveness of appearance. It is the articulation of this modern nightmare, of the loss not of the capacity for truth but of the *certainty* that formerly went with what educated people believed to be true.[8]

Descartes expressed this despair in the *Discourse*, in the *Principles*, and in the *Meditations*. In all these works he reminds us of how untrustworthy the senses are, concluding that the wise truth-seeker starts from the premise that "all the things that [we] see are false (fictitious); [he will] believe that none of those objects which

6. Edwin Arthur Burtt, *The Metaphysical Foundations of Modern Physical Science*, p. 5. Emphasis added.

7. Quoted by Hannah Arendt, *The Human Condition*, p. 274n31. Galileo, in the *Dialogues concerning the Two Great Systems of the World*, thus expresses his admiration for Copernicus and Aristarchus (a Greek philosopher who also conceived the sun as the center of the universe).

8. Arendt, *The Human Condition*, p. 277.

[our] fallacious memory represents ever existed." Correct thinking should, in fact, proceed on the assumption that "we possess no senses."[9] A tool of knowledge far more reliable than sense perception exists.

Since childhood, Descartes was absorbed in mathematical studies to the exclusion of everything else. By the age of twenty-one he was in command of what was then known on the subject. Shortly afterward, he himself pushed the frontiers of mathematics forward with the invention of analytical geometry. Perhaps as a result of this invention, he conceived the notion that mathematics (or geometry, since in analytical geometry the worlds of space and numbers are one) may provide the key to understanding nature. To do this, one must reduce all physical reality around us to geometrical properties and concepts.

Reason does reveal that, in fact, the essence of reality is extension, an obviously geometrical concept. Descartes illustrates this with his well-known example of the bee wax. A lump of wax has certain empirical qualities, odor, color, flexibility, temperature, etc. But when it is placed by the fire, all these qualities undergo change. Nothing remains of the original sensuous elements, except a "something extended." Extension is, therefore, the *ultima ratio* to which the wax can be reduced. Now, Descartes concludes in his *Second Meditation,* the realization that extension is the essence of a ball of wax is "neither an act of sight, of touch, nor of imagination . . . but is simply an intuition (*inspectio*) of the mind."[10] What is intuitively grasped must be true.

What is intuition? "The conception which an unclouded and attentive mind gives us so readily and distinctly that we are usually freed from doubt about that which we understand."[11] There are other propositions which share this quality of clearness and distinctness of ideas: two plus two makes four; triangles have three angles; and (according to Descartes) thinking entails existing. Intuition provides the concepts, the raw materials of thought; deduction provides the engine to sew concepts to each other and to push them forward toward a proof. The pre-eminent example of deductive reasoning is given by mathematics, which, therefore, becomes the

9. *The Meditations* (Second Meditation).
10. Ibid., First Meditation.
11. Descartes, *Rules for the Direction of the Mind,* Rule III. Most of the doctrines contained in this work are also met in the *Method* and *Meditations.*

prototype of correct thinking. However, in order to place the mathematical chariot in the service of truth, two initial premises—both false, although, naturally, Descartes did not regard them as such—must be laid down: that all reality is reducible to essences, and that essences are extended magnitudes. Descartes and his followers conceived practically everything in mathematical terms—the universe, the body politic, the human body, even human impulses and morality. The Benthamite calculus is the offspring of this epistemology. Naturally, the insights of intuition (introspection) are above the standards of truth and falsehood established by the very epistemology that such insights were setting up. The "primary qualities" (extension, motion, number) are axioms.

It is now well understood that Descartes' reduction of all reality to extended matter was necessitated by his desire to attain that utmost degree of certainty which his skeptical contemporaries had destroyed but which he felt a mathematical handling of reality could restore. In the case of the wax, Descartes justifies his choice of extension over all other sensuous qualities by asserting that extension is "more permanent" than they are. But, as Burtt asks, are not color and resistance equally constant properties of bodies? "The fact is . . . *Descartes' real criterion is not permanence but the possibility of mathematical handling.*"[12] This point cannot be emphasized too strongly: the empirical qualities—color, resistance, smell, etc.—are suspect. The mind sees them as "obscure and confused." Having thus softened the citadel of what William James would call "stubborn and irreducible facts," the Cartesian mind can proceed to draw out of its own consciousness exactly those qualities that make a mathematical handling of the problem possible.

The same characteristic of inventing something of a geometrical nature in order to bring some phenomenon under mathematical relationships was illustrated by Descartes' famous "vortex theory," which resulted in a novel conception of the universe. Galileo had attempted to describe the movements of the heavenly bodies mathematically but was hampered by a lack of empirical data. Descartes, who had a low opinion of facts, solved the riddle of the universe by intuition. Intuition indicated, clearly and distinctly, that one of the basic "simple natures" is a "something extended" which he called "first matter," or "ether," occupying the space between the various planets. The universe thus consisted of the stars, and the planets,

12. *Metaphysical Foundations*, p. 110. Emphasis in the text.

and their satellites swimming in "extremely fine splinters" (the ether). This primary matter, once set into motion by the Creator, fell into a series of whirlpools or vortices which carry within themselves the planets. Objects on earth fall toward certain points because of the laws of vortical motion. The vortices themselves communicate motion to each other by sheer mechanical impact, much as in a well-constructed system of gears.[13]

What interests us in this conception is the role of ether. *This invention was demanded by Descartes' implicit desire to bring planetary motion within the laws of mechanical impact, a desire dictated by his epistemology.* Through impact, the movement of the celestial bodies is made amenable to mathematical treatment, but impact needs a physical medium in order to be transmitted. This interjection of something new and fictive within the interstices of mathematical thinking is rather common in economics. Leontief has detected it and decried it as "implicit theorizing."[14] We know now the reason for this phenomenon. Having abjured empiricism as a way of attaining truth (we are to seek the "certain principle of material things—not by the prejudices of the senses, but by the light of reason"[15]), the way is opened to the creation of that which is not but which enables us to link concepts with each other mathematically.[16]

The jejune nature of Cartesianism is well illustrated by Descartes' own *Tract on Man.* There he "imagines" the body as "nothing else than a statue or machine of clay," and he explains its functioning logically without calling on any but those simple principles of mechanics "used in making clocks, artificial fountains, mills and

13. Ibid., pp. 102 ff. Arendt reminds us that both Spinoza and Karl Jaspers have been struck by the "strange ineptitude of Descartes' 'scientific' ideas, his lack of understanding for the spirit of modern science, and his inclination to accept theories uncritically without tangible evidence" (*The Human Condition,* p. 272n27).

14. "Implicit Theorizing: A Methodological Criticism of the Neo-Cambridge School."

15. Descartes, *The Principles of Philosophy,* Part III, Principle I.

16. Another signal advantage of the ether which pleased Descartes very much was the fact that it enabled him to assert that the earth is motionless relative to its vortex (it is the vortex that moves, carrying the earth along). Descartes was, quite frankly, afraid that the Inquisition would deal with him as it had already dealt with Galileo. The reader will recognize that he "solved" the theological problem with a sheer "play on words." As many foes of Cartesian rationalism (Bentham, Kierkegaard, Dewey) recognized, plays on words are inevitable when thought proceeds unchecked by observation.

other similar machines." This approach claims to explain everything that modern psychology despairs of ever being able to uncover, including the "interior motions of the appetites and passions," and the "imprinting of ideas upon the memory."[17]

But did Descartes really think that the world can be grasped by mathematical forms of thought starting from wholly psychic axioms? He himself dichotomized the world into *res extensa* (the things outside the mind) and the web of concepts created by the mind (*res cogitans*). Did he implicitly assume that the products of the latter must "reflect" the former? To put it differently, on what was ultimately based his confidence in the power of *inspectio* to correctly portray reality? Descartes did address himself to this crucial point and, as in centuries past, relied on the traditional handmaid of philosophy for an answer. The mind, following geometrical ways of thinking, must correctly portray the world outside; otherwise, nature and man would be the playtoys of a *Dieu trompeur* (a deceiving God). This to Descartes—who was a good believer— was inconceivable. God exists, His nature is goodness, hence He cannot lead man into error.

Quite clearly, this solution to the mind-matter dualism, as it came to be called, attained by introducing a veritable *deus ex machina*, ran counter to the whole positivist, antitheological current that Descartes himself had pioneered in his scientific work. His contemporaries and followers tended to ignore it, *thereby truncating the only connecting link between thought and objective reality.* Ignoring Descartes' theological argument is tantamount to asserting that one cannot distinguish between dream and reality, as Berkeley pointed out later.

Descartes was probably aware of the weakness of introducing theological considerations in a work purporting to aid science. This realization, coupled with his low opinion of sense perception, finally led him to look for the highest degree of certainty within the realm of psychic, contentless concepts, which are not derived from observation and which, therefore, do not need to be supported by theological considerations. Not even a Dieu trompeur can change the fact that two and two make four: "Physics, Astronomy, Medicine, and all the other sciences that have for their end the consideration

---

17. In this brief essay, Descartes, quite in keeping with his dualism, explains that all bodily processes can be accounted for mechanically and without making reference to thinking, emotions, etc.

of composite objects, are indeed of a *doubtful character*; but . . . Arithmetic, Geometry, and other sciences of the same class, which regard merely the simplest and most general objects, and *scarcely inquire whether or not these are really existent*, contain somewhat that is certain and indubitable: for *whether I am awake or dreaming*, it remains true that two and three make five, and that a square has but four sides; nor does it seem possible that truths so apparent can ever fall under a suspicion of falsity."[18]

Recent scholarship—studying Descartes from the viewpoint of a non-Euclidean world—has discovered that Descartes unwittingly confines certainty and truth to only that which *man himself has created without borrowing anything from nature* (nature being Another's creation). In pure mathematics, as in Aristotelean logic, man sets up the concepts, the rules of thinking, the nature of the relations, the boundaries and meaning of truth. Within this wholly man-created framework, there is formal truth, internal consistency. But let man give empirical content to these or any other concepts, let him claim that he can portray the world, and the results are "of a doubtful character."

Descartes might have sensed this. In a letter to Henry More, he wrote, "Though our mind is not the measure of things or of truth, it must assuredly be the measure of things that *we* affirm or deny."[19] Grasping on these and similar statements, Whitehead maintains that Cartesian reason is entirely based "on the implicit assumption that the mind can only know that which it has itself produced and retains in some sense within itself."[20] Cartesian thought is "the playing of the mind with itself." Introspection is "the sheer cognitive concern of consciousness with its own content. . . . *Cogito* always means *cogito me cogitare* [I think about my own thoughts],"[21] as Hannah Arendt says.

Had Descartes held this truth consistently and clearly, his insight would have been remarkably profound. Modern philosophers of science—as shaken by recent revolutions in our understanding of the world as Descartes had been shaken in his day—have returned to it. As Einstein put it, in a lecture delivered at the Prussian Academy in January 1921, "In so far as geometry is certain, it

18. Descartes, *The Meditations* (First Meditation). Emphasis added.
19. Quoted by Alexandre Koyré, *From the Closed World to the Infinite Universe*, p. 117. Emphasis added.
20. *The Concept of Nature*, p. 32.
21. *The Human Condition*, pp. 284, 280.

says nothing about the actual world, and in so far as it says something about our experience, it is uncertain."[22] Or as Bertrand Russell wrote not too long afterward, "mathematics can be defined as the subject in which we never know what we are talking about nor whether what we are saying is true," true, that is, by reference to some standards outside the mathematical frames themselves.[23] But Descartes certainly did not intend to limit knowledge within psychic, man-made concepts. This is why, in his *Second Meditation*, he speaks of using the introspective method to surmount the "difficulties of the other sciences." His *Essay of Man* and his view of the universe all show that he used the method of *inspectio* to grasp reality.[24] Even the famous *cogito ergo sum* is vitiated by the error of assuming that thought entails existence. Having started out from universal doubt, Descartes cannot take man's existence for granted. Neither observation nor feelings prove existence. An amputee, for instance, continues to feel pain in a limb that has been lost. However, a modicum of intuition showed Descartes that the very act of doubting entails existence: I think (that is, I doubt), therefore I exist.

It is now widely agreed that Descartes' conclusion is erroneous. From the act of thinking, one can logically infer only the existence of thought, not of physical being. All that can be extracted from cogito is the existence of cogitation. As Kierkegaard put it, "From the logical point of view the Cartesian formulation: 'I think, therefore I am' is a play on words, because the 'I am' logically signifies nothing more than 'I am thinking' or 'I think.'"[25] To think is to think: this is the fundamental intuition of Descartes. It is the basic tautology, the *fons et origo* of the tautologies of those who followed his method. And the crux of the matter is that Descartes' own stringent standards of "clearness and distinctness of ideas" compel

22. Philipp Frank, *Einstein: His Life and Times*, p. 177.

23. *Mysticism and Logic*, p. 75.

24. Even this, however, is not certain. Copernicus, it will be recalled, is the originator (at least in modern times) of the "as if" fiction. He prefaced his work on astronomy by writing, in effect, that although everyone knows the sun moves around the earth, let us "suppose" that the opposite is true, and let us see what the results will be. It may well be that Descartes never claimed to explain the world as it is, but was engaged in a mental experiment, testing, so to speak, how far his mechanistic viewpoint would carry him. (Copernicus' fiction, too, was apparently dictated by a desire not to antagonize the censor.)

25. *Søren Kierkegaard's Journals and Papers*, para. 1033. For a modern statement of the same conviction, see, for instance, Hans Reichenbach, *Experience and Prediction*, para. 28.

this interpretation. And just as Descartes' "proof" of his existence leads him into tautology, so the hypotheses and theories that derived from his methodology remained forever imprisoned in the original axioms that they postulated. Regardless of how complex the chain of derivation, such truths all collapse, as Hegel noted, to the statement $A = A$.

Let us summarize: (1) "The work of Descartes had an enormous influence throughout all Europe." Modern thinking began with his *de omnibus dubitandum est.*[26] (2) Especially to be doubted is the world portrayed by the senses. (3) The possibility of certainty exists only by reducing nature to geometrical concepts, and by linking them mathematically so that theorems can be derived. (4) Whether the result of this procedure is true "discovery" of something "outside the mind" or whether it is rather an *invention* of the mind—a mode of perception and a way of coherently organizing one's ideas about reality—is not unequivocally clear in Descartes, but the weight of evidence favors the first interpretation. (5) This, however, is certain, and for the purposes of our study, this is the only relevant point: regardless of what Descartes meant, his contemporaries understood his method to produce a *coincidence* of thinking and being. And how could it have been otherwise? If Descartes himself, in a work on pure theory (epistemology), did not realize how circumscribed geometrical thinking is, what could be expected of men whose primary interest was in political and economic (that is, practical) matters? They found it impossible to avoid falling victim to the Baconian idols of the cave. They inevitably gave substance to what was purely mental. They hypostatized their psychic creations.

Thus a most amazing thing happened. Descartes, the man who aspired to put human knowledge on a secure and firm basis, actually succeeded in encouraging the most unrestrained flights of the imagination. Thought turned megalomaniac in that it claimed to explain wider and wider aspects of reality starting from the narrowest basis. His obsessive doubting led to the most naïve theorizing, his ingenious critique of knowledge to the most ingenuous constructs, all ending in tautology. Cartesianism severely limited both the universe and man. Just as thought was freed from whatever reins the objects outside provided, so the bounds of correct thinking

26. Burrt, *Metaphysical Foundations*, p. 117; Arendt, *The Human Condition*, p. 273.

were severely limited. Rapture, love, sympathy, mysticism, animosity, self-pity, and a host of other feelings have often been the source of important truths (in Descartes himself, as mentioned, his extreme sensitivity probably played a role in shaping his theory of knowledge). But Descartes naturally regarded these states of mind with Calvinist suspicion, as "pathological," since they hardly display geometrical qualities. Indeed, reason had no more determined and powerful foe than passions and feelings. They are the source of "obscure and inadequate ideas." Thus the severe limitation of the nature of the object (*any* object is extension) is balanced by as severe a limitation of the nature of right thinking. Despite his superficial emphasis on thinking, Descartes really assigned to thought only a very meagre role. The roads to discovery are many, but he acknowledged only one—the mathematical one. Descartes' ego has clearly nothing to do with whatever psychology now means by this term. As William James put it, it is the name of a nonentity—as unreal as his wax (which is pure extension, without any sensible qualities).[27] Paralleling this narrowing of intellect is a narrowing of our conception of man. These are the roots of the *homo economicus,* as narrow a concept of man as can be imagined. Yet the refashioning of reality out of geometrical categories is not unilinearly simple. Neither Descartes nor his followers would have gone very far had they adhered to the mathematical method *consistently.* Mathematical thinking has to be provided with ever new "intuitions" to accomplish its task of passing from discovery to discovery. We shall elaborate later on this quality of rationalistic thought in connection with economics, the most mature offspring of the Cartesian ego. Descartes' imagining of a space among the planets full of "extremely fine splinters" is exactly one of these purposeful fictions needed by that mathematical medium which had previously demanded that all reality be reduced to geometrical concepts.

This demand made by mathematics is so insistent and so neglected that it may pay to emphasize it with reference to Newton. Although emphatically not a Cartesian,[28] Newton, too, had to acknowledge the existence of an ether enveloping the planets. He conceived the propagation of light as analogous to the propagation

27. See chap. 11 for a fuller presentation of the nineteenth-century case against the method of the ego.

28. See chap. 4 for a brief summary of Newton's method.

of sound. Sound, as is well known, is not transmitted in a vacuum. Therefore, neither is light. There must be something between the sun and the planets through which light "waves" can travel. With this fiction, Newton was able to apply the mathematical formulae tested against sound phenomena to light phenomena. The conception of the ether did not die until Einstein found that it stood in the way of his own theory. By then, however, the constant repetition of that which does not exist had given reality (i.e., body) to a pure invention of the mind. The word had been hypostatized. Einstein had difficulty reminding his colleagues that ether was just a word, a will-o'-the-wisp.[29]

It is not mathematics by itself that enables one to interpret the world, but mathematics aided by what we may call analogical fictions, names of non-entities to which we attribute those properties that enable us to use the mathematical method to advantage. We may compare Descartes' rationalism to a ship. The original inspectio will carry one only so far; then the ship will go aground. Eventually, a high tide (a bold stroke of imagination) comes which will free it from the shoals and the journey can continue. Mathematical modes of thinking *and* the necessary fictions that enable these modes to function are the materials of which are made the seven-league boots which allow rationalism to travel through and refashion the universe.

The Cartesian dualism with its emphasis on thought and logic and de-emphasis of matter and sensations is also a prominent characteristic of such diverse philosophers as Locke, Berkeley, and Hume. Voltaire praised Locke highly and endeavored to popularize his works on the continent. On the surface, Locke's theory of knowledge restores what Descartes' had taken away. This is what the popular characterization of Locke as an empiricist seems to suggest. Upon closer scrutiny, however, Locke's epistemology places as much emphasis on the primacy and certainty of pure ideas over mere sensations as Descartes' did.

In *An Essay Concerning Human Understanding*, Locke sets up a hierarchy of sources of knowledge. The highest is intuition, then demonstration, and sensations are the lowest.[30] Intuition affords the greatest degree of certainty, for it consists in the grasping of self-

29. Frank, *Einstein*, pp. 53–56, 168.
30. *An Essay Concerning Human Understanding*, 4:ii.

evident truths. The theorems of mathematics are self-evident. In economics, the statement that, given the quantity theory of money, an increase in the money supply will, other things equal, lead to an equi-proportionate increase in prices, is an intuitive truth. Demonstration affords the second highest degree of certainty since it consists of showing the connection among intuitively grasped ideas "by the intervention of other ideas." The statement that, under perfect competition, optimum resource allocation follows is a demonstration, the last link in a fairly complex chain of reasoning starting from intuitively grasped axioms. The main difference between intuitive and demonstrative knowledge is that the latter entails greater intellectual labor and man can thus more easily be led astray if the rules of logic are not strictly followed. In reality the process of demonstration is often not unilinearly simple, hence the necessity for "other ideas." When links are found missing in the mathematical chain, they are forged *ex novo* by the ego following non-logical (e.g., analogical) rules. We saw this process of creation in connection with Descartes' splinters and Newton's ether.

The certainty afforded by sensations of external objects is on an altogether lower plane. Paradoxically, the idea of the object *in the mind* is an intuitive certainty, but "whether there be anything more than barely that idea in our minds, whether we can hence certainly infer the existence of anything without us which corresponds to that idea is that whereof some men think there may be a question made" (4:ii, 14). The customary "bifurcation of nature and mind" is, then, present in Locke too. Descartes bridged the gap by assuming an identity of the two worlds. Locke hesitated. He seemed to have been caught between common sense and the professional desire to be lucid, logical, and critical. He paid homage to common sense by asking the reader whether there is not a difference between our dreaming ourselves to be in a fire and our actually being in it, but this is a purely rhetorical trick used innumerable times before and since, one which hardly addresses itself to the philosophical question. This sudden appeal to experience in a philosopher who first denigrated it is contradictory. A shift of methodology from rationalism and lofty speculation to the common sense reasoning of the layman is the surest indication of the failure of rationalism. And, at length, professional honesty compelled Locke to admit that "since the mind, in all its thoughts and reasoning, hath no other immediate object but *its own ideas,* which it alone does or can contemplate, it is evident that our knowledge is only conversant about them" (4:i, 1; emphasis added). And later, "The having the idea of anything in our mind, no more proves the existence of that thing than the picture of a man evidences his being in the world, or the visions of a dream make thereby a true history" (4:xi, 1). This remarkable admission on the part of the so-called empiricist can only mean that, when we reason along Cartesian-Lockean lines, we never know whether we are talking about real things or our own inventions; any hope of comparing our ideas with reality is dashed.

Locke often seems to imply that not the highest but the only certain knowledge we possess is that attained intuitively and demonstratively. This conclusion is confirmed by his distinction between "primary" and "secondary" qualities of objects, a dichotomizing device that, as in Descartes, has the purpose of laying down categories through which reality is handled mechanistically and mathematically. Primary qualities are extension, figure, motion, solidity, and number. Secondary qualities are odor, color, warmth, etc. The latter may be quite false despite the testimony of the senses (2:viii). Like Descartes, Locke argues that trustworthy conclusions can be attained only when the mind works with the primary qualities and their interrelations.

It seems that Locke had a clear realization of the true nature and purpose of the rationalistic method. He acknowledged that "General and universal concepts belong not to the real existence of things, but are the inventions, and creatures of the understanding, made by it for its own use, and concern only signs, whether words or ideas" (3:iii, 11). When we leave particulars, the general concepts we use are only "creations of our own making," subjective constructs of the psyche (3:iii, 11). Locke even recognizes that they are often illogical, that they "carry difficulties with them." A triangle (a general concept) "must be neither oblique, nor rectangle, neither equilateral, equicrural, nor scaleon; but all and none of these at once," which is a contradiction in terms. That certain rationalistic concepts are not even logical (since they involve the mind in the infraction of the fundamental rule of thinking, the law of identity) we shall illustrate with reference to economic theory. Their illogical nature goes undetected, Locke adds, because thought "has need of such ideas and makes all the haste to them it can for the conveniency of communication and the enlargement of knowledge" (4:vii, 9).

The British philosopher already possessed the building blocks necessary to understand the development of economic theory. He realized that general concepts do not bear on reality and may even be self-contradictory, but are nevertheless useful, at least when employed with full knowledge of their true nature. The danger arises, as Lange points out in his summary of Locke's position, when words are treated as adequate pictures of things, while they are really only arbitrary signs for certain ideas which must be used with great care. When this is forgotten, concepts and theories cease to be useful and may, in fact, become a source of strife.[31]

Locke's pragmatic considerations apparently did not please Berkeley, perhaps the most consistent of the epistemological writers of this period. He reaffirmed the chasm between the idea and the object, and concluded that ideas are the only entities known to thinking man. Coherence, coincidence, and truth are only qualities of ideas in their mutual relation.[32] Truth is not coincidence of ideas with the object, but of ideas with each other.[33] "When we do our utmost to conceive the existence of external bodies, we are all the while only contemplating our own ideas."[34] Driving home his point, Berkeley notes ironically and pointedly that the "very patrons of Matter" have not proved that there is a *necessary* connection between objects and our ideas of them,[35] a judgment which, as we saw, is true of Locke. Epistemologically, the empiricists never established a *nexus* between ideas and reality. Nevertheless, in contradiction to their pure speculations, they often assumed such a connection in their more practical works since they found it difficult to live in a sign world. Having given up the heuristic fiction of God as an explanation of nature, the rationalists enthroned geometrical fictions. They replaced God with consciousness, or, we may say, God with Euclid. By effectively divorcing ideas from their objective substratum, the seventeenth-century philosophers caused the emergence of a world view framed by mathematics for the use of mathematicians.[36]

31. Lange, *History of Materialism*, sec. 3:322.
32. George Berkeley, *A Treatise Concerning the Principles of Human Knowledge*, sec. 8.
33. It is remarkable that pragmatism, which has a realistic ("tough-minded") view of the process of discovery, defines truth in the same way. See chap. 11.
34. Berkeley, *Treatise*, sec. 23.
35. Ibid., sec. 24.
36. Whitehead, *Science and the Modern World*, p. 81.

Descartes was not only the "legislator of modern science," as Whitehead calls him. He also determined the mode of analysis in social matters. His viewpoint encouraged what we may call intellectual adventurousness. The imaginative creations of the "state of nature," of "social compacts," of historical *"corsi e ricorsi"* are eloquent examples. Freed from the necessity to describe the world as it appears—for appearance is deceptive—thought began its long and distinguished career of fiction-building. The objective fact was almost never the starting point of analysis. In attempting to explain aspects of society, social thinkers began by laying down an axiom which was beyond analysis: a universal characteristic of "human nature" or a "natural state." Indeed, their aspiration to go back to fundamentals precluded historical research, for no research on prehistoric conditions is possible. Appropriate theorems were then derived from the basic axiom, aided by useful fictions. Finally, an unequivocal conclusion stood out. Thought that proceeds in this fashion may be called purposive rather than explicative. Hitherto, it has been criticized as the expression of a political bias on the part of the thinker. We think rather that the appearance of bias was forced by the very methodology employed. The method of the ego is singularly unfit to portray the shadows and nuances of life. It is inherently dogmatic (like mechanicism must be) and strives to show the cold inflexibility of everything. Not the least paradoxical result of the Cartesian epistemology is this: it aspired to make thinking independent from feelings but it only created deeply ethical, political, and pedagogical works. It is no accident that the enlightened thinkers discovered the value of political freedom.

Hobbes' writings are a good illustration of Cartesianism in social thought. To him, philosophy is the attempt to go beyond appearances to the first causes and, since all reasoning is computation, it follows that "ratiocination . . . is the same with addition and subtraction. . . . So that all ratiocination is comprehended in these two operations of the mind."[37] Diderot might decry the mathematical method, warning, as Cassirer puts it, that its very "perfection will necessarily remain its immanent limitation. For [mathematics] cannot reach out beyond its own self-made concepts: it has no immediate access to empirical concrete reality."[38] But the most ex-

37. Thomas Hobbes, *Concerning Body.*
38. Ernst Cassirer, *The Philosophy of the Enlightenment,* p. 74.

treme philosophers of the seventeenth century evidently thought they had solved the riddle of the universe. To build a science of the state it was sufficient to apply to the field of politics the principles of Cartesian thought. The fact that mathematical models have been brought to perfection in our own days in political theory testifies to the strength of this methodology.

But Hobbes himself did not live by algebra alone. At age forty, on the eve of the English revolution of 1628, he brought out a translation of Thucydides into English with the express intent of showing his conationals the folly of democracy by the experience of Athens in the Peloponnesian Wars. Later, in the *Leviathan*, he provided a legal basis for absolute authority. The unhistorical and fictional nature of the method that he used enabled him to do this easily. He first manufactured a "general inclination, a perpetual and restless desire of power after power, that ceaseth only in death."[39] Hobbes presents this craving after power as the *primum mobile* of the human species and it is the axiom on which the argument is based. Wealth is the precondition of power, and since wealth is scarce, men fight over it and live in perpetual fear of being robbed. The misery of this situation led primitive men to enter into a "social compact" abdicating their freedom to absolute authority in exchange for an orderly and peaceful civic life. Hobbes very meticulously reports verbatim the formula of man's abdication of freedom: "I authorize and give up my right of governing myself to this man, or to this assembly of men, on the condition, that you [the other members of the commonwealth] give up your right to him and authorize all his actions in like manner."[40]

It is remarkable, however, that, despite his literary punctilio, Hobbes himself regarded the description of the state of nature, of the nature of man, and of the compact as pure fantasy. His descriptions, he felt, were philosophically and logically, but not historically, accurate. The formula for the abdication of freedom reported above is introduced with the words "*as if* every man should say to every man, I authorize," etc.[41] The old fiction by which many thinkers tried to avoid troubles with the Inquisition, by artificially asserting their works to be philosophically true but theologically false, became philosophically true but historically groundless, which

39. Part I, chap. 11.
40. Ibid., chap. 17.
41. Ibid. Emphasis added. See also chap. 13.

means logically consistent (given its premises) but beyond the realm of experience. And we should not forget Hobbes' own warning not to confuse mere names for real things, since names are signs not of things but of our cogitations.[42] We are thus warned not to accept his own theory as anything other than a literary reflection of his political opinions.

By Hobbes' own admission *Leviathan* must be interpreted as a fable, a story with a moral, a work of rhetoric that, it is hoped, will teach man something. Its worth lies not in the description of reality but in the expression of an outlook, in the pointing of a moral. It definitely teaches public authority to act as if men were acquisitive cowards and as if they preferred order and peace over everything, including freedom. Innumerable other writers of this period allowed their imaginations to run loose creating fictive "states of nature." Milton notes that man's primitive state was that freedom and bliss that Adam's sin forfeited. An age of violence followed (Cain and Abel) from which men emerged by entering into a compact whereby they "agreed by common league to bind each other from mutual injury, and jointly to defend themselves against any that gave disturbance to such agreement. Hence came cities, towns, and commonwealths."[43]

Spinoza's conception is a variation on the same theme; desire is the spring of human actions, but it is better to live by reason than by desire. Hence, men decided to come into an agreement to live together as securely and as well as possible in order to enjoy as a whole the rights which naturally belong to them as individuals.[44] G. B. Vico complicates the story somewhat by dividing mankind into Hebrew and Gentile, the latter passing through a state of barbarism and savagery after the Fall and the Deluge. Vico identifies these "ignoble creatures" with the Homeric Cyclops and the Titans. Mighty thunderstorms followed which induced them to seek refuge in caves. Here forced inactivity caused domestic life to emerge and appears to have stimulated what we may call the search for identity. They were overcome by a sense of shame for their brutality, lust, and degradation and, lo, the monogamic family emerged, followed by the clan, the tribe, arts, and civilization.[45]

42. *Concerning Body*, chap. 2, sec. 5.
43. John Milton, *The Tenure of Kings and Magistrates*, reprinted in F. W. Coker, *Readings in Political Philosophy*, p. 425.
44. *A Theological-Political Treatise*, chap. 16.
45. Robert Flint, *Vico*, pp. 200–204.

The state of nature conjured up by the eminent German social philosopher Pufendorf is avowedly "speculative," the product of the author's method of "abstracting from all the rules and institutions, whether of human invention, or of the suggestion and revelation of Heaven."[46] Descartes abstracted and found extension: Pufendorf abstracts and finds "a mute and ignoble animal, master of no powers or capacities, any further than to pick the herbs and roots that grow about him."[47] Man emerged from this vicious state through cooperative effort and social intercourse. But intercourse necessitates order, and order calls for laws and public authority. Pufendorf acknowledges that this state of nature never existed historically.[48]

It is a characteristic of thought that proceeds unchecked by reality that diametrically opposed conclusions can be easily reached by a sheer change of the original fiction. Thus it was easy for Montesquieu to imagine original man to be a timid, frightened creature, rather than a brutal, cruel one. A "natural" fear and a just as "natural" instinct of self-preservation compelled him to associate with his fellows, after which he shed his timidity and became bellicose. The tables are now turned on Hobbes; far from bringing about stability and peace, society is responsible for wars and social strife.[49]

As for Rousseau, he held both views of the natural state, the pessimistic and the optimistic. In his *Discourse on the Origin and Foundation of Inequality among Men,* he pictures natural man as an easy-going, happy being. In the *Social Contract,* he portrays man as so savage and barbarous that the human race would have perished if it had not entered into a Covenant.

Bossuet, Blackstone, and Locke also contributed "models" of society all based on a primitive state of nature from which pertinent "derivations" were made. The Cartesian method is unmistakable in all of them: they begin by drawing from their own minds, a priori, the "innate" qualities of primitive man. From this axiom eventually followed certain characteristics of modern society (those that they wished to emphasize, e.g., its brutality or its intrinsic order). To go from the axiomatic innate qualities to the conclusion (order, civility, or wars), fictions had to be created—con-

46. *The Law of Nature and of Nations,* 2:ii, 1.
47. Ibid., 2:i, 8.
48. Ibid., 2:i, 3.
49. *The Spirit of Laws,* 1:ii.

tracts, fears, thunderbolts, which triggered the natural response of the innate qualities.

Some modern scholars have understood these writings to be historical. E. Sidney Hartland, for instance, in his book *Primitive Law*, criticizes the notion of the Enlightenment that primitive man was free. On the contrary, he asserts, the savage is "hemmed in on every side by the customs of his people; he is bound in the chains of immemorial tradition. . . . These fetters are accepted by him as a matter of course; he never seeks to break forth. . . ."[50] This criticism of enlightened thought is uncalled for: most *philosophes* knew that they were indulging in myth-making. This is not to deny that some of their educated contemporaries mistook these allegories as true, historical narratives of an age long gone. In 1724 in Hanover, a boy was discovered who could not speak and had only the most rudimentary intelligence. "Wilde Peter" set the intellectual world ablaze. In London, where he was sent, the luminaries of that empirical country and the contemporaries of the skeptical Hume engaged in heated philosophical and naturalistic discussions of his origins. At length, a consensus emerged that he was a specimen of some primordial natural state transplanted to Europe by merchants. His discovery was deemed as important as that of the planet Uranus, just then added to the family of bodies circling the sun. Alas, many years later, painstaking empirical research demoted Wilde Peter from the lofty pedestal where scholarship had put him. He was found to be a widower's dumb child whom the stepmother, as in the story of Hansel and Gretel, had thrown out of the house.[51]

More clearly imaginative were some mental constructs arising in the same enlightened age, for "scientific" reasons. They all partake of the nature of mental experiments—"let-us-suppose" games —a technique that was to become the mainstay of economic theorizing. Condillac envisaged an imaginary statue similar to a human being but as yet devoid of ideas. The statue is enclosed in a marble case which prevents it from using its senses. Conceptually, in his own imagination, the philosopher allows the statue to use one sense organ at a time (just as the economist keeps everything but one variable constant), first the sense of smell, then hearing, etc., in succession. Accordingly, he creates an olfactory man, an auditory man, in each case showing which ideas would be associated with

50. Page 138.
51. A. C. Haddon, *History of Anthropology*, pp. 27–28.

this particular fraction of a man. Apparently, Condillac was trying to study the origin of ideas from a materialistic standpoint—one that assumes that the environment is the sole cause of ideas. But his standpoint was really ideal, the experiment being a *mental* act of imagination which, among other things, severed what is whole. Naturally, his Cartesian methodology led to absurdities, like the fact that language arises before the ear is opened.[52]

We noted how Lovejoy credits Cartesianism as the source of both idealism and mechanism or materialism. This apparent paradox is solved by distinguishing between the mode and the *substance* of thought, i.e., between its form and its ethics. The mode of thinking was imaginative and idealistic. The conclusions were materialistic. This dichotomy is illustrated by the thought of Lamettrie, probably the most extreme of the eighteenth-century materialists but an acknowledged follower of Descartes' method. He tried to undermine his master's notion of innate ideas by *imagining* (the idealistic method) a baby to be nourished in a faintly lit cellar by a silent nurse. When, at a later age, the boy is allowed to step into the world, society, words, concepts have no meaning for him, or so the philosopher thinks. From this, Lamettrie draws the not trivial conclusion (a materialistic one) that all knowledge comes through the senses.[53] The stage for such conclusions was set by Descartes' own method as illustrated, for instance, by his essay on man.

It was inevitable that the skepticism that arose as a reaction against the nimble scholastic mind should eventually have turned against the creations of the *philosophes*. Hume's doubts of the ability of the mind to know anything suggest that the denigration of the sensuous world eventually brought about a revolt against reason, for the latter was depreciated by the very fables it created. Hume's skepticism swept nearly everything away, even the logical necessity of an effect following a cause. Only one thing survived, the conclusions of psychic-tautological reasoning, which he held to be undeniably true. He provided an example of such reasoning in the specie-flow mechanism of trade and prices, which we will examine later.

It is well known that Hume cast doubt on the fundamental premise of knowledge, the belief in the logical necessity of cause

52. Cited by H. Vaihinger, *The Philosophy of 'As If': A System of the Theoretical, Practical and Religious Fictions of Mankind,* pp. 190–91.
53. Lange, *History of Materialism,* sec. 4:63.

and effect. In the *Abstract of a Treatise of Human Nature*—which was for a long time attributed to his pupil Adam Smith—Hume argues that our belief that an effect follows a cause is ultimately only founded on "custom," which alone induces the mind to expect that the future will conform to the past. Instead of seizing upon this insight to reaffirm the importance of custom (in enlightened thinking, a neglected category which would not be disinterred until Hegel), Hume uses it to denigrate empirical reasoning (as Descartes had done) on the novel ground that it is founded on a sheer act of faith: the "supposition," that is, that "the course of nature will continue uniformly the same." As J. M. Keynes noted, Hume's skepticism was primarily directed against arguments by induction.[54] But his acute critique of induction pushed him into the ranks of the geometers: his skepticism then became naïveté.

Echoing many other thinkers of the period, Hume asserted that the theorems of mathematics do not rely on cause and effect. Instead, they carry their proofs within themselves. "If any term be defined in geometry, the mind readily, of itself, substitutes on all occasions the definition for the term defined." Only geometrical and mathematical reasoning expresses necessary, not merely probable or expedient, connections; such reasoning does not proceed with the notion of cause and effect, but merely develops the implications of the fundamental axioms. And this is the "great advantage of the mathematical sciences above the moral."[55] For Hume, as for Descartes, skepticism led to an emphasis on the tautological and, therefore, the unexciting. One's fame can hardly be based on uttering true statements like "a triangle has three angles," although it is often based on reminding us how true such banal statements are. And Hume, like everybody else, succumbed to the blandishments of the method explicated by this statement to derive important conclusions about the behavior of real men and real nations. He did so in his writings on money and trade which the Mercantilists had tried to approach statistically and historically, and as men of feelings and men of action. Before we see how Hume solved their confusions, we must briefly indicate the main characteristics of Mercantilist, that is, prescientific, economic thought.

54. *A Treatise on Probability*, p. 272. See also Whitehead, *Science in the Modern World*, p. 63.

55. David Hume, *An Inquiry Concerning Human Understanding*, sec. 8, part 1.

Herbert Heaton's observations on Heckscher's standard study on Mercantilism immediately suggest the fundamental characteristics of this early "school" of economics: "Heckscher makes a generalization and then discovers at least one contradiction or exception that demands attention; but having given this intruder due consideration he decides it is not really important, and struggles back to his first proposition."[56] And again: "It is fascinating to watch a twentieth century scholar drip perspiration in his efforts to build a 'system' out of pamphlet polemics."[57] Undeniably, Mercantile literature is a chaotic mass of special pleadings, naïve arguments, insight, facts, hypotheses, dogmas, prejudices, acute observations, and sheer guesses. The writings of this period belong to the pre-Cartesian age. They lack the main engines of rationalist thought, the abstract concepts, the universals, the generalizing fiction, the ability to go beyond the surface (monetary) manifestations of a phenomenon to its ultimate ("real") essence. The Mercantilists could not imagine what does not exist, a closed economy, a barter transaction, money as a mere *numeraire*, a Robinson Crusoe type of society, labor as the essence of value. They could not abstract. In their arguments they kept too close to reality to see that they must "pierce its veil" in order to attain truth.

The Mercantilists could not discover "laws": the detached view that is expressed by the many classical comparisons of economics with astronomy was not theirs, for they felt that they were not spectators but actors in the economic drama. Their wish was to manipulate reality, not simply explain its "natural" (that is, imaginary) workings. They looked at the state realistically, as the tool of their political passions and the power that they must try to influence. Businessmen, financiers, jurists, literateurs, adventurers, politicians, physicians, divines, moralists, novelists, and prospectors —the Mercantilists did not form a school in a sociological sense. They lacked the prerequisite of the school, a common methodology. The strongest tie that united them, the belief that the richer the country is in gold, the wealthier and more powerful it is, was simply the reflection of the popular, down-to-earth lore of the Golden Calf worshippers of any age. By a natural transition, the presumed beneficial effects of bullion were later transferred to paper money as well, the glories of which they often sang lyrically: while goods

56. Heaton, "Heckscher on Mercantilism," p. 371.
57. Ibid., p. 388.

perish in the act of consumption, "money still lives" as if "it were immortal."[58] Money was viewed unphilosophically in its time-historical context, and hence dynamically. The Mercantilists felt that it stimulated trade and production. It took the philosophical imagination of Locke and Hume, following Cartesian mechanicism and idealism, to transform this vital agent of production into a dead numeraire, a mere unit of account.

The Mercantilists lacked generalizing ability, their categories were the categories of human action, of politics, not those of detached intellect. Their economics was disaggregative: *certain* goods should not be imported, *certain* prices should be kept down, *certain* outlays of certain classes of individuals should be discouraged. Universals like exports, imports, and the price level were not used. Neither did they feel constrained to divorce economic matters from the rest of human affairs. Their suggestions were frequently justified on ethical and on expedient grounds. Their thinking being unspeculative, it is not surprising that they often advocated contradictory policies, for reality *is* often contradictory, and they had not annihilated it by laying down an axiom. In relation to labor, for instance, they were of two minds; laborers shared with gold the honor of being a source of wealth and power, yet the most innocuous pleasures were denied them. The habit of drinking tea, especially with sugar, was a particularly heinous crime, more serious than "snuff-taking" or "wearing ribbons."[59] Gathering at the alehouse was believed to be debilitating to health or morals or both, and thus was an enemy to industry deserving to be counterbalanced by the discipline of the workhouse and by subsistence wages.

By the early eighteenth century, however, Mercantilist thought displayed symptoms of moving away from life toward abstractions. The glittering metals were de-emphasized and labor clearly emerged as the "source of wealth," "the chiefest, most fundamental and precious commodity."[60] This suggests the beginning of an ability to look beyond the surface into first causes. Teleological strains, the surest indication that thought is moving away from the real, also began to appear, as, for instance, in Mandeville's celebrated *Fable of the Bees* (the word "fable" is suggestive), which implied that

58. Jacob Viner, *Studies in the Theory of International Trade*, p. 28.
59. Edgar S. Furniss, *The Position of the Laborer in a System of Nationalism*, p. 153.
60. Ibid., pp. 17 ff.

egoism led to public good. This suggestion later entered economics via Adam Smith.

It is mainly in the area of prices and the balance of trade that the clamping of the Cartesian approach on economic reasoning can be seen. From their earliest writings, Mercantilists had concluded that a favorable trade balance could be obtained by keeping prices at a level lower than in foreign countries. They knew that such a balance brought in gold and they knew also that an increase in the stock of money tended to raise prices. The individual, single pieces of the specie-flow theorem were thus well known before Hume. Why were they not placed in their *right* relation to each other to conclude that a favorable balance of trade is ephemeral because it brings about "its own corrective"? The inability of the Mercantilists to do so is an indication of their activistic, non-Cartesian outlook, for it takes a rather detached philosophical and mechanistic mentality to arrive at the equilibrium concept. The Mercantilists were not so detached: they found truth in action and action determined their discovery of truth. To have asserted that all their policies pertaining to money matters, all their efforts to increase the country's gold stock, were self-defeating, thwarted by a "law of nature," would have been tantamount to acknowledging the futility of activism.

A new spirit had to emerge before the stoic, fatalistic conclusion of the specie-flow theorem could be drawn—a spirit rising above the vulgarity of politics and experience and moving away from the substance of the relations among nations to their mere form. Cartesian detachment provided such a spirit. It contributed a skepticism toward those fragments of reality which statistical investigations yield, and a childlike admiration for deductive, mathematical thinking. Hume expressed both of these characteristics: "The custom-house books are allowed to be an insufficient ground of reasoning; nor is the rate of exchange much better. . . . Every man, who has ever reasoned in this subject, has always proved his theory, whatever it was, by facts and calculations."[61] But facts and calculations are "very uncertain" by their nature. Objective reality is untrustworthy: no laws can be derived from it, especially since such laws would have to rely on the discredited cause and effect. It is much safer to trust consciousness. Consciousness must become a substitute for the unreliable custom-house books, for exchange

61. *Essays,* "Of the Balance of Trade."

rate records, and for facts. But the ego clearly can only reason hypothetically: "*Suppose* four-fifths of all money in Great Britain to be annihilated in one night [Hume asks the reader]. . . . Must not the prices of all labour and commodities sink in proportion? . . . In how little time, therefore, must this bring back the money which we had lost and raise us to the level of all neighboring nations? [Thereupon] we immediately lose the advantage of the cheapness of labour and commodities and the further flowing in of money is stopped by our fulness and repletion."[62]

It is noteworthy that no proof is provided for this important conclusion; indeed none is needed. That the destruction of a certain proportion of a country's stock of money reduces the price proportionately, thus encouraging exports and discouraging imports and bringing in exactly that stock of money that was originally destroyed (thus restoring the old price level)—this "truth" follows solely by virtue of certain arithmetic properties of ratios and because of the mind's ability to see analogies. A proof of the theorem in the empirical, experimental sense is impossible by Hume's method: "events" occur only in Hume's mind, and his mind proceeds from conclusion to conclusion analogically and rhetorically. Money, whose vital role in the economic body Mercantilists compared to that of the circulation of blood in the human body, was henceforth viewed as perfectly neutral. Elsewhere, Hume states boldly that "the size of the money stock of a nation is of no consequence since the prices of the commodities are always proportioned to the plenty of money."[63] Abundance or scarcity of money "can have no effect," either good or bad, for a closed economy or for one having international transactions, a view shared not only by Locke but by Berkeley.[64] That the alleged skeptic, the so-called empiricist, and the idealist were united in their theory on money is proof that they were all under the sway of the same epistemology, at least with regard to economic thinking.

The theorem of the specie flow is the first economic example of reasoning in "real" terms, of going behind the phenomenon with the aid of number, extension, etc. It is a fine example of what Locke called "demonstrations." The theorem proceeds by stringing together a few propositions, whose inner tautological relations, di-

62. Ibid. Emphasis added.
63. *Essays,* "On Money."
64. Joseph A. Schumpeter, *History of Economic Analysis,* p. 296.

vorced from facts and viewed with the mathematical *forma mentis,*
are "intuitively" obvious. The same methodology that governs "I
think, therefore thought exists" is also responsible for "given free
trade, a balance of trade surplus brings about its own corrective
through the specie inflow and concomitant reciprocal price movement." We may note, incidentally, that Hume's relationships must
occur instantaneously: the destruction of four-fifths of the money
supply, the collapse in prices, the rise of exports, the inflow of
foreign gold, the rise in our prices, and the reattainment of balance
of trade equilibrium must all occur in the blink of an eye. Following the Cartesian road to certainty via purely mental deductions,
Hume's successors eventually produced static equilibrium analysis.

Hitherto, we have implicitly assumed that Hume meant his
economic theories to be explanations of economic reality. But is
this interpretation consistent with his broader methodological beliefs? We know that he referred to the various state of nature arguments as "poetic fictions" ("This state of nature, therefore, is to be
regarded as a mere fiction not unlike that of the golden age, which
poets have invented"[65]). Isn't it possible, therefore, that Hume regarded his specie-flow theorem as a derivation based on purely
subjective axioms, of no value for understanding the dynamics of
trade, prices, and economic relations?

But even if Hume had seen his theories in this light (and we
are not saying that he did), the climate of educated opinion of his
century would have sufficed to interpret his writings in economic
matters as realistic portraits of historical relations. "There is nothing
that requires more to be illustrated by philosophy than trade does,"
Dr. Johnson complained. Hume's trade theorem was exactly what
the educated mind—educated by Cartesianism—was craving.

The thinkers of the seventeenth and eighteenth centuries felt
that they had the method to unlock the secrets of the world. In
reality, the very nature of this method led them into supposing the
existence of more order and regularity in the world than there
really is. In applying the mathematical method to political and
economic matters the Enlightenment merely confirmed the keenness of Hegel's insight: "if one looks at the world rationally [that
is, with the categories and thinking cap of geometrical reason],
the world looks rationally back."

65. Hume, *A Treatise of Human Nature,* Part 2, sec. 2.

3

The Epistemological "Underground"

> Reason does not derive its laws from Nature but
> prescribes them to Nature.
>
> *Kant*

In CHAPTER 2, it was pointed out that many of the Cartesian theorists understood their own "state of nature" creations as heuristic fictions, that is, as logically correct but historically untrue accounts of the rise of civilization. Their thought is thus positive and critical at the same time: positive insofar as it built theories and hypotheses; critical insofar as it doubted the realism of its own creations. From these doubts arose the epistemological works of Bentham and Kant, who saw clearly that the order the rationalist mind had discovered was rooted in sources other than objective reality. Bentham, for instance, cannot be regarded as the geometrizing child portrayed by economic theory. His and Kant's critiques of knowledge were at least a century in advance of their times, resurfacing, in particular, in the nineteenth-century attack on the ego. To the extent that these thinkers saw more clearly than anyone else the true nature of the mind which was to create economics, their insights are insights into the modus operandi of economic theory.

41

Bentham's positive thought is exemplified by his conception of the "Springs of Human Action," an early example of that mathematical reasoning which soon pervaded all of economics down to the present. The whole conception is fictional (as Bentham was aware), and displays the fundamental characteristic of all fictions, one already detected by Locke: contradictoriness. Bentham was a libertarian; like many enlightened thinkers, he fought for the widening of man's freedom. But consider the definition of man he has to adopt in order to build his theory of human action: "Man is the *slave* of two sovereign masters, pleasure and pain." Opposed to obedience to an external master such as a monarch, Bentham made man the slave of the abstraction of pleasure and pain. Philosophically, this radical thinker believed that man was a free agent. But the Cartesian theory of truth he adopted forced him into a rigidly deterministic position.

This conflict between ethics and method has plagued economic theory throughout its evolution. The premise of all economic thinking is that the economic actors (workers, entrepreneurs) are free beings. Yet, faced with a certain event (a change in taxes, a cut in wages), they act with remarkable uniformity, one may even say with robotlike thoughtlessness. Why is this so? Because the ethical desideratum of freedom clashes with the epistemological longing for certainty. True freedom is the ability to do as one pleases. As such, true freedom is the foe of the certainty that Cartesianism sought so diligently. Predictable and precise reactions can hardly be expected of individuals and groups that are truly free. Uniform "laws" of behavior could not be discovered. In the conflict between ethical and methodological convictions, the latter won. In economic theory freedom is spoken of, but in reality the economic agents act as slaves, just as Bentham noted. This betrayal of the assumption of freedom proceeded at the same pace as the adoption of mathematics as the medium of analysis. Mathematics, the perfect product of a mind wholly free from the constraints of the environment, is also the most deterministic tool of reasoning: given a, then b; not c or d, but b only.

The mathematical medium of analysis—chosen because it gave the possibility of attaining certainty—even led the theorist to make practical suggestions strangely at odds with his libertarian ethics. For instance, the classical reaction to a depression was an overall wage cut. Keynes rightly detected the clash between this practical proposal and the political ethics of classicism when he asked, "Who is to administer such a cut?" He went on to point out the obvious fact that an across-the-board reduction in wages of the type theorists advised was characteristic of totalitarian rather than democratic countries.[1] The narrower the degree of freedom enjoyed by the community, the more appropriate the classical prescription.

Cartesianism's craving after certainty also accounts for the classical economists' view of money as a mere "unit of account," a numeraire, having no influence on the "real" sector of the economy. In life, money is much more than this: it is the embodiment of a passion, "money-making," but we saw that Cartesianism ruled passions out of existence. Once again, the classical conception of money can more truthfully be applied to the Soviet system than to a freer economy. It is in the Soviet system that money is closer to being merely an accounting unit. It is easy to solve the paradox of a concept which, though devoted to explaining the nature of the free economy, comes closer to explaining the nature of a planned economy. Modern Russia's economy is avowedly "scientific" and "rationalized." Soviet leaders display the same characteristic bias that the Cartesian ego has, a bias in favor of order, regimentation, predetermined (programed) responses that leave no room for surprises. Passions, at least economic ones, have been brought under a modicum of control in the Soviet Union, so that mathematical thinking about social questions reflects their reality better than it reflects that of a freer country.

Conflicts between ethical preconceptions and methods of analysis are rather common. For instance, many Marxists are caught between their belief in man's inherent ability to shape his destiny and the methodological determinism they read in Marx. If Marx asserts that the evolution of the "modes of production" shapes the thinking and behavior of men, then the alleged ability of the workers to move history is a mockery. Party leadership, propaganda, the "forging of the intellectual weapons of the proletariat" are all futile exercises. The materialistic method logically compels one to assert that "when the times are ripe," the new order will emerge "with the ineluctability of scientific laws." We shall see later that Marx, who was well grounded in philosophy, sidestepped this contradiction into which fall those who stress his determinism.

Returning to classical economics, we saw that freedom (a

1. Keynes, *The General Theory*, p. 269.

basic axiom of economic theory) is actually overruled in the conclusion of the theorem, where the economic agents behave with the
utmost uniformity because they are all the "slaves" of higher forces.
They exercise no choice in any meaningful sense of the term. In
view of this contradiction, it is not idle to ask why the freedom of
economic agents is mentioned at all. Hitherto, commentators have
answered this question by noting the political qualities of the centuries of Adam Smith and John S. Mill. The realm of political freedom, they argue, was widening after centuries of Mercantilist and
ecclesiastical regulation, so it was natural that social thought started
with this premise. Our stress on the "Cartesianization" of economics
can give an alternative answer. The various economic freedoms
(e.g., freedom of contracts, of movements) which underlie economic theory are actually *demanded* by that mathematical medium
of analysis which Cartesianism regarded as the tool of absolute
truth. Mathematical reasoning is reasoning *free from constraints*.
It needs agents (workers, entrepreneurs) who respond instantaneously to given stimuli—instantaneously because mathematics abstracts from time. Swift, frictionless responses of social beings to
given occurrences (a change in prices, in wages) are essential if
mathematical forms of reasoning are to be employed. And how can
there be swift responses without freedom from both outer (e.g.,
legislative) and inner (e.g., habit-rooted) constraints? As noted,
the assumption of freedom does not prevent economics from *denying* freedom in the conclusion: ultimately, economic agents act as
they must, i.e., as the *rules* of logic demand.

Thus, the concept of freedom in economic theory displays that
quality of self-contradiction that Locke had noticed in general concepts. To emphasize this point, we may note that freedom in economics has the same purpose and characteristics that it has in the
administration of justice, human or divine. Only the reason for the
adoption of the concept differs: in law and religion it is practical,
in economics it is theoretical. The fundamental assumption of justice
is that the evil-doer is a free and responsible agent. It is clear that
under no other assumption could he be jailed[2] or threatened with

2. We may note in passing that this fiction, like so many others, has recently been called into question as armies of psychiatrists take the witness
stand and testify to the power of the "unconscious," of the environment, or of
genes to determine action. The resulting movement away from the fiction of
individual freedom has thrown the administration of justice into confusion.

eternal damnation.[3] But it may be argued that the very act of sentencing a man (and the very awareness that jails and hell exist) severely restrains that freedom of choice that was predicated at the outset. Likewise, the very dogmatism of the "if . . . then" statements of economic theory is the negation of that free behavior which economic agents are supposed to possess.

Even Bentham's "felicific calculus" involved itself in a self-contradiction, but Bentham recognized this. The mathematics of the springs of human action is well known. Pleasure and pain are opposite poles of a magnet, the one attracting, the other repelling, and both compelling a definite response. Each has seven dimensions: intensity, duration, certainty (or uncertainty), propinquity (or remoteness), fecundity (i.e., the ability to generate another sensation of the same kind), purity (or the likelihood of its being followed by sensations of the opposite kind), and extent (determined by the number of persons experiencing it). The individual considering a certain action will calculate the prospective pleasure and/or pain to be derived and will decide so as to maximize the former and minimize the latter. "Men calculate," Bentham asserts, "some with less exactness, indeed, and some with more; but all men calculate."[4]

Bentham applies such a calculus to the reforming of the criminal code. All punishment itself is evil, therefore, the only rationale of punishment is that it promises to exclude some greater evil, such as a recurrence of the crime.[5] But since men calculate with varying degrees of exactness, who shall perform the computation in a practical, real case? Reflecting the atomism of the political thought of the age (which can be related to the Cartesian epistemology, since Descartes found truth in the most *solitary* act of man—thinking), Bentham could not recognize any entity above the individual (in our case, above the criminal): "every man is nearer to himself than he can be to any other man. . . ." And so he had to admit that "no other man can weigh for him his pains and pleasures."[6] It follows

3. Calvinism, as is well known, largely dispensed with the assumption of man's inherent freedom of choice. Man is "predestined." Perhaps this is why this and related faiths opened up an era of relative anarchy (relative to the Middle Ages). If man is "predestined" he can as well do whatever he wishes.

4. Jeremy Bentham, *An Introduction to the Principles of Morals and Legislation*, chap. 14, sec. 28.

5. Ibid., chap. 12, sec. 1.

6. Bentham, *Deontology: Or, The Science of Morality*, 1:18.

that a jury's sentence is hardly "scientific." Only the one who experiences pleasure and pain can judge.

This breakdown of Benthamism in the area of jurisprudence is paralleled by a similar breakdown in the field of public finance and welfare. Here the fiction of atomistic man as the sole judge (upon which all value theory is based) is a source of difficulties. A new actor is introduced, the state, but the theory cannot acknowledge it to be above the individual. Thought, then, becomes enmeshed in problems such as who can weigh another man's pains and pleasures in paying taxes and receiving benefits. Within the framework of economics nobody can, since economics recognizes no entity higher than the individual's consciousness. Attempts to get out of this impasse have made welfare theory a fertile field of contradictions and of fictional creations. I. M. D. Little might have detected this when he wrote, "I know of no serious attempts to test the realism of welfare theory, *perhaps because there are no obvious tests.*"[7]

Had Bentham advocated only utilitarianism, he would have gone down in history as the man for whom had already dawned Leibnitz' ideal day (when all men would solve their differences by sitting around a table saying, *"Calculemus"*). But in fact, Bentham had radical intellectual leanings. He provided a linguistic critique of knowledge which has been given systematic presentation by C. K. Ogden's *Bentham's Theory of Fictions.* In the light of this critique, it is not possible to think of Bentham as an enthusiastic and naïve follower of the Cartesian method. On the contrary, he emerges as its antagonist, the precursor of such determined foes of logic à outrance as Nietzsche, Kierkegaard, and Dewey, but a man who, like Kant and Nietzsche, saw that fictions are unavoidable.

Bentham's interest in fictions seems to have been aroused by his dislike for the law. In his *Fragment on Government,* he applauded the change of the legal medium from Latin to English, but despite this reform he found that "tautology, technicality, circuitry, irregularity, inconsistency remain. But above all, the pestilential breath of Fiction poisons the sense of every instrument it comes near."[8] What gives Bentham's work a universal character is that he rose above a narrow, dogmatic criticism of legal fictions: he ana-

7. *A Critique of Welfare Theory*, p. 4. Emphasis added.
8. C. K. Ogden, *Bentham's Theory of Fictions*, p. xvii (from *The Works of Jeremy Bentham*, 1:235).

lyzed the roots of fictions in political, scientific, and philosophical discourse. His theory is a tool to cope with the symbolic elements of language in all its ramifications.[9] And it had prophylactic power. It prevented him from taking seriously the mental products of the age, including his own "felicific calculus." The psychological roots of fictions he found in a well-known human tendency, which Francis Bacon had already emphasized: "What we are continually talking of, merely from our having been continually talking of it, we imagine we understand; so close a union has habit connected between words and things, that we take one for the other."[10] When laboratory experimentation is impossible, verbal repetition creates laws.

Let the magic "principle of diminishing returns" be alleged in explanation of a (mental) economic relation and the intellect is suddenly benumbed. This supposed principle has been talked of so often that it is seen as independent of both the phenomenon to be explained and of the conceiving mind. Constant repetition and a certain uncritical outlook have made it a veritable Pillars of Hercules of the mind. Bentham's theory of fictions clears up the confusion and renders every entity its due. All entities, he asserts, can be divided into "real" and "fictitious." A real entity is a substance the existence of which is made known to us by one or more of the senses. A fictitious entity is an object whose existence is "feigned by the imagination—*feigned* for the purpose of discourse—and which when so formed, is spoken of as a real one."[11] Bentham's distinction thus acknowledges that our tendency to give a material basis to purely psychic creations is partly caused by the sheer necessity of discourse. Language, he asserts, is unsuited to conveying modern legal, philosophical, and scientific subtleties.[12] It is as if our intellect and our interests had run ahead of the medium in which ideas must of necessity be expressed, a point which William James was to make later.[13]

Bentham acknowledges that fictions are unavoidable: fictitious entities could not be spoken of at all if they were not spoken of as real ones. We refer to them as if they were real, but we must not

9. Ogden, *Bentham's Theory of Fictions*, p. xxvii.
10. Ibid., p. xx (from *Works*, 10:74).
11. Ibid., pp. 10, 2. Emphasis added.
12. Ibid., p. cxxi.
13. See chap. 11.

think so in a literal sense.[14] Although language conspires to blur
the distinction between the fictive and the real, the critical intellect
must rise above this barrier, otherwise the results are catastrophic:
"lamentable have been the confusion and darkness produced by
taking the names of fictitious for real entities,"[15] Bentham writes,
echoing Locke. Confusion, error, dissension, hostility, and, above
all, unyielding dogmatism stem from this fundamental tendency to
give a material reality to the purely psychic. Bentham's own
"felicific calculus" would perhaps have generated less enthusiasm
among economists and less animosity among its critics had it been
understood in the light of his *Theory of Fictions*. Then, it might
have been judged as a practical fiction of great utility in reforming
the administration of justice along more humane lines, but not as a
reflection of the way men behave.

The confusion of words with things, abstractions with concrete
reality, fictitious with real entities is encouraged by conventional
logic. Logic claims to be an instrument for the attainment of knowledge, but Bentham, anticipating the nineteenth-century attack on
logic, says that in reality it has been unable to add "the smallest
particle of knowledge." By working outside a frame of reference
bounded by observation, experiment, and action, logic encourages
the sheer fabrication of words and symbols which are then related
to each other according to rules. Not only does this technique not
advance knowledge, but, given the dominance of Aristotle, it has
actually retarded it by preventing mankind from entering the "only
instructive track of study—Experience, Observation, Experiment,
Reflection."[16] The first three of the above "tracks," we may add,
have not been used by economic theorizing so that reflection could
only use psychic, not historical, entities as its raw material.

Next only to logic as a source of fictions is rhetoric, Adam
Smith's forte. Rhetoric is "a perpetual vein of nonsense, flowing
from a perpetual abuse of words. . . ."[17] It is an engine for the
creation of abstract phrases—the Court instead of judges, the Law
instead of lawyers, Property instead of rich men—all the more
dangerous because it deludes the people into accepting the dominance of the few as part of the Order of Nature. The effect of

14. Ogden, *Bentham's Theory of Fictions*, pp. 12, 16, 37 (from *Works*,
8:126, 198).
15. Ibid., p. lxiii.
16. Ibid., p. lxviii (from *Works*, 8:238–39).
17. Ibid., p. lxxii (from *Works*, 2:497).

such flowery language is to eliminate any unpleasant ideas the reader may have in regard to, say, rich men, by actually portraying them as non-concrete, spiritual, and thus venerable, everlasting, and worthy of respect.[18] In an analysis that would have greatly pleased Marx (had he been familiar with it), Bentham goes on to observe that the rhetorical fiction of property inculcates in the naïve reader the belief that this institution is natural, sacrosanct, and ordained by God, "as if man were made for property, not property for man. Many indeed have gravely asserted that the maintenance of property was the only end of government." Many were to assert it again repeatedly, including economists who acknowledged Bentham as their intellectual father. By the same token, "rights" are commonly understood to stand alone, to be above man-made law and above experience. They are spoken of as being "discovered" by the law. The truth is that a right is only a creature of the law, and hence an artificial creation of man. "A right without a law is an effect without a cause"—in order to create a right, one must first create a law. Not until Holmes' *The Common Law* (1881)—the product of the American revolt against formalism—did such an interpretation enter conventional legal thought.[19]

The critical aspect of Bentham's works hardly affected economics. As a methodology, it is opposed to Descartes, not only in its emphasis on the value of sense perception but also in its awareness that much that goes under the names of positive science is only a subjective creation. But Bentham suffered the fate of many geniuses; his ideas were sifted through the social consciousness of the age, sterilized, and made conventional. In point of fact, Bentham's theory of knowledge complements Marx' theory of ideology. The latter stressed the class origins of the fictions, the former their psychological and linguistic bases. Like Marx, Bentham peels off the surface of the conscious and looks for the bases—"the moral, the inward, the secret causes"—of the fictional mode of thinking. He finds them not only in the shortcomings of language but also in a general intellectual laziness that expresses itself in the preference for commonly used but deceptive metaphors. By their very nature, Bentham notes, fictions have little stability. They are vul-

18. *Works*, 9:76.
19. Legal fictions are still with us. They were the objects of at least three non-legal books in the 1930s alone. Thurman W. Arnold, *The Folklore of Capitalism*, and *The Symbols of Government*; and Edward S. Robinson, *Law and Lawyers*.

nerable to every speech and pamphlet and to other imaginative creations. When they cease to be useful they are discarded.

Just as many social contract theorists saw clearly the mythical nature of their own cogitation, so Bentham makes no mystery of the fictive character of his *Springs of Action.* He plainly says, "The words here employed as leading terms are names of so many *psychological entities,* mostly *fictitious,* framed by necessity for the purpose of discourse."[20] Thus, we find Bentham recognizing that fictions do not reflect reality but are nevertheless useful. And this realization is the difference between him and the more dogmatic Cartesians. He recognized fictions for what they were and was able to place them in the service of a higher ideal.

Unhappily, the tendency of the mind to reify pure categories of thought by constant repetition induced many readers to view pleasure and pain as two computers weighing, pondering, and solving equations. Keynes' criticism of Benthamism in the *General Theory* suggests how pervasive its influence has been in economics, but it is less a criticism of Bentham than of his admirers. They borrowed his pleasure/pain calculus because it fit their Cartesian molds. They christened it hedonism. The pernicious effects, the dissensions that Bentham had noted, followed as a matter of course. They are called "methodological disputes."

No other philosopher of the eighteenth century summarizes the two tendencies of the Enlightenment, the conservative and the radical, better than Kant. And it is exactly this quality of his thought that has given commentators so much difficulty in presenting his philosophy. Many have shied away from even considering the revolutionary element of his writings. Thus, P. F. Strawson admits that the German philosopher so often emphasized the belief that it is inherently impossible for man to know things as they are that we may be tempted to see the whole *Critique of Pure Reason* in this light. We may, that is, easily conclude that Kant sees "the whole model of mind-made nature as simply a device for presenting an analytical or conceptual inquiry in a form readily grasped by the picture-loving imagination." But to subscribe to such interpretation, Strawson continues, would entail "reading into much of the *Critique* a tone of at least half-conscious irony quite foreign to its char-

20. Ogden, *Bentham's Theory of Fictions,* p. cxiii (from *Works,* 1:205). Emphasis in the text.

acter."[21] This is not a very strong defense: Kant might very well have viewed human knowledge as largely imaginative and subjective and yet meant no irony by this. Moreover, Kant did see redeeming quality in man-made constructs, a quality which we who worship only "positive" science tend to ignore: Kant deemed fictions to be justified on ethical grounds.

A "balanced" interpretation of Kant is beyond the scope of this book and is, in any case, impossible. We are interested in emphasizing a few passages that show him as an early exponent of the viewpoint we are using to interpret the nature and evolution of economic theory.[22]

A flavor of Kant's radical theory of truth is obtained from the section entitled "The Ideal of Pure Reason" in *The Critique of Pure Reason*. There, after defining an idea as something "which exists only in the mind," Kant examines the question of the nature of God. He finds it to be a concept, a "transcendental ideal," in particular the embodiment of the idea of "all reality."[23] Reason has always needed a concept through which to bring unity into the manifold complexity of reality. The *idea* of God arose exactly to fulfill such a need. From this idea we can deduce all things. The medieval "chain of being" through which the lower led to the higher through the intermediate is probably the best-known example of the unifying power of the concept of God. Nevertheless, God is a mere concept and the concept-God is "a mere fiction."

Kant's interpretation of the origin of the concept of the deity immediately raises an intriguing point. In the beginning, Kant says, there was a need, the need to unify what, on the surface, is complex, chaotic, and apparently meaningless. Through many centuries, God proved to be an exceedingly useful unifying invention, both in natural thought (e.g., in cosmology) and in social thought (as in political philosophy, economics, and ethics). Later, battered by Averroist philosophy, Byzantine free-thinking, Renaissance naturalism, and innumerable other trends, the concept of God became more and more outmoded. But might it not be possible that some of the concepts that took the place of the idea of God are of exactly

21. *The Bounds of Sense: An Essay on Kant's Critique of Pure Reason*, p. 22. See also p. 35.
22. The reader who wishes to explore this facet of Kant's theory of knowledge may well start with Vaihinger, *The Philosophy of 'As If,'* esp. Part III, chaps. 1–4. Vaihinger is the founder of a journal on Kantian studies.
23. Kant, *The Critique of Pure Reason*, A580/B608.

the same nature? Might it not be that theology and science are two manifestations of the same need, using the same imaginative creations to explain the nature of the world around us? Kant was not averse to answering these questions positively (at least occasionally), but before turning to this aspect of his work, we call attention to another interesting observation of his. The mind, he asserts, as if uneasily cognizant that it has created God solely to satisfy a "base" emotional desire (for the desire for unity is lower than the desire for truth), immediately attempts to provide dogmatic proofs of the objective reality of its own idea (God). In the end what was a "mere idea," albeit a useful one, is hypostatized. God the idea becomes God the Father. The concept is personified, it is given reality independently of, and prior to, the thinking mind. But even in this hypostatization (this "natural illusion"), Kant sees something desirable: it frees the mind from doubts which would otherwise paralyze its creativity.

Equaling the heuristic value of the idea of God as an organizer of reality is its ethical value, since, together with the notions of soul, eternal reward and punishment, and so on, it encourages men to live morally. Thus, the idea of God proves as useful as a principle of behavior as it does as a principle of truth. In both the realm of ethics and the realm of (medieval) science, God (the idea) is a force defeating anarchy. The theme that we should act "as if" there were a Supreme Being who kept an account of our actions is developed in *The Critique of Practical Reason*. It led priests and ministers to name their dogs after the German philosopher.

As Strawson suggests, it is possible to interpret the whole of Kant's theory of ideas along the lines of these theological considerations. In the section "The Discipline of Pure Reason in Respect to Hypotheses" in the first *Critique*, Kant distinguishes between "hypotheses" and "rational concepts." Only the former are based on the certainty of *perceived* reality.[24] "Rational concepts" instead are "mere ideas," "regulative principles of pure reason." They are rules for the understanding to follow. They serve reason as a canon of usage and are capable, not so much of enabling reason to gain cognition of objects, but of furnishing it with a framework within which phenomena can be squeezed. Many of the basic ideas of enlightened philosophers in political and social matters could perhaps be regarded as "regulative principles," providing thought with

24. Ibid., A770/B798.

beacon lights. The very intuition that life can be interpreted mechanistically is a heuristic idea of great value for the organization and systematic presentation of thought.

The ultimate value of these regulative principles is pragmatic: "Reason has, in respect of its *practical employment,* the right to postulate what in the field of mere speculation it can have no kind of right to assume without sufficient proof."[25]

The Cartesian split between subject and object now becomes the dichotomy of theory versus practice. The standards of truth that satisfy the latter do not satisfy the former.

This insight is very important for an accurate understanding of economics. Even economic theory is actually a practical branch of study. It, therefore, takes some liberties with the "field of mere speculation," namely logic. (Locke, as will be recalled, made the same point.) Milton Friedman might have understood this when he insisted that economics can and should make unrealistic assumptions, the important thing being the practical applications of a theorem. The emphasis on practice suggests that economics is a practical not a merely speculative science, and, as such, it may well start from axioms that would not pass the more stringent tests demanded of true speculation.[26]

In the "Appendix to the Transcendental Dialectic," Kant stresses again the regulative use of the ideas of pure reason.[27] These ideas have the "excellent" purpose of directing the understanding: like highways, one may say, they allow one to go through a country swiftly, but the one who follows them will gain no understanding of the country. Employing this insight, we may say that the notion of the Invisible Hand is an example of practical fiction: it did not originate from even the most superficial observation of reality. It is rather a "standpoint," a "mere idea," whose justification lies elsewhere than in "reflecting" reality. The belief that society has been arranged for the purpose of achieving justice and order gives meaning and direction to public policy, allowing policy to orient itself in the otherwise chaotic reality. Moreover, on an intellectual plane, from the postulated harmony of interests, Smith derives the laws of exchange, at least in an embryonic form, and the existence of what came later to be called Say's Law. Through

25. Ibid., A776/B804. Emphasis in the text.
26. Milton Friedman, *Essays in Positive Economics,* esp. part I.
27. *The Critique of Pure Reason,* A643/B671 ff.

these discoveries, the value of the original fiction is enhanced, for it suggests very strongly that the regulations of the Mercantilist state are not only unnecessary but positively harmful. Ethically, the fiction of harmony portrays an ideal: the same ideal that Marx found lacking in his day but saw emerging in the future.

Whether fictions coincide with reality (whether they are true in the common-sense meaning of the word) is a trivial question to the moralist. What matters is the power of fictions to shape behavior. Monotheism obviously wrought profound changes in society. In the face of these changes, it is picayune to worry whether the idea of the one God is true or false. Likewise the moralist does not worry whether Smith's notion of the Invisible Hand is a true portrayal of reality. He is satisfied with its power to influence politics.

It is probably a measure of Kant's own intellectual greatness and self-discipline that, toward the end of his studies, he turned his criticism against his own peculiar creation, the thing-in-itself. Originally conceived as the stable reality behind the "appearances," in the *Posthumous Papers* (published in 1881–84), Kant held it, too, to be a "mere thought-entity," a "standpoint," a "point of view" only "subjective" and "ideal" whose value must be sought elsewhere than in adherence with reality.[28]

With Kant, the mind, freed by Descartes from its subjugation to the world of sense-data and from religious authority, turned against itself. Kant recognized the contradiction of denigrating reality and, at the same time, appealing to it for confirmation of its creations. In an act of intellectual courage, he resolutely faced this contradiction and refused to subscribe to the fiction of the "copy theory" of truth. But his critical idealism was ignored. He himself wrote that he was a hundred years ahead of his times. Immediate acceptance of his critical standpoint, as acceptance of Bentham's, would have paralyzed the new disciplines and intellectual creations which, instead, proceeded with the boldness characteristic of the young.

While Bentham and Kant acknowledged that fictions could be useful and even desirable (if they serve a moral purpose), Mill strove to eliminate them from correct thinking. Writing two centuries after Descartes, he could survey the excesses of abstract thinking. His uneasiness about the method of the ego led him to set up innum-

28. Vaihinger, *The Philosophy of 'As If,'* pp. 313–18.

erable warning signs in the path of thought, warnings that he, like all Cartesians, found impossible to follow in his more practical works.

Truth, Mill asserts in his *System of Logic*, is known to us in two ways: directly, or through some other medium. A directly grasped truth is one that stems from the consciousness of the individual. Whatever consciousness makes clear is known beyond the possibility of question.[29] Does the ego reflect an object external to the mind? Mill knows that thought can conceive non-existent beings (as mythology, fables, and states of nature do), so he warns that by thought is to be understood what passes in the mind itself, and not any object external to the mind. The conventional dualism thus reappears: thoughts are separated from sensations. The former may be conceived without any object exciting them (1:55, 56). Not only is the mind free from dependence on matter, but matter provides no test of the validity of our ideas, for all we know of objects are the ideas we have of them. This view, Mill asserts, unites Kant, Berkeley, and Locke. It is tantamount to a reassertion of the tendency of thought to "contemplate itself," rather than the world outside (1:65).

To slide into the easy belief that thought reflects reality, Mill severely warns, is the source of a whole "tribe of errors." Only by an "illicit assumption" can subjective ideas be mistaken for objective facts, "laws of the percipient mind for laws of the perceived object, properties of the ideas or conceptions for properties of the things conceived." A large proportion of erroneous thinking has this root: that the same order must obtain among the objects in nature which obtains among our ideas of them (2:315). This disposition to hypostatize concepts ("to suppose that what is true of our ideas of things must be true of the things themselves") is actually a lowly intellectual vice or superstition, comparable to the belief that the devil will appear if you talk about him.

Like Bentham, Mill finds that the tendency to present an argument by stressing analogies between the phenomenon investigated and a more familiar one is the mark of the unimaginative and narrow-minded person. "Metaphors, for the most part . . . assume the proposition which they ought to prove." They dull the reader's critical powers by their being poetical (2:377–78). Moreover, inso-

29. John Stuart Mill, *A System of Logic, Ratiocinative and Inductive,* 1:5–6.

far as an idea is metaphorically related to a fact, the objectivity of the latter is transferred to the former.

Mill did not appreciate, as Bentham did, the inevitability and usefulness of metaphorical thinking. He did not grasp that, faced by the new and perhaps the inherently unknowable, wedded to the attainment of ultimate knowledge through "clear and distinct" ideas, the only option open to the mind is to bring the new under the rubrica of what, by being old and familiar through repetition, we think we understand. Economic theory is full of analogies, no less today than a century ago; indeed all economic "occurrences" (which really "occur" in the mind and are only alleged to belong to the realm of men) are explained as the result of "forces" through an analogy with the phenomena of mechanics. To this day, elementary and advanced theory textbooks are crammed with diagrams indicating the "direction" of "forces" by the use of vectors.[30] It was not a puerile desire to imitate the "more successful" physical disciplines that forced such analogy on a large scale, but rather the adoption of the method of Descartes. Such were his standards of truth that only by recasting a phenomenon in the peculiar language of the mind, that is, by assimilating it into mathematical molds, would it be "understood."

The erroneous metaphysical belief that "a thing conformable to the idea must really exist" is the "cause of two-thirds of the bad philosophy . . . which the human mind has never ceased to produce" (2:319–20). Nor is this fallacy the monopoly of philosophers, for scientists, too, are often its victims. For instance, Mill notes, Newton was so impressed by the Cartesian a priori that "a thing cannot act where it is not" that he deemed it necessary "to invent" a material substance, the ether, to justify and make possible action at a distance of the sun on the planets. Actually, it is probable that the great scientist knew that ether was only a word, a name for "nothing," whose existence was required exactly by the metaphysical considerations noted by Mill. Accordingly, it was not Newton but more conventional scientific and philosophical minds that hypostatized the word "ether."

Mill's *System of Logic* contains radical seeds. He clearly saw the schism between the psychic world and the material. He saw

30. These vectors ignore one of the characteristics of the vectors of physics, i.e., the *duration* of motion. They only portray *direction*, and that is always toward equilibrium.

that the mind had no moorings and that a large amount of theorizing was fictive. He ridiculed those who "by watching and contemplating these ideas of [their] own making . . . read in them what takes place in the world without" (2:326). But he was like a man throwing stones in a glass house, for he did not understand that the source of the "errors" and "abstractions" was the split of ideas "in the mind" from objects "outside" to which he, too, subscribed. Like Bentham, Mill saw certain political consequences of excessive reliance on concepts produced by "inner consciousness." Being frozen and lifeless, such concepts subtly inculcate a belief that "human nature and society will forever revolve in the same orbit, and exhibit essentially the same phenomena." The opposite is rather true, so that a theory of society "best expressive . . . of the general result of observation" should stress change and temporal sequence (2:366), a statement which elevates Marxian economics as much as it condemns static, conventional theory.

Another important fallacy is noted by Mill, that of asserting a proposition to be true with a qualification, but then losing sight of the qualification in the conclusion. Scholarly thought provides many examples of this fallacy. The qualifications and special assumptions of the perfectly competitive model are familiar to all economists. But they are easily forgotten and the conclusions of the theory are transferred to reality without qualifications. Thus, the model is alleged to "prove" the advantages of atomistic competition, the impossibility of planning, etc. The fallacy of neglecting the qualifications in the conclusion of an argument, Mill relates to the error of hypostatization: what is true only in the realm of mental relations, where subtle qualifications can be made and reality can be suspended, becomes "true absolutely" because of the error of assuming that everything thought of exists somewhere or in some form. It is an error, Mill warns, that very frequently mars reasoning on politics and society (2:384 ff.).

These considerations throw light on Mill's view of the method of economics as expressed in the 1830 essay "On the Definition of Political Economy; and on the Method of Investigation Proper to It." Economic theory does not deal with "the whole of man's nature." It views man "solely as a being who desires to possess wealth, and who is capable of judging of the comparative efficacy of means for attaining that end. . . . It makes entire abstraction of every other human passion or motive; except those which may be regarded as perpetually antagonizing principles to the desire of wealth, namely, aversion to labour, and desire of the present enjoyment of costly indulgences." Does such a being exist? No, says Mill, and no political economist "was ever so absurd as to suppose that mankind are really thus constituted." The laws derived from this abstract method must then be interpreted as true only in this society of non-existent beings. Political economy "aims at showing what is the course of action into which mankind, living in a state of society, *would* be impelled, *if* that motive, except in the degree in which it is checked by the two perpetual counter-motives above adverted to, *were* absolute ruler of all their actions."[31] Mill further clarifies the nature of the economic method by distinguishing between the modes of thinking of the "practicals" and of the "theorists." He conveys his ideas analogically. Faced with the question "Are absolute kings likely to use their power for the welfare or for the oppression of their subjects?" the practicals would draw conclusions from an examination of the conduct of actual monarchs in history. But the theorists (who can be identified with the builders of economics) "would contend that an observation of the tendencies which human nature has manifested in the variety of situations in which human beings have been placed, and especially observation of what passes in our own minds, warrants us in inferring that a human being in the situation of despotic king will make a bad use of power; and that this conclusion would lose nothing of certainty even if absolute kings *had never existed,* or if history furnished with no information of the manner in which they conducted themselves."[32] This explication of the way of thinking of the theorist is somewhat confused: Mill's theorist seems to refer to experience ("an observation of the tendencies which human nature has manifested in a variety of institutions . . ."). But this empiricism cannot be taken too seriously. It cannot represent an important part of the method used to ascertain the behavior of kings. Why should one examine a multiplicity of men in different institutions to answer a query specifically pertaining to the behavior of one class of men in one institution only? The zoologist who wants to study the behavior of cockroaches and can do so would not dream of studying

31. John Stuart Mill, *Essays on Some Unsettled Questions of Political Economy,* pp. 137–38. Emphasis added. This essay is also quoted verbatim in *A System of Logic,* vol. 2, book 4, chap. ix, para. 4.

32. Mill, *Essays,* pp. 142–43. Emphasis added.

monkeys, whales, lizards, and spiders, although he recognizes that they are animals.

Mill's other source of truth is the true and only one. It is "especially observation of what passes in our own minds" that allows us to infer that despotic kings are oppressive. This testament of faith in man's ability to detect and confess to himself his own evil tendencies is very charming. It is the naïveté to which the axiom of a rational ego led: surely, if man is rational, his own soul is an open book. The axiomatic nature of the whole argument is given away in the last part of the quotation. The conclusion that despotic kings make bad use of their power would not be impugned even if absolute kings had never existed. Just as ideas held with Cartesian clarity would be true even in a dream, so Mill's conclusion that despotic kings are bad is true even if kings belonged to the same realm of reality as witches. Everybody knows that beings riding on broomsticks and meeting around a "charmed pot" do not exist, and yet everybody also knows that they *are* evil. Similarly, Mill is saying, though despotic kings may never have existed, they *are* bad. Indeed, given the meaning of "despotic," this is so by definition, while at least the evil nature of witches is rooted in the tradition and lore of many lands. Transferred to economic theorizing, Mill's argument thus becomes "Economic man desires wealth, even though such a man does not exist." One who is unaware of Mill's Cartesian ancestry might conclude that the only justification for his argument is Seneca's dictum *Nullum exstitit magnum ingenium sine aliqua dementia* (no great genius exists without a touch of madness).

The seventeenth-century paternity of economics accounts for the major characteristics of that discipline: its tautological nature, its divorce from the empirical, its axiomatic quality, its atomism, its total neglect of what may be called the "realm of chance," and its clear bias in favor of certainty and necessity (for mathematics can leave nothing to chance). Following the Cartesian method, economics was able to proceed through the social universe with lightning speed. But it also absorbed the weaknesses and contradictions of Cartesianism, the most important of which was its aspiration to explain the whole of reality without even looking at it. Paradoxically, Descartes' rationalism became the irrationalism of "cast my eyes away that I may see better." Just as man created an anthropomorphic God, so Cartesian man—all-rational, all-knowing, all-calculating—created an egocentric world, a world spun out of orderly mathematical relations, mechanistic reactions, and predictable results. Ethically Cartesianism created a world of exquisitely balanced justice of which, in economics, the marginal theory of distribution is the epitome.

Thanks to the sway of the geometrical method, thinking retained that unity which in previous centuries the Revealed Word had provided and which in later centuries would be lost. But this unity was purchased at the price of applying to life those categories and forms of reasoning which are more useful in understanding the lifeless. Extension, quantity, number do succeed in explaining inert matter and its laws of composition. Thinking naturally runs spatially and mathematically, perhaps because (as Bergson suggests) it has been formed largely in man's relation with matter: "Put one of those little cork dolls with leaden feet in any posture, lay it on its back, turn it upon its head, throw it into the air; it will always stand itself up again, automatically. So likewise with matter: we can take it by any end and handle it in any way, it will always fall back into some one of our mathematical formulae, because it is weighted with geometry."[33] Matter flows into our mathematical mental grooves and has no way of rebelling against our way of handling it. The movements of the heavenly bodies can be explained by such opposed formulae as Ptolemy's, Newton's, and Einstein's. Only minute *observation* tells us that one formula is superior to the others.

But matter and life are not identical: matter is moderately stable;[34] life is flux. Being stable, matter can be viewed independently of time; life cannot. Matter can be uprooted from the whole and treated as an independent entity; man cannot. Matter has no will of its own; man does. Matter has no consciousness and so its behavior is repetitious: electrons circled the nucleus even in Pericles' days. Not so with man's behavior. Yet following the Cartesian method, the intellect treated life, including economic life, as it treated matter. It viewed life as stable; it uprooted it from its time-space continuum; and it dealt with men as if they were will-less.

33. Henri Bergson, *Creative Evolution*, p. 240.
34. It is interesting that mathematics is of little assistance in those branches of the physical sciences where matter is not stable, e.g., in meteorology.

This outlook has been called mechanistic. When we attempt to apply its framework to encompass life, "we feel the frames cracking," as Bergson says. We become vaguely and uncomfortably aware that mechanicism deceives us in direct proportion to its scientific trappings. This is implicitly recognized by economists who, in practical writings like the reports of the Council of Economic Advisers, in congressional testimonies, and in industrial and trade monographs, abandon nine-tenths of the unbelievable complexities of their craft, those mechanistic "nuts and bolts" that comprise the universe of discourse of economic theory. That notorious *pons asinorum* of the beginning student—the distinction between the movement along and the shift of the function—is unceremoniously ignored. The distinction between independent and dependent variables is not considered. We hear nothing of elasticities. The whole field of "real" economics is neglected. And whatever is left of economic theory after these surgical operations have been performed carries the mind up to a point. Soon the economist has to appeal to common sense, and even use concepts and relationships that never entered economic theory, such as capacity utilization, mark-up pricing, or the Dow-Jones stock averages. Faced with life, the economist has to ignore a large part of mechanistic thinking and bend the remainder along the sinuosities of life aided by the common sense available to the layman.

In his practical work the theorist senses that the logical-deductive method is to life what the tangent is to the curve. We would expect deduction (primarily an operation of the mind) to be most successful in the study of the mind itself (i.e., in psychology) and in the study of those forms of behavior where thought is the precondition for action, e.g., in economics or politics. But the opposite is true: it is exactly in psychology and in the social sciences that deduction proves to be a feeble guide, while in the study of the thoughtless (minerals, celestial bodies, molecules) mathematical deduction, aided by observation, triumphs. Does this not suggest that deduction is an operation governed by the properties of the lifeless which are not the properties of the living?[35]

Cartesianism treated social reality as if it were lifeless. Objective reality is movement and even chaos. But a sleight-of-hand transformed it into stillness and order. Cartesianism, when it reflected on its own work at all, did acknowledge that reality (the *mundus*

35. Ibid., p. 233.

sensibilis, as it was called) confronts us with often unintelligible change. But higher than it and more real still was the *mundus intelligibilis,* the intellectual world. This hierarchical view is not so very different from that which dominated intellectual discussions in the Middle Ages. And just as in the Age of Faith the energies of scholars were largely devoted to the study of theology (the hidden kingdom), so in the Age of Reason intellectuals were naturally drawn to the study of the "more real"—that which lies "behind" the phenomenal world. The mundus intelligibilis was a world created by the intellect. Once intellect—under the aegis of the Cartesian epistemology—recognized the essence of all things to be quantity and extension, the way was clear to linking these "things" (which in reality were only verbal symbols) with each other in a geometrical fashion. Few among the architects of rationalism doubted that, in entering more and more deeply into the world of mind-made symbols, they were thereby also explaining the mundus sensibilis. Most thinkers assumed that this was so as a matter of course. And who could impugn their conviction? The world, after all, speaks to us only through our interpretations. We are as deeply reliant on our world view as we are on the oxygen around us. The one who has been brought up with a heavy dose of Marxism will easily detect the economic ("real") factor "behind" the Protestant Reformation, Shakespeare, and the impressionist school of painting; he will interpret the character and troubles of Willy Loman (of Miller's *Death of a Salesman*), of Gregor Samsa (of Kafka's *The Metamorphosis*), and of Cinderella as the result of economic exploitation; and he will see the dialectic at work in the germination of seeds and in the development of mathematics. The object (the Reformation, Loman, or seeds) does not complain at being so interpreted in Marxian-deterministic terms. The same inability to escape his own categories is the characteristic of the Cartesian. Man's intellect is "the measure of all things" created by man, as Descartes knew.[36]

From the standpoint of explaining the realities of life, it was indeed regrettable that the "positive" skepticism of Bentham and Kant was ignored. But what was lost by social science (whose sole aim should be to explain the world) was gained by ethics and art, as we shall illustrate later.

36. See chap. 2.

The standpoint of economic theory is, then, Cartesian. Geometric fictions are the *termini a quo* analysis starts: the propensity to truck and barter, diminishing returns, the balancing of pleasures and pains are all idea-bound, unempirical conceptions. Fictional, also, are those contrivances of thought that allow economic theory to surmount obstacles in its path and to carry on its derivations. The Marshallian notion of "effectively constant real income" must be viewed as an ingenious and, on the whole, successful invention (similar to Newton's ether) to overcome obstacles in the way of pure thought. And thus the same epistemology that explains the origins of economic theory also explains its dynamics and development. Wholly self-reliant in the production of its axioms, the ego also provides the power to keep itself going. Since it has no goal external to itself (the betterment of mankind, the explanation of reality), it turns inward and strives toward self-perfection. Its highest aspiration is to create a "well-rounded" system, or "model," whose qualities will be symmetry, internal consistency, simplicity, economy of axioms, and "elegance." Forced by its epistemology to "contemplate itself," the rationalistic mind acquires a narcissistic quality. It sets basically esthetic goals for itself.

Striving, however, is not necessarily followed by success. In fact, the ego's products have certain qualities that make them singularly unfit to reach perfection. First, as Locke noted and as we showed in our example of the administration of justice, they tend to be self-contradictory. Second, as we shall see later, their very mathematical nature creates special problems and inconsistencies. Third, as Bentham pointed out, being unrelated to anything material, fictions are basically very vulnerable creations. No sooner are they discovered than some intellect will delight in knocking them down. The goal of perfection is never given up, however. Every setback only stimulates higher intellectual flights.

This process of refining and perfecting tools of expression is familiar to students of certain fields of intellectual endeavor. Just as familiar is the result: the progressive refining of means stifles content, the philosophy and the ethical-political *meaning* of a work or system of thought. Some forms of literature, for instance, display such lavish care on stylistic modes and techniques that content is almost smothered. This has occurred, notably, in some of the seventeenth-century so-called metaphysical poets (apparently, men of letters have recognized the *metaphysical* quality of their seventeenth-century ancestors) whose poems were sometimes mere vehicles for elaborate conceits. Another example may be provided by Paul Verlaine, whose primary interest in musical, sensual combinations of words led him to a deliberate deemphasis of content. Architecture provides a similar example. In the Renaissance its techniques aimed at serving man or God. Later, techniques acquired a life of their own and architecture entered the rococo stage. Technical virtuosity to the exclusion of anything else is also apparent in certain musical schools. So strong is the power of the medium to suffocate the substance of thought that, in the arts and in literature, we practically define a genius as one who is able to bend the literary or artistic medium to his own purposes. If this definition of genius is correct, one is forced to conclude that between Smith and Keynes conventional economics had no geniuses. As we shall show, the very problems that economists studied were determined and defined by the mathematical method. What was not amenable to being handled by that method was simply ignored.

Smith's economics was part of a system of morality. He was concerned with the end, the purpose, the ethical values of society, and was not averse to shaping them. Within a few generations, however, the medium wrested itself from these goals, acquired a life of its own, and became a collection of techniques. Economists came to view their work as the forging of "tools" divorced from ends or even meaning. The remarkable thing is that there is absolutely no break in the movement of economics away from content toward contentless techniques. No single economist can be credited with turning away from Smith's concerns. The flight was progressive, continuous, and practically imperceptible. Economic theory *non facit saltum*. Does this not prove that the perfecting of techniques stemmed from the dynamics of the ego?

And how could this have been otherwise? In addition to the already emphasized qualities of rationalistic Cartesianism, another factor contributed to the progressive neglect of content. The very ethics and substance of economics was, from its beginning, inherently shallow, collapsing to the proposition that money-making is the great hinge holding society together. Just as a strong-willed individual often stifles the personality of a weakling mate, so the marriage between geometry, which is a powerful, creative, swift medium of expression, and economics left no room for the development of the philosophy itself.

The original means employed for the expression of ideas (the physiocrats' *tableau œconomique* and Smith's rhetorical fictions) were primitive. But they held the promise of refinement which eventually came with Ricardo's arithmetic tables and ratios, with differential calculus, difference equations, input-output tables, "simulations," etc. Trying to "cash in" the promises of the mathematical medium arrested the development of the vision, of the substance of economic theory, which remained unchanged for a century and a half (abstracting from Marx' and Veblen's contributions which were a reaction to this state of affairs). The explanation for this growing dominance of means illustrates another vicious circle of rationalistic thought. The philosophy itself held little promise of development (indeed many economists were uneasy and not a little ashamed of such creations as the "economic man," and perhaps this is why they asserted that such an animal does not exist). So intellectual energies were devoted to the impossible task of achieving perfection of means and techniques. The ethical essence was more and more ignored, occasionally resurfacing only because of dissenters' criticism, and then only to be disavowed. The lopsided development of content and form the reader will recognize as a by-product of the uneven importance accorded objective reality in the subject-object equation of Cartesianism.

The archetypal forms of thought that have no object but themselves are logic and mathematics. And they are the oldest areas of systematic study of Western man. As Bentham recognized, any science that relies too heavily on them runs the risk of being emptied of meaning by them. In the physical sciences (which also use the mathematical medium of expression), this has not happened because matter (the object) has exercised a counterbalancing power to mathematics: experiments are made with things and observation of things plays a role. But in economic theory, experimentation was purely conceptual and imaginative (recall Condorcet's, Lamettrie's, and Hume's "let us suppose"). Thus, economics progressively shed its own substance and ethics and became mere form—viz., mathematics.

From an esthetic point of view this was good. Opera-goers are seldom bothered by their inability to understand the language of the libretto. They may even thank their ignorance because they know that the words, the plot are shallow, superficial nonsense. Yet the overwhelming attention given the medium of analysis subtly influenced the outlook of the economist. Under the sway of the infinitesimally small, for instance, thought became oversubtle. It was blind to the most obvious factors of social change; these were considered "data" and hence were left unexplored. Sometimes the effects are humorous. Fisher, the foremost authority on financial markets in America, assuaged the fears caused by the first stock market tremors in October 1929 by asserting that the economy was inherently strong, that thanks to prohibition, labor productivity was soon to go up.[37] Presumably, abstemiousness eliminates the adverse effects of a Monday-morning hangover with therapeutic effects throughout the economic body.

And yet everyone knows that economic theory did influence the economic policies of many countries (though not as much as is commonly thought). Does this not show that the web of ideas that make up economic theory is correct? This conclusion, though fairly common, is nevertheless inaccurate. That the success of a certain action proves the correctness of the underlying theory is the epistemological equivalent of the moral dictum that "might makes right." The nineteenth century saw in practically every Western nation a blossoming of racial theories stressing the innate intellectual and moral superiority of the white man and his "burden" to civilize the "lesser races." These theories stimulated far-reaching political action which was eminently successful in enabling England to extend its political dominion over 4½ million square miles, France over 3½ million, Germany over 1 million, and Belgium over 900,000 square miles.[38] But few scholars today would maintain that the racial theories that supported imperialist expansion represented a correct understanding and evaluation of the white vis-à-vis other races. Nations, like men, may be moved to action by beliefs which they may later find erroneous, if they are fortunate. The history of practical intellectual creations is little more than the history of errors.

Constructs of social thought that add nothing to our understanding of reality have clear advantages over genuine understanding in promoting political action. True understanding is, by its very nature, aware of the possibility of many interactions and reciprocal relationships to which narrow rationalism is blind. Admitting the

37. John Kenneth Galbraith, *The Great Crash: 1929*, p. 102.
38. Carlton J. H. Hayes, *A Generation of Materialism*, p. 237. The figures cover the period 1871–1900.

possibility of everything, true intellect is not dogmatic and often leads, therefore, to an unpolitical paralysis of action.

Dogmatic and simplistic schemes free the mind from these shackles and facilitate action. Not only has Kant recognized this characteristic of "practical" (fictive) thought, but Keynes, too, detected its existence and usefulness. Decision-making, he wrote, rests on the false assumption that tomorrow will be like today, that the institutions and values of society will remain as we now know (or misunderstand) them.[39] Nietzsche was even more explicit: "I am convinced that *the most erroneous assumptions are precisely the most indispensable for us,* that without granting the validity of the logical *fiction* [that the world of logic captures *Existenz*] . . . man could not live: and that the negation of this fiction is equivalent to the negation of life itself."[40]

All creations of the mind, regardless of how they arise, crave to be reunited with the real. Even the most idealistic system of thought has practical implications. Everyone is, at heart, a pragmatist. Mathematics, whose development owes nothing to observation of the ways of nature, eventually builds bridges and fortifications. Tools, once born, want to be put to use. Thought systems, once hypostatized, become the framework within which actions are taken. Their raison d'être lies in enabling man to tamper with reality. Thus the seventeenth-century epistemological chasm leads to another conflict, that between understanding and manipulating. Just as fictions (e.g., the conspiracy view of history) are created in politics for the sole purpose of facilitating certain actions, so Cartesian rationalism unwittingly created an economic world that deflects understanding from its true object but that is eminently suited to encourage behavior by its dogmatism and mock precision. That nineteenth-century economic practice was based on classical theory proves the correctness of that theory as much as imperialistic adventures prove the correctness of the racial theories on which they were based. And the record of economic policies, for whatever it is worth, is not as good as the imperialist record. Periodic crises have continued to plague capitalism, crises which economists, despite their aspirations, have been no more successful in forecasting and controlling than anybody else. This mixed record has been recently

39. See chap. 13.
40. Quoted by Vaihinger, *Philosophy of 'As If,'* p. 354. Emphasis in the text.

documented by Friedman and Schwartz' study of Federal Reserve policy.[41] But their explanation for the central bank's indifferent stabilization record is erroneous. Central bankers are not incompetent: they are economists.

In this and in the preceding chapter we have reviewed the two aspects of the seventeenth-century epistemological background, the dogmatic and the critical. Both are necessary to attain a true understanding of the nature and development of economic theory. It is to dogmatic Cartesianism that economic theory owes its birth and from which it inherited its qualities. Critical Cartesianism (the writings of Bentham and Kant and the doubts of Locke) provides us with a number of insights into the true nature and dynamics of theory. Alternatively, one may say that dogmatic Cartesianism explains why economists followed the method they did to achieve their intended goal (i.e., the explanation of economic reality). It is critical Cartesianism, supplemented by the views on the nature of knowledge of some nineteenth-century philosophers, that exposes the true methodology of the dogmatic Cartesians and shows that they actually attained goals that (to paraphrase Adam Smith) "were not part of their original intentions."

Behind all of economics stands the peculiar creation of Descartes, the ego. Its qualities are the qualities of economics. The ego was a mathematical *enfant prodige*. So was the economics fathered by the physiocrats (recall the tableau œconomique), by Locke and Hume, and brought to an ephemeral "perfection" first by J. S. Mill, later by the marginalists, and later yet by the neo-classical synthesizers. The ego had the boundless aspiration to uncover the secrets of nature and man. The ambition of economists was to discover the laws of distribution, production, exchange, population growth, etc. The ego was necessarily dogmatic about its abilities. And so were economists in their pronouncements. The ego was eternal; it had been slumbering in man since the Creation, though only in the seventeenth century had it been discovered and exploited. Economists, too, claimed to be able to attain eternal truth, independent of space and time. The ego was above the storms of passions. Economic theory was unaffected by whatever political pre-

41. Milton Friedman and Anna Jacobson Schwartz, *Monetary History of the United States: 1867–1960.*

conceptions the theorist had. The ego was stability. It created the supreme embodiment of stability, equilibrium.

The ego's qualities were eventually attributed even to the subjects of economics; indeed, this is the inevitable result of hypostatizing economic theorems. The ego's omniscience became the "perfect foresight" of the entrepreneur. Its mathematical bent became a quality of every economic agent who computed with lightning speed. Its "aloofness" (because it was above passions) became the stoicism of economic agents whom nothing could deter from taking a course of action other than the one dictated by a statistically weighted calculation of pains and pleasures.

But the ego does not exist and thus one may say that, *on a logical level*, economic theory does not exist. As a fact of history and as a force of civilization, it owes its existence to the perfectly human error of supposing that anything spoken of exists. Created by actual men who were hardly possessed of divine attributes, born of the erroneous separation between thinking and observing, economic theory, *on a logical basis*, is a congery of logical errors: hypostatizations, false analogies, neglect of qualifications in the conclusions, the error of subsuming heterogeneous elements under one mind-bound symbol. These very errors provided the fuel for the development of economic theory. Just as a humble grain of sand entering the *maleagrina margaritifera* is presently converted into a beautiful pearl, so what starts as a "hunch," a vision, an apparently trivial intuition (whose psychological bases must forever remain a mystery), when bathed by the psychic juices of the extralogical mind, emerges as a monumental system of arresting quality. For a century and a half, economics followed these extralogical principles of the mind, mistaking them for the principles of objective reality.

In the light of these remarks, we may lay out the plan of the following chapters. Stemming from the Cartesian ego, economics has been propelled by the tendency of means to perfect themselves. Accordingly, four stages can be distinguished in the development of economics. The first is pre-Cartesian and represents the "realm of matter." This confused, policy-oriented, often unintelligible stage is represented by Mercantilist thought, with which we have dealt. It was eminently realistic in its emphasis on power, a fact of political life. Economic theory as such did not exist; arguments existed, and they were a mixture of intuition and self-interest pleading. At best, economics was the handmaiden of the state, a means for the attainment of higher ends. This stage of development was guided by Bacon's warning: "Matter rather than forms should be the object of our attention."[42]

The Cartesian promise of certainty stood in stark contrast to the confusion of reality. And it was instrumental in causing a revulsion against economic matter. The confused analyses of Mercantilist economics obviously did not meet the standards of "clearness and distinctness" of ideas. With the assistance of the new method of derivations, the Gordian knot of the balance of trade problem was cut and the specie-flow mechanism emerged, its dazzling clarity standing in stark contrast to the inept discussions and murky conclusions of the Mercantilists. For the next century the method of economics faithfully followed Cartesianism, its political content, its substance becoming fainter and fainter because thought was rapidly moving away from reality. This is the phase of classical economics.

Formalistic thought, borrowing little or nothing from reality, has the remarkable characteristic of maintaining itself "pure" and self-sufficient for centuries. Certain basic tricks of thought (to be examined later) will ensure enough raw material for such thought to keep itself busy. Economics between 1870 and 1930 attained near perfection of tools in the stage that we shall call hyperclassicism.

It had its grandeur but also its weaknesses, the greatest of which was that even the most clear-minded economists of the period misunderstood the very method they were using. An inadequate appreciation of the epistemologic roots of their thinking made them feel that they were explaining the world. By the 1930s it became impossible to uphold this view as matter suddenly and forcefully reasserted its sway.

Just as a revolution is often necessary to overthrow parties and constitutions, means which have grown to suffocate the very ends they were supposed to serve, so a "revolution" in the realm of ideas was necessary to dethrone hyperclassicism. Keynes effected this methodological revolution. He brought conventional economics as

42. Francis Bacon, *New Organon*, Book I, aphorism 50. The same aphorism starts with the sentence "The human understanding is of its own nature prone to abstractions and gives substance and reality to things which are fleeting."

close to matter as it has ever been, before or since. Form once
again was made subservient to ends. Economics became holistic
and, as in Mercantilism, a tool to serve higher social ends. The use
of mathematics was denigrated, the realm of chance was greatly
enlarged, the science/art dichotomy was overthrown. Man was
viewed as fundamentally free—free even from the rules of Cartesian geometry. But such is the power of means over ends that the
economics of Keynes soon became Keynesian economics. Hyperclassical modes of thought were reinthroned in the ensuing "synthesis," our fourth stage.

The following chapters are devoted to an examination of the
modus operandi of dogmatic Cartesianism in its economic aspects
from the standpoint of the principles presented in this chapter. The
primary thesis of our work (the dogmatic Cartesian origins and
nature of economic theory) is confirmed by an examination of the
systems of thought of Marx and Keynes. They are at odds with
orthodox economic theory because they derive their sustenance
from two epistemologies that are inimical to Cartesianism, that of
Hegel and that of what we may loosely call Existentialism.

4

Classical Economics I

> The individual and isolated hunter or fisher who
> forms the starting point with Smith and Ricardo,
> belongs to the insipid illusions of the eighteenth
> century. They are Robinsonades which do not
> by any means represent . . . a reaction against
> over-refinement and a return to a misunderstood
> natural life. They are no more based on such
> a naturalism than is Rousseau's contrat social. . . .
> They are the fiction and only the esthetic fic-
> tion of the small and great Robinsonades.
>
> Marx

THE *Wealth of Nations* has long been a "puzzle" to many readers.[1]
Extreme libertarianism is quickly followed by invectives against
businessmen, which, as Viner notes, could provide material for
several socialist orations.[2] Historical analyses follow on the heels
of descriptions of an imaginary "rude state of nature." At times a
trivial fact is examined in detail while important aspects of economic life (i.e., Watt's invention or the many contrivances that
revolutionized textile manufacturing) go unmentioned. Those who,
following well-established principles of criticism and exegesis, go
to Smith's other book, *The Theory of Moral Sentiments*, in order to

1. See, for instance, A. H. Cole, "Puzzles of the Wealth of Nations."
2. Jacob Viner, "Adam Smith and Laissez Faire," in *The Long View and
the Short: Studies in Economic Theory and Policy*, pp. 213–45.

understand *Wealth of Nations*, meet with the ultimate puzzle. There Smith makes sympathy the great hinge that holds society together, while in *Wealth of Nations* it is sympathy's negation, egoism, that is cast in the same role.

The observations of the preceding chapter go some way toward dispelling the mystery. The conflict between the two principles disappears if both books are viewed as exercises in the Cartesian method. After all, apparently neither economists nor anybody else has been disturbed by the obvious conflict between, say, Hobbes' bellicose and brutish state of nature and the peaceful and bucolic one of so many other philosophers of the same period. The fact that one author, Adam Smith, provided alternative and opposite explanations is unimportant. Behind Smith was a higher entity called the ego which, for over a century, had been indulging in an examination of how society would behave if it were ruled first by one principle, then by another. The fact that it is ruled by neither is immaterial.

It is time to call attention to a characteristic of Enlightenment raisonnement. The writers in this tradition were deeply conscious of having ushered in a new intellectual era, of being trail blazers. Of such individuals we might logically expect a desire to test their newly discovered method on small problems first, before attempting a grand synthesis. This in fact has been the procedure of the physical sciences which study the world of matter (mechanics, the movements of the celestial bodies, the phenomena of light and sound, the structure of the human body) piecemeal before attempting to bring together some of these phenomena in the Newtonian synthesis. But in dealing with man, the ego immediately tested its method on the macrocosm, that is, on the larger issues of the nature of society. In particular, it was obsessed with the question "What holds society together?" This concern with society stems directly from the paradoxical and contradictory qualities of the Cartesian method on which we have already commented. This method is, by its nature, introspective. It draws the thinker into the position of solipsism—the viewpoint that the mind and its states are the only thing the self does and can know. (Bentham came close to recognizing this when he asserted that nobody can, logically, assess another man's pleasures and pains.) Obviously, the Enlightened thinkers did not want to be cornered in this position, which, among other things, strongly implies that society is continually on the verge of disintegration. They wanted to stress the order and harmony of the social body, not to expose its weaknesses. The ensuing tension between the desires of the theorists and the nature of the method they had chosen to follow is responsible for both the concern with society's "centrifugal force" and for the peculiar thought-contrivances that were created to answer a question within a methodology that was inappropriate to portray cohesion. The concern with society, in other words, may be taken as reflecting the need (perhaps felt unconsciously) to move away from the uncomfortable conclusion to which their method led.

Those who follow the accepted methodology of the times do not feel compelled to lay bare the fundamental presuppositions on which their thinking is based. Adam Smith was no exception. His major works contain no important methodological remarks. After his death, however, an essay of his was published ("The Principles which Lead and Direct Philosophical Enquiries: Illustrated by the History of Astronomy") which addresses itself to the problem of method. It reflects the views dominant in the eighteenth century.

To Smith philosophical enquiries were evidently investigations into the world of men, but he used astronomy and mechanics as his *falsa riga*. Just as Descartes tried to explain man's physical and psychic impulses by viewing him as a mechanical device (so that those principles "used in making clocks, artificial fountains, mills and other similar machines" could be applied), so did Smith look at the social world as an immense machine. Accordingly, intellectual "systems in many respects resemble machines. . . . A system is an imaginary machine invented to connect together in the fancy those different movements and effects which are already in reality performed."[3] Smith makes no effort to prove that the principles of mechanics (as known to the ego) are reflected in social reality, perhaps because almost every educated European of his day believed this to be true. And, in fact, it is as unfair to demand such a proof as it is impossible for a mind under the sway of rationalism to provide it.

Smith pushes the analogy with machines further. The first industrial contrivances, he goes on to say, are the most complex: later, fewer "wheels" and fewer "principles of motion" are generally

3. This essay has recently been reprinted by A. M. Kelley in *The Early Writings of Adam Smith.*

found to perform the task even better: "The first systems [of thought], in the same manner, are always the most complex, and a particular connecting chain, or principle is generally thought necessary to unite every two seemingly disjointed appearances: but it often happens, that one great connecting principle is afterwards found to be sufficient to bind together all the disconnected phenomena that occur in a whole species of things."

This passage is remarkable both in what it says and in what it suggests. The whole argument is conveyed analogically: indeed, when one aspires (as Smith did) to address all men, the new and unfamiliar must be clothed in "principles familiar to all mankind."[4] Like many of Smith's analogies,[5] this one is not only misleading but incorrect: later, up-to-date machines are characterized not by fewer but by more "wheels," whether we think of a loom or a steam engine, a typewriter or locomotive. Smith confuses elegance with simplicity. Industrial designing does tend to produce *esthetically* more pleasing machines, but it certainly does not check their "perfectionist" tendencies toward greater complexity. Economic theory, too, has followed these principles. Conceived as a "box of tools" it has grown not less but more complex. It has also become more elegant exactly through the discovery of the one principle (the margin) toward which Smith groped.

In the essay on astronomy, Adam Smith makes no mystery of the fact that appearances are "seemingly disjointed." Later economists were even clearer on this point. Menger regrets that "there is not a phenomenon of the real world which does not offer us the spectacle of constant change,"[6] while von Mises, quoting Heraclitus, laments that "everything is in flux."[7] But Smith rightly suggests that man has the capacity to connect "in the fancy" what is "disconnected" in reality. And the "fancy," as noted in chapter 3, strives toward monism: its ideal is to replace the ad hoc, varied principles that operate the prototype (literally, the first, original model) with

4. Ibid. Smith's desire to address all men is reminiscent of Marshall's wish "to be read by businessmen." In both cases these hopes might have encouraged the use of false analogies.

5. Recall, for instance, the analogy between the family and the state: "What is prudence in the conduct of every private family can scarce be folly in that of a great kingdom" (*Wealth of Nations*, 4:2). For a century and a half this maxim has been quoted in support of a balanced budget, although Smith uses it in pleading for free trade.

6. Carl Menger, *Problems in Economics and Sociology*, p. 109.

7. Ludwig von Mises, *Ultimate Foundations of Economic Science*, p. 1.

one great connecting principle that will account for as many phenomena as possible.

Smith's ideal was, then, to produce in the realm of intellect something comparable to any of today's engines. If we open up, say, a toy airplane, we see that motion is imparted to the wheels and propellers by a system of gears, shafts, and small wheels that, in turn, are operated by the master shaft coming out of the motor. Sympathy and egoism are, alternatively, the two "master shafts" that Smith discovered and through which he aspired to explain all the characteristics and movements of the social organism. His error was to believe that it is a relatively simple matter to transmit the master shaft's motion to the outer concepts more or less in touch with the real. That it is not simple is evidenced by the fact that the economists who succeeded him worked for two centuries on producing subsidiary shafts, wheels, and linkages through which self-interest explains the economic phenomena of society.

Smith's mechanicism is expected to yield all sorts of desiderata. Through it, the ambition of all idealism ("to give the ceaseless change in the stream of time something of a permanent and unchangeable nature to support it," in Fichte's words) is satisfied. Through it our ethical sense is also satisfied. For, Smith writes in the *Theory of Moral Sentiments*, "Human society when we contemplate it in a certain abstract and philosophical light, appears like a great, an immense machine whose regular and harmonious movements produce *a thousand agreeable effects*."[8] Let us consider some of those imaginative creations that simultaneously yielded both the Beautiful and the Agreeable.

His first machine prototype is the *Theory of Moral Sentiments*, whose subtitle is *An Essay towards an Analysis of the Principles by which Men Naturally Judge Concerning the Conduct and Character, First of their Neighbors and Afterwards of Themselves.* "Naturally" is the key word in the subtitle: it suggests that human motivations are rooted in innate, not acquired, traits. The *Theory* deals with man in the abstract, in his "natural" state, not a rude state, but an unhistorical one nonetheless. No attempt is made to outline the emergence of ethical feelings by considering the role of customs, events, accidents, etc. The *Theory* is concerned with

8. W. Schneider, ed., *Adam Smith's Moral and Political Philosophy*, p. 52. Emphasis added.

discovering why moral feelings arise despite the obsession with the self implied by the method of Descartes.

Smith finds the answer in the existence of sympathy, which enables the bystander to share the sentiments of those involved in an action and thus to partake in the social approbation and disapprobation that meet them. But what stimulates sympathy? Prisoner of its own self, the mind cannot reach outside itself: "as we have no immediate experience of what other men feel, we can form no idea of the manner in which they are affected," a problem which, as we saw, baffled Bentham. The senses, predictably, are of no use: "Though our brother is upon the rack as long as we ourselves are at ease our senses will never inform us of what he suffers." Where the senses fail, the intellect triumphs. By sheer force of "imagination," we can form a conception of what are his sensations (p. 73), that is, we can sympathize. Imagination allows Smith to build a theory of ethical society. What holds society together is each man's ability to sympathize with others. Through sympathy, the subject appropriates the object (as Hegelians would say) and the original schism is bridged. Since this solution is built upon a static, abstract conception of man, Smith's ethics do not evolve. They are not shaped by customs, traditions, laws. The ego becomes the alter ego and vice versa in a kind of swinging movement to and fro which leads nowhere.

Smith himself was half aware of the imaginary origins of his concept of sympathy: "Sympathy [he asserts] is very properly said to arise from an *imaginary* change of situation with the person principally concerned, yet this imaginary change is not supposed to happen to me in my own person and character, but in that of the person with whom I sympathize" (p. 53, emphasis added). When I condole with a person for the loss of his son, Smith goes on to say, it is not that I think how I would feel if I lost my son, but I consider "what I should suffer if I was really you." This subtle distinction is needed to allay the accusation that sympathy is synonymous with selfishness; Smith was a severe critic of writers like Mandeville who turned men's most generous motives into vanity, egoism, and frivolousness (pp. 43 ff.).

Imagination, apparently, does not by itself suffice to guarantee moral social intercourse. And, in the end, Smith has recourse to a dialectical device—that of the "impartial spectator." This impartial spectator is not a physical person in the sense that Mannheim's "detached intellectual" is. Smith clearly indicates that this, too, is an imaginary being. He refers to it metaphorically as "the great inmate of the breast," or the "man within the breast." This abstraction is the ethical equivalent of the epistemological ego: from the latter sprang truth, from the former springs morality. And just as the ego is besieged by passions that threaten to deflect it from its geometrical path, so the "man within the breast" can, unhappily, be bribed or killed altogether.

We have already noted the Sisyphean nature of Enlightened thought: despite its claim to originality, it often ended up by restating quite old beliefs. Smith, it seems to us, painfully rediscovered the ancient idea of "conscience." It is, however, a hybrid conscience, half Old Testament, half New. It is guided neither by the principle of an eye for an eye nor by that of turning the other cheek. In an action arising from a feeling of revenge, for instance, the impartial spectator sympathizes both with the actor (who wants to avenge a wrong done him) and with the victim (the one who committed the wrong). The man within the breast strikes a neat average between Jehovah and Christ and approves of only moderate punishment. This solution (mindful of Bentham's minimum punishment) forces Smith to view life as a gentle comedy. One thing is certain: his observations are hardly confirmed by the behavior of the Parisian mobs howling around Marie Antoinette's scaffold.

Despite the loftiness of the subject, it seems probable that Smith's attitude toward his first book was half-hearted. For although sympathy is the source of many desirable sentiments (love, gratitude, friendship, etc.), even if this power of man's imagination should falter and disappear altogether, "society, though less happy and agreeable, will not necessarily be dissolved: [it will exist] from a sense of its utility."[9] The one who expects consistency in the whole of Smith's works must regard the *Theory* as a first draft, later repudiated. In the *Wealth of Nations*, what holds society together is not sympathy but its negation—self-interest. For sympathy did not succeed in bringing all social phenomena under one great principle. It had to be supported by many other devices to accomplish this goal and, finally, it had to be shored up by the notion of the impartial spectator. This was very unsatisfactory. So Smith built an-

9. Ibid., p. 124.

other prototype based on self-interest. Just as he had foreseen, however, the first machines *are* clumsy and unnecessarily complex. And the *Wealth of Nations* is no exception. Later generations of economists (starting with Ricardo) took only the gravitational point around which men and institutions revolve (self-interest) and attempted to make the whole machine more esthetically pleasing.

It is tempting to interpret the whole of *Wealth of Nations* as the offshoot of that natural law philosophy which we have traced back to the sway of the Cartesian epistemology. But this interpretation, although fairly common, does not do justice to Smith. The answer is more complex. Smith set up two worlds, the intellectual and the sensuous, and shuttled back and forth between them, attempting to use the former to explain the latter. But he often realized that a wide gap existed between the two and he could not bridge it fully. The final outcome is that the book as a whole lacks coherence. Certain insights (generally those pertaining to the "rude state of nature"[10]) are not exploited in advancing understanding of empirical phenomena. They stand alone. The "natural" order of laissez-faire is surrounded by so many qualifications that a modern liberal would have little difficulty living with it. Smith's failure has been recognized by economists who abandoned the descriptive, historical part of the *Wealth of Nations* and refined and elaborated only those parts of his book that comprise "real" economics.

The meaning of "real" in economics may appear mystifying to the one who is unaware of the Cartesian methodology from which theory arose. Etymologically, real comes from *res*, meaning a material thing. In common parlance we speak of real persons and facts as opposed to mythical ones, acknowledged products of the imagination. But it is clearly not in this sense that the term is used in economics. We see an act of buying and selling, but real analysis detects "behind" it what is not there, namely a barter transaction in which buyers and sellers exchange labor for labor. Likewise, we see a saver setting aside a portion of his money, but real economics detects behind it an act of "abstinence," a calculus of "time preferences," or the building up of the stock of machines in the country. Real in economics then means exactly the opposite of what it means in everyday language: it stands for qualities and characteristics

10. "State of nature" arguments appear in *Wealth of Nations,* pp. 47, 161, 259, 653, 859, and passim.

which are invisible and abstracted from experience but which, *eo ipso,* are permanent and unchangeable.

The theory of value illustrates this conflict between the fact of movement and the desire to anchor this (unpleasant) fact on something unchanging. Common observation suggests that market prices fluctuate. But, Smith says, these fluctuations tend to gravitate toward a "natural" level given by the labor content of commodities. But does not labor itself vary in value at different places and times? This is only "the employer's view" and it is wrong. In reality, "equal quantities of labour, at all times and places, may be said to be of equal value to the labourers."[11] This homogeneity of labor effort is illustrated by conditions existing in the "early and rude state of nature" where land is free and capital nonexistent. Here, relative prices are "clearly" governed by the respective labor content of the commodities. Yet one beaver will not exchange for two deer if the hunters' efforts differed radically, if it took more cunning and speed to kill a deer (with one's bare hands, for no capital exists) than a beaver. Hence Smith was forced to imagine a unit of "toil and trouble," a kind of physical and psychic minimum common denominator to which actual effort and intelligence can be reduced as a multiple (a kind of ancestor of the I.Q., it would seem). Labor thus becomes "homogeneous" in all respects, and *units* of toil can be compared with each other. The problem of the exchange ratios of commodities is brought within the category of Cartesian extension. If it takes ten units of effort to hunt a deer and twenty units to hunt a beaver, intuition dictates that the "natural" price between the two animals will ("should"?) be two to one, or that two deer must be given up for one beaver.

It is worthwhile to note the mind's procedure in arriving at this truth because it is typical of many other cases. The result is arrived at by draining from the concept "work" all those attitudes, aptitudes, and skills that make it unique and historical, i.e., real. Only the Lockean primary quality is left—namely, number—and on this basis a theory of value is erected. That such a childlike reasoning set into motion the whole theoretical train that culminated in Rodbertus' and Marx' labor theory (which was to act as

11. Ibid., pp. 32–33. Why did Smith substitute the unequivocal "are of equal value" which appears in the first edition with the hypothetical "may be said to be of equal value" of the later (standard) edition? Did he recognize that his theory only reflects a *subjective* standpoint, to be interpreted on an 'as if" basis?

one of the most powerful yeasts of modern history) is clearly an example of the power of fictions to affect reality. Methodologically, the essence of the theory consists of transforming the heterogeneous into the homogeneous, the dissimilar into the similar, the unique into the abstract and hence self-identical. The engine behind these transformations is the "regulative power of reason" in Kantian language. The problem of value, brought within the Cartesian methodology, acquires clearness and distinctness.

Something else is worth noting in this procedure. The relation between the hunter and his prey can be viewed as one between the subject and the object. But while Adam Smith goes to great lengths to examine the former, he totally ignores the latter, just as Cartesian methodology dictates. He renders labor homogeneous but, in effect, regards beavers as identical to deer. If he had stopped to consider that beavers have characteristics different from deer (less tasty meat but richer fur, smaller bulk but possessed of kidneys valuable to the medicine man, etc.), then he would not have been able to conclude that labor is the measure of value even in the hypothetical state of nature. He would have been forced, in other words, to consider the influence of demand upon value and he would have seen demand for what it is: a complicated web of relations between qualities of the object (the commodity) and the desires of the subject (whose outlook, in turn, is largely shaped by society). In this case, Smith's state of nature fiction would have been a useful device, holding the key to understanding real economic relations. Economics (if we may be allowed to speculate) might have attained Veblen's insights. But the demands of clearness and distinctness precluded this avenue of investigation.

When Smith tried to pass from his state of nature to modern society, he realized that his method was a feeble guide. He recognized that homogeneous labor does not exist. This "realization" induced him to turn his back on his beaver/deer reflections. There has been continuing debate on the significance of this illustration. Some economists argue that Smith meant it applicable only in the natural state. But that a pupil of Hume was concerned with the state of nature *as such* is unthinkable. He certainly knew this state to be a fiction. The truth seems to us that Smith attempted to use his imaginative reconstruction of the state of nature to provide a substratum of permanence to the chaotic phenomena of value. When he faced reality with his labor theory, he was intelligent enough not to try to force eighteenth-century England into it. He did not even take the obvious step of defining capital as nothing but past labor, a step which Ricardo and Marx did take. As it is, his machine, like all prototypes, has some wheels circling independently of the others, creating much inefficient heat. But he certainly enabled his successors to improve on it.

Even had Smith taken the step of subsuming capital under labor, other realistic considerations would entitle one to question the relevance of this "natural price" in Smith's own system. For in Book I, chapter 10, he launches into an examination of what labor really means in a modern society. The homogeneity of effort that he had postulated at the outset is now abandoned. We are told that employments differ in agreeableness, in the cost of acquiring skills, in the extent of responsibility entrusted to the individual, and in scores of other factors. The unit of toil and trouble is exposed as a useless will-o'-the-wisp. If this were not enough, Smith in Book I, chapter 8, even put his finger on a problem later economists were happy to neglect: wages arise out of a struggle between the workers and the entrepreneurs and the outcome cannot be forecast a priori.

Observation suggests that goods have an exchange value. But just as the transaction of commodities for money actually hides an exchange of labor for labor, so behind exchange value is use value. But here again Smith was incapable of transcending the empirical fact. He makes no use of his insight (use value) because he could not conceive of objective measurability of utility (after all, "anybody is closer to himself than to any other person"—Bentham) and was therefore unaware of the significance of his own discovery. After the faux pas of the labor theory of value was forcefully brought to the attention of economists by the Marxists (it led to such revolutionary conclusions as to embarrass the scientific claims of the ego), orthodox economics turned inward (as the nature of the ego demanded) and use value became the ultimate determinant of price.

From the standpoint of later economics, Smith is more notable for the questions he posed and for the hints he threw out than for anything else. The Cartesian outlook had succeeded in solving the narrow problem of the specie flow. It was another story to produce an all-encompassing system with the hallmarks of clearness and distinctness. The advantages of mathematics had not yet been recognized. Rhetorical analogies were the main engine of thought in Smith's days. Smith never understood supply and demand in a schedule sense but solely as willingness and ability to sell and buy *at the existing price,* that is, in a popular sense.[12] Smith could visualize hunters in a primordial forest but could not imagine businessmen (consumers) worrying themselves to death as to how much they would offer (buy) if prices were other than they now (empirically) are.

All-encompassing systems do not spring full-blown from the head of a single thinker. System-builders are usually people who come at such junctures in the development of an idea that they are capable of amalgamating the insights of their predecessors. What previous economic writers gave him, Smith skillfully wove together. But they did not give him enough. That is why he is considered the father of economics. Smith's fault was a certain inability to subsume the objective under the subjective, coupled with the desire to explain too wide a "species of things." He did not see that by narrowing the focus of attention (by treating customs, techniques, tastes, etc., as data) one could advance greatly toward the abstract solution of the value problem. Neither did he see the merit of the great scholastic adage that advises whoever meets a contradiction to make a distinction. Later economists made quick progress in value theory by artificially distinguishing the question of how to measure value from what determines value. The first question (of great practical importance in problems of inflation, etc.) is solved by the admittedly expedient index numbers. Having shaken off practical interests, the ego can now devote itself to the purely metaphysical quest of the logical justification of value.

Smith failed in providing a well-rounded social system—his answer to Hobbes' authoritarianism. That selfish conduct which motivates the baker and the butcher to provide us with bread and meat is, unfortunately, also responsible for their wicked tendency to conspire against the public good. And even if private economic motives did tend to maximize welfare, Smith recognizes that "defense . . . is more important than opulence," which is why the navigation acts are "perhaps the wisest of all commercial regulation of England." Considering that Great Britain was at war with someone at least half the time in the preceding two centuries and that (then

12. This comes out most clearly from his discussion of prices in Book I, chap. 7 of *Wealth of Nations.*

as now) government regulations of economic life were often justified from a military-political point of view (the Mercantilists used
this argument methodically), not much room was left for the "obvious and simple system of natural liberty" to take root and flourish.
To make matters worse for those who like unequivocal answers,
Smith finds merit in the "infant industry" argument for protection,
and in retaliation against foreign tariffs.[13] It seems that the Invisible
Hand suffered from congenital arthritis.

Of Smith, one can say what can perhaps be said of many
geniuses. He was confused. He knew the limitations of the mind
and was willing to perform intellectual somersaults up to a point.
The methodological remarks in the essay on astronomy, after all,
must be viewed in juxtaposition with his criticism (in the *Theory*)
of Epicurus and philosophers in general. They try to "account for
all appearances from as few principles as possible." And this is a
"natural vice"![14]

Smith's youthful essay on astronomy shows how, like all intellectuals
of his days, he was awed and thrilled by that architectonic synthesis of natural phenomena—the Newtonian system. As we saw, he
failed to do for social theory what Newton had done for the realm
of nature. But since his days it has become a commonplace to compare the mechanicism of economic theory with the mechanics of
Newton's universe.[15] This often conveys the impression that the
method of economics and that of Newton are basically the same.
Thus it may be useful to see what modern scholarship understands
by Newton's method.

Let us stress at the outset that even if there were a perfect
identity between the method of Newton and that of economic
theory, this would prove nothing. The objects of the analysis of
economic life differ so deeply from those of the world of nature that
the success of the Newtonian method in its sphere hardly guarantees
success in the totally different social sphere. But the truth is that

13. All these arguments are presented in Book IV, chap. 2 of *Wealth of
Nations*.

14. *Smith's Moral and Political Philosophy*, p. 33. If "natural" means
here what it means in all Enlightenment thought, then Smith must be classed
with Bentham, Kant, and Nietzsche as one who realized that fictions (stemming
from a "natural vice") are unavoidable and perhaps desirable.

15. David Hamilton, *Newtonian Classicism and Darwinian Institutionalism: A Study of Change in Economic Theory*.

Smith and subsequent economists simply misunderstood Newton's method. They transformed the scientist's extreme and vigorous empiricism into a metaphysics. And they did so without being aware of it.[16]

In opposition to Descartes, Newton does not distinguish between sensible and ultimate reality, between what the senses portray and the primary qualities. If the senses deceive, it is because they are imperfect instruments to detect the infinitely distant or the infinitely small. There is no universal doubt in Newton. In fact, there is no mind-matter dualism. But perhaps the major characteristic of Newton's thought is an unwillingness to divest bodies of all qualities but those required by the mathematical method. He held that "our business is with the causes of *sensible* effects," the purpose of science being to explain the observed phenomena of nature. "For Newton there was absolutely no *a priori* certainty such as Kepler, Galileo, and preeminently Descartes believed in, that the world is through and through mathematical, still less that its secrets can be fully unlocked by the mathematical method already perfected."[17] The world is what it is, and the senses portray it correctly. It is not to be fitted in the Procrustean bed of mathematics. At best, it can be described in mathematical terms, thus attaining clearness and conciseness. If it cannot be so described, we can either invent a mathematics to fit the observed facts or resign ourselves to a descriptive, less exact method. And this clearly illustrates the relation between facts and mathematics in Newton vis-à-vis Descartes. The latter conceived mathematics as the unquestioned mistress of the mind-matter relation; indeed, in a sense, there was no relation, for the French thinker had driven sensible reality underground by his basic a priori—matter is extension. Newton held facts to be supreme, to the point of even dictating the speculative interest of the pure mathematician! That is, mathematics itself is to be modeled on experience. In his *Universal Arithmetic* he even held the he-

16. Perhaps we should remark that we find nothing derogatory in metaphysics, understood as the final implication of any proposition or set of propositions. "The only way to avoid being a metaphysician is to say nothing." But metaphysics does become a vice when the thinker is not aware of the method he follows and of the extent to which he shares the ideas of his age. These intellectual qualities, unfortunately, are especially common exactly in those who claim to be "emancipated" from metaphysical presuppositions, i.e., to be "positivists." See Edwin Arthur Burtt, *The Metaphysical Foundations of Modern Physical Science*, pp. 224 ff.

17. Ibid., p. 208. Emphasis added.

retical view that some problems cannot be properly translated into mathematical language. And in the preface to his *Principia,* he compares his method to that of the ancient inventors of mathematics, who had advanced mathematics to come to grips with practical problems (this view of the evolution of mathematics is, interestingly enough, shared by Engels).

Students of the Newtonian method conclude that his "ultimate criterion was more empirical than mathematical."[18] His writings are certainly full of polemics against "hypotheses" (*"hypotheses non fingo"*), by which he attacked the "dilettantism very widespread in his day of formulating entirely arbitrary and phantastic hypotheses, impossible of verification."[19] In squabble after squabble with his contemporaries, Newton fought a losing battle against those who misunderstood his method. So incensed was he by unrestrained flights of imagination that he became convinced that the only way of escaping falsehood was to ban hypotheses entirely from science. In a letter to Robert Hook he makes this point and concludes by saying, "I do not think it needful to explicate my doctrine by any hypothesis at all. . . . You see, therefore, how much it is besides the business in hand, to dispute about hypothesis."[20]

In the *Principia,* Newton sets forth a "Rule of Reasoning in Philosophy" (read: natural science): "we are certainly not to relinquish the evidence of experiments for the sake of dreams and vain fictions of our own devising." Not only are facts conceded a primary place in Newton's methodology, but careful experimentation must occur at the beginning and end of every scientific reasoning, since it is always the world of senses that we are trying to comprehend. To do otherwise is to run the risk of overturning the natural relation between ends (an understanding of the physical world) and means (the mathematical imagination). Newton was aware of the power of *idola theatri,* of the weakness of the human mind to substitute a ready-made metaphysics for a dispassionate examination of facts.

The dread of a prioris naturally led Newton to emphasize the importance of induction, while his emphasis on facts and experi-

18. Ibid., p. 209.
19. Vaihinger, *The Philosophy of 'As If,'* p. 41. Karl Jaspers in an essay on Descartes asserts that "Newton's *'hypotheses non fingo'* was directed against Descartes, who reasoned but did not investigate" (*Three Essays: Leonardo, Descartes, Max Weber,* p. 173).
20. Burrt, *Metaphysical Foundations,* p. 213.

ments caused in him a lively awareness of the possibilities of exceptions appearing even in the most widely accepted theorems. This is why experimentation holds such an important place in his methodology. It is, partly, a way of nailing down what we already know, of convincing ourselves that we do not live in a dream world.

But does this not contradict what we have already said about Newton's ether? Obviously, this "matter" could not be grabbed by the tail, observed, or reproduced in a laboratory. In fact, it could only be inferred by analogy with the way of behaving of other phenomena. It is, therefore, something imposed on the universe by the need to explain certain aspects of physical behavior. The whole conception represents the surreptitious inserting of a non-fact between observable facts. How Newton conceived the ether is subject to debate even today. Burtt asserts that it never occurred to Newton to doubt the existence of this medium performing the function of transmitting light. Vaihinger, on the contrary, believes that to Newton the ether was a conscious fiction whose only justification lay in its practical scientific value.

Even if Burtt is right, one must keep in mind the alternative "hypothesis" which Newton's contemporaries set forth and which Newton fought. This alternative consisted of regarding certain needed qualities (needed, that is, to explain the phenomena at hand) as inherent in bodies. Just as Descartes had assumed that there were "innate ideas," so bodies were assumed to have innate qualities (e.g., gravitation), through which action at a distance was possible. This way of thinking struck Newton as "a great absurdity," a remnant of scholasticism. Belief in an ether was obviously the lesser of the two evils. For, though pushed to accept the ether, Newton's natural suspicion of anything not directly observable caused him to add, "Whether this agent be material or immaterial, I have left to the consideration of my readers."[21]

The method of economic theory is diametrically opposed to that of the Newton portrayed by philosophers and intellectual historians. Even if economists had correctly interpreted Newton, it is difficult to see how they could have imitated his method and still come up with a "system." Quite plainly, the heirs of Newton's method are the humble descriptive historians.[22]

21. Ibid., p. 266.
22. By descriptive historians we mean, for instance, the members of the

Let those who find parallels between Newton's method and the practice of economic theory ask themselves how "springs of human action" or "psychological propensities" can be observed in a dispassionate examination of the available facts of social behavior. In economics the possibility of using mathematical ways of thinking has always been the controlling factor in attributing qualities to human behavior and in setting the limits to the discipline. Newton invented a mathematical tool (the fluxional calculus) to describe observable phenomena. Economists invent facts to fit them into their mathematical knowledge. One example of this mathematical metaphysics (of which Descartes was the founder in modern times) will suffice, for now. It is well known that the theory of the collectivist state was developed by Pareto and Barone. Their path-breaking studies were published in 1897 and 1908, respectively. *It is an incontestable fact that, at that time, no collectivist (socialist) state existed.*[23]

What Smith and his colleagues saw in Newton was a confirmation of their Cartesian outlook, to wit, that the universe (including the social universe with which, after all, they thought they concerned themselves) is, at bottom, incomparable beauty, order, and harmony.

German Historical School. And by humble, we mean those members of the school who realized that no system can be erected out of a mountain of true but contradictory facts.

23. Burdened by these precedents, economists were doomed to misunderstand the nature and workings of the socialist state when it did appear. Many years after the viability of the Soviet system had proved itself they still debated whether economic calculations were possible in a social order where the means of production are owned by the state.

5

Classical Economics II

Our logic is pre-eminently the logic of solids.
Bergson

SMITH FAILED to solve the problem of value, which, in any case, was only of peripheral interest to him. It was left to Ricardo—the most unphilosophical and yet most imaginative of all orthodox economists—to convert the Smithian rough draft into a full-fledged system by the ruthless exploitation of inspectio. Thomas de Quincy unerringly detected the nature of Smith's problem and of Ricardo's solution of it. De Quincy says in his emphatic style that while Ricardo's predecessors "had been crushed and overlaid by the enormous weights of facts, details and exceptions, Mr. Ricardo had deduced, *a priori, from the understanding itself,* laws which shot arrowy light into the dark chaos of materials, and had thus constructed what hitherto was but a collection of tentative discussions into a science of regular proportions, now first standing on an *eternal basis.*"[1]

And this, in fact, is what Ricardo did. He peeled off the *Wealth of Nations* the various layers of facts, details, and exceptions and discovered Smith's value theory a priori: that the exchange ratio of goods is determined by their labor content. Overthrowing the hesi-

1. *The Confessions of an English Opium Eater,* p. 203. Emphasis added.

tations of his predecessor, he then translated Smith's conclusion at least to contemporary England, although de Quincy and his contemporaries had no difficulty detecting the "eternal" basis of his theorizing.[2]

But the passage from a "rude state of nature" to a modern capitalist country is beset with problems. For instance, in the former there was no capital stock and land was free, while this is not the case in modern conditions. What the senses detect and common sense cannot ignore, inspectio annihilates. Ricardo did what many other thinkers did before. He set up an intellectual world in which, although land and capital were acknowledged to exist, they were so defined as to have no bearing on the problem of value which was, therefore, brought within the mold of Cartesian certainty. His procedure provides a good example of the tendency of means to perfect themselves, following the elusive goal of clearness and distinctness of ideas.

To eliminate rent, Ricardo has to view land as in fixed supply and subject to diminishing returns (to be considered later). Unlike labor, land is a heterogeneous input, each plot being unique in terms of fertility, location, etc. One would suppose that this heterogeneity is ideal to produce a variety of crops: after all, some plants thrive better in dry, others in rich soil, some do well in shade, and others demand sun. But no, all land yields just one product, "corn" (wheat) and this product is of identical quality regardless of soil! The market price (whatever it is) is such that it allows the least productive plot (marginal land) to receive an infinitesimally small rent, i.e., in practice, a zero rent. Ergo, "rent does not enter into price." The uninitiated may well be baffled by this conclusion until he realizes that the category land which Ricardo employed had peculiar but very serviceable characteristics. First, it was barren of man-made improvements (drainage, fencing, fertilizing, etc.), although it was heterogeneous by virtue of "natural" differences. Thus the income received by an actual landowner was split "in the mind" (exactly what Smith could not, in another context, bring himself to do) between profits and rent proper. Rent arises solely because someone has a monopoly of a scarce resource. Second, this land had no alternative uses. The owner of the "mar-

---

2. It is the characteristic of logical and mathematical a prioris that they portray a "world of essences" wholly autonomous of shiftless facts. De Quincy's remarks confirm the correctness of our interpretation.

ginal" land which is brought under cultivation, being an economic man, is clearly happy to accept one pence rent a year, because the alternative is no rent at all. Therefore, the market price of wheat includes (practically) no rent payment.[3] Owners of so-called intra-marginal rent do, of course, receive a rent which is in direct proportion to the fertility of their holdings, but Ricardo had discovered the miraculous properties of the margin. The market price must be such as to cover factor costs on marginal land but marginal land itself receives (practically) no rent.

Having eliminated rent, Ricardo tackles capital. Observation suggests that capital takes a bewildering variety of forms—needles and steam engines, ships and bank accounts, spades and windmills. Heterogeneity (which was serviceable in the case of barren land) is now a hindrance to theorizing. But appearances are misleading. All forms of capital share one characteristic: it takes time for the businessman who uses them to recoup their cost. He who uses machines to produce something will have to "wait" for the completion and sale of the final product before he can recover his money. Curiously enough, hiring labor also entails "advancing" wages to the workers and "waiting" to recoup the money. By the "waiting" it is not just capital that is transformed into a homogeneous mass (the equivalent of our theoretical K), but the very difference between labor and machines is totally obliterated.[4] Time swallows all.

It would seem that Ricardo has now solved the problem of value: If it takes one year of total (direct and machine) time to produce commodity x and two years to produce y, two units of x will have to be given up for one of y, exactly as in Smith's deer/beaver illustration. In reality, that wonderful category "time" that allows Ricardo to advance so rapidly toward clearness and distinctness now plays a trick on him. If one worker produces a bushel of wheat in one year, while it takes one worker two years to produce a yard of cloth, the exchange rate cannot be two to one. The entrepreneur who has to wait two years wants a profit somewhat larger than twice as much as that reaped by the wheat entrepreneur.

3. On a logical basis, there is, of course, a wide difference between zero and almost zero. The contradictions of the calculus will be examined in the following chapter.

4. This obliteration continues in modern theory where it is customary to speak of "human capital."

He wants to earn a profit[5] on the sum he advanced in the first year but which would not be covered by the sale until the end of the second. In other words, a compound interest problem appears. "It follows that we can no longer predict relative prices from the labor coefficient alone [from a comparison of time, we would say] unless $t_1 = t_2$," unless, that is, the production periods of the two goods are identical.[6] In pure mathematics, two is twice as large as one, but in the world of finance a sum lent for two years at a given yield returns more than twice as much as a sum lent out for only one year. The value problem once again eluded inspectio, and certainly not for lack of imagination.

Actually, Ricardo's interest in pure theory was in inverse proportion to his capacity for abstractions. Value theory he did not view as an end in itself: through it, he wanted to discover the laws that regulate the distribution of the national output.[7] The share of the landowner is easily determined, with the assistance of Malthus' population theory. The size of the population determines "the margin" and hence total rent share. As population increases, inferior land is brought under cultivation and the once marginal (no rent) land now earns a rental. We are now left with a rentless national product: How is it shared between labor and entrepreneur? Time which absorbed all before is too broad a category now. So fixed capital is made to disappear altogether by assuming a one-year production cycle for all goods. Machines destroy themselves in the act of producing goods. Capital then consists only of "circulating" capital, that, is of "advances" to workers, the wage bill. Now wages gravitate toward subsistence level (thanks to Malthus' population theory again), and since full employment prevails (thanks to Say's axiom) the total wage bill is easily discovered. Subtracting this figure from the rentless national output cannot but yield the share of profits. This is why, when wages go up, profits go down.[8] Given a fixed sum divided between two groups, an increase in one share must mean a decrease in the other. The truth is certainly such as to be independent of observation and experiment: "eternal," as de Quincy put it.

---

5. It is well known that classical economists made no distinction between profits and interest.
6. Blaug, *Economic Theory in Retrospect*, p. 87.
7. David Ricardo, *Principles of Political Economy and Taxation*, p. 1.
8. Ibid., chap. 6.

But Ricardo is not yet satisfied. He wants to be able to prove unambiguously that a rise in the price of wheat is caused by rising input requirements under conditions of diminishing land yields. Empirically, an increase in the price of wheat might, of course, be due to inflation, so money disqualifies itself from consideration. The search for an "invariant standard of value" begins afresh. It must clearly be a unit independent of factor rewards, otherwise an increase in wheat prices may be attributed to an increase in wage rates. Ricardo decides that gold is the invariant standard of value and attributes to gold these characteristics. First, it was produced at all times and places with a constant quantity of capital and labor (gold is thus reminiscent of Smith's "unit of toil and trouble"); second, it has a period of production which happily coincides with that of wheat: for both goods the "waiting" is one year.[9] Now Ricardo can unequivocally conclude that the price of wheat is determined by the "quantity of labor necessary to produce it" and, moreover, that "the only adequate and permanent cause for the rise of wages is the increasing difficulty of providing food and necessaries for the increasing number of workmen."[10]

The whole of Ricardo's work clearly illustrates the ambivalent nature of the rationalistic mind: no matter how high it soared from abstraction to abstraction, it eventually wanted to be reunited with existence, from which it never derived sustenance. For from his ego-spun system, Ricardo drew conclusions of cosmic importance, for instance, that, as population rises, money wages must go up (though they remain at subsistence), and profits fall until a point is reached which is incompatible with capitalist institutions. That, in the process of solving the value problem, Smith's famed harmony of interests met an inglorious death illustrates a point we made in chapter 2. Just as different and largely contradictory conclusions were derived by many political philosophers from the various state of nature a prioris, so widely different conclusions are reached by such thinkers as Smith and Ricardo. A prioristic thinking follows its own dynamics. Interested in attaining clearness and distinctness of ideas, it passes from fiction to fiction without knowing where it is headed until it reaches its destination. It is customary to assert that Ricardo's model originated from an antilandowner bias. But

9. Ibid., chap. 1, sec. 6.
10. Ibid., p. 64.

nobody has ever explained the roots of this bias, all the more in-credible since Ricardo himself was a landlord.[11] It is rather more likely that Ricardo's only goal was purely intellectual: to place political economy on a sound scientific basis, as he himself as-serted.

Not only are Ricardo's implications fundamentally contradic-tory of Smith's, but the model is even in contradiction with itself. This is most apparent by a comparison of the body of the *Principles* with chapter 31 ("On Machinery," added to the third edition). While in the bulk of the book the only glimmer of hope is pro-vided by technological improvement in manufacturing (it can de-feat the "relentless margin"), chapter 31 pessimistically concludes that innovations may cause a permanent displacement of labor: "The opinion entertained by the labouring class, that the employ-ment of machinery is frequently detrimental to their interests, is not founded on prejudice and error, but is conformable to the cor-rect principles of political economy."[12] Previously, Ricardo had found labor and business united against a common exploiter—the landowner. Now it appears that there is a natural disharmony of interests between labor and capital, too. It is no wonder that Mc-Culloch tried to do his best to suppress a paper written by his mas-ter a few weeks before his death touching on the machinery question with the same catastrophic implications for harmony, for Say's law, and for the so-called Ricardian system as a whole.

Ricardo knew that he had followed a will-o'-the-wisp. In a let-ter to McCulloch in 1820 he readily confessed his dissatisfaction with the heart of his system—the theory of value: "I sometimes think that if I were to write the chapter on value again . . . I should acknowledge that the relative value of commodities was regulated by two causes instead of one, namely by the relative quantity of labour necessary to produce the commodities in ques-tion, and by the rate of profit for the time that the capital remained dormant, and until the commodities were brought to market." Monism, seriously maimed by this confession, receives a further jolt when Ricardo continues: "After all, the great questions of Rent, Wages and Profits must be explained by the proportions in which the whole produce is divided between landlords, capitalists, and

11. He might have argued, however, that he was an entrepreneur. After all, his land was not unimproved swamp.
12. Ibid., p. 383.

labourers, and which are not essentially connected with the doctrine of value."[13]

His contemporaries were dissatisfied, too. "The solution of the 'machinery question,'" Charles Babbage wrote in 1832, "depends on facts, which unfortunately have not yet been collected."[14] Every time expectations are disappointed, the methodological pendulum swings the other way. The factual analysis of trade by the Mercantilists gave rise to the call for a more "philosophical," a priori approach; the failure of the a priori caused a demand for a return to observation. In any case, Babbage's request went unheeded; the Cartesian ego was only in its infancy.

One of the most characteristic fruits of the "understanding" of this period is the law of diminishing returns, which soon became one of the pillars of economic theory. Schumpeter calls it "an empirical statement" to be verified by the normal scientific method.[15] We call it a fictional one, for testing is not only impossible in the world of reality but self-contradictory even within thought itself. The law states that additions of more labor to a given plot of land and size of capital stock will, "after a certain point," yield a smaller and smaller extra output. Who is to perform this presumed experiment? Clearly not farmers: the economist himself admits they are motivated by profits, not by scientific considerations, sheer idle curiosity, or a desire to solve the problems of economists. Thus the task must devolve on those who are interested in the law in the first place, i.e., economists. But despite the fact that many outstanding economists, including Ricardo, have been gentleman farmers, none of them has troubled himself to do what Schumpeter and accepted scientific canons require.

This is no accident, for the law, the product of pure thought, cannot be tested in the world with which we are acquainted. Only homogeneous labor inputs are to be added, but men are hardly identical in physical and psychological qualities. Furthermore, how many decades or centuries of experimentation on one and the same plot are necessary? Many agricultural outputs are obtained only once a year and the introduction of existential time into the experi-

13. Letter of David Ricardo to J. R. McCulloch, quoted by Eric Roll, *A History of Economic Thought*, p. 193.

14. *On the Economy of Machinery and Manufacture*, p. 337.

15. Schumpeter, *History of Economic Analysis*, p. 588.

ment plays odd tricks. For instance, it is impossible to maintain the original qualities of the labor force: by the time the second worker is added, the first one is one year older, perhaps more skilled or perhaps weaker. It is similarly impossible to prevent weather changes from year to year. Frosts, droughts, rainfalls, pests, etc., all affect agricultural output and no precise "adjustment" can be made for them. It is a contradiction that all through such experiments land retains its original qualities (as it must, for otherwise any change in output will be the net result of adding the variable input *and* of a change in the quality of the fixed input land). Since time immemorial it has been known that the yield of land tends to fall the more intensively it is used. One cannot freeze in a time context what is inherently changing. Finally, the belief that diminishing returns set in only after a vague "certain point" has been reached complicates the called-for experiment.

In reality, the process whereby a statement becomes or fails to become a law in economics is not empirical verification. The touchstone is heuristic usefulness, its fruitfulness in bearing more fictions and supporting a huge superstructure. A law often begins its career as a guarded vague suggestion, with many qualifications and a warning of its weakness. If the statement is useful, however, the Cartesian mind abjures its methodological doubt, for doubt is psychologically painful to bear, and slides progressively into dogmatic certainty. Bentham and Mill and Kant called attention to this phenomenon. Then thought proceeds to make the original statement more and more stringent, thus precluding more and more the very possibility of testing. This is what happened to the law of diminishing returns. Ricardo put it to use to eliminate rent. By Senior's time it was an axiom. Economics since then has always found a place for it: in value theory, in cost theory, in capital theory, in public finance, in welfare theory, in international trade theory, in population theory, in the long run and in the short, diminishing returns in one of its infinite themes was to prove its indispensable value. Indeed, without it economics would have been impossible. It provides much of the scaffolding on which equilibrium, the offspring of reason, stands.

In his essay on Malthus, J. M. Keynes highly praised the respect for facts of Ricardo's friend, the fundamental expression of which is presumably his rejection of Say's Law. But in his work on population Malthus follows faithfully the main Cartesian current. He sets up an institutionless world, a world beyond history, and assumes an original "population" devoid of all attributes but mathematical ones. He then shows how poverty, crime, war, etc. "naturally" follow unless mankind "decides" to adhere to true rationalistic principles of morality and keep its numbers in check.

Blaug notes that despite the fact that the second edition of the *Essay on the Principles of Population* was published two years after the census of population, Malthus "barely examined its findings,"[16] a fact that reminds one of Adam Smith's neglect of the revolution of production methods going on around him. Why should Malthus have run the risk of being "crushed and overlaid" by the elusive facts of demographic changes when the geometrical method of the age promised so much with so little effort? The procedure followed by Malthus is unempirical and a fine instance of rationalism at all costs. By the method of abstraction he succeeds in bringing life and death into a mechanistic mold. He abstracts from all causes of death except the natural cause, old age. He further asserts that the progress of technological advance is (and would continue to be) such as to effect a growth of agricultural output every twenty-five years in the arithmetic ratio of 1, 2, 3, 4, while men, subject only to "natural" death, double themselves during the same intervals according to the geometric ratio 2, 4, 8, 16. A corollary of this relation is that if population fails to double every twenty-five years, it must be due to a shortage of food and to the attendant evils stemming from such shortages, e.g., illness, pestilence, wars, etc. Thus cast, the law not only defies testing, but is true by definition. It is idle to question Malthus' two ratios: the pace of technological advance is inherently unknown and unknowable as periods of slow growth suddenly give way to outbursts of invention, discoveries, and industrial advances. To unlock the secrets of technological growth and stagnation is to forecast the rise and fall of civilizations —a task well beyond Malthus' interests, preparation, or methodology.

The birth rate of population is arrived at by shearing from historical man all feelings, beliefs, and customs imposed by culture and civilization, and exposing his presumed essence, his hard-core nature. This essence is basically that of a brute, a prey to basic

16. *Economic Theory,* p. 62.

drives only, of which the drive to procreate is the most powerful. It is not by accident that Darwin found the theoretical thread underlying the evolution of animal life in Malthus' *Essay*, for between Malthusian man and the lower animals with which Darwin was concerned there is no difference.

The reduction of man to the minimum common biological denominator is the logical result of the methodology of the times. Malthus had to portray a totally predictable nature and man, or he would have been unable to derive any conclusion—hence, the fixed ratios of population and food growth. This deterministic outlook led to a paradox. While believing that every mystery gives way in front of man's reason, Malthus found a thorough *lack* of reason in the common run of the human race. Malthusian man is evidently bent upon a mechanical and thoughtless multiplication of the species. Such is the characteristic of the fiction-producing mind that, as we noted, it is involved in perennial contradictions with itself.

One of the distinguishing characteristics of a fiction is its utter inability to submit to the test of empirical verification: facts can neither confirm nor deny a fiction. Malthus' theory is no exception. Whether a certain country has a high or low density of population, it is always possible to assert that, but for the operation of the positive and/or preventive checks, it would be higher. High density proves Malthus right, low density does not prove him wrong. The observable population level of a country can hardly be compared with what population "would have been" in the absence of those checks that make population what it is. The rewriting of history on the assumption of no wars, no pestilences, no crime, no moral checks, seems a useless task. Yet those who regard Malthus' theory as empirical can check it only by comparing the existent with what might have existed in the absence of history. Wittingly or unwittingly, all rationalism is led to this standpoint. Born of reason, it is unreasonable in its disregard of the real.

The Malthusian method is typical of the broader economic method. The latter, too, sets up an ideal ex post world, and it interprets movement (which is itself purely mental, not observed) as caused by people "changing their minds," institutional devices suddenly changing, attitudes breaking off from past ones. Instead of observation and experience being used to check the hypotheses, the hypotheses become the substitute for true understanding. This is the necessary result of having not true hypotheses but fictions incapable of being tested. The naïve believer in, say, the Marxist theory of history does not need to study events to find their cause: he knows it to be the "economic factor." In its own theoretical domain, economic theory does the same. Shifts in psychological attitudes (or "propensities") are seldom seen; but they *must* have occurred, otherwise the phenomenon would not have occurred. Both naïve Marxism and orthodox economic theory, being allegedly alternative ways of "looking" at the world, do not "look" at it; they interpret it according to their own axioms.

Malthus' population theory shared the fate of the law of diminishing returns. Its parallel characteristics of lack of verifi*ability* and practical (ethical and heuristic) usefulness turned it into a universal postulate. Senior's second postulate, on which economics is based, reads, "That the population of the world, or, in other words, the number of persons inhabiting it, is limited only by moral or physical evil, or by fear of deficiency of those articles of wealth which the habits of the individuals of each class of its inhabitants leads them to require."[17] Senior's formulation is so broad that it is beyond denial; *all* factors influencing population are covered by the axiom. And this, of course, is no accident. For in an effort to attain "clearness and distinctness," even statements that start their careers containing that shadow of empiricism which makes them mildly vulnerable must turn into ironclad tautologies. Even the fear of losing (by excessive procreation) certain "articles of wealth" that the individual has come to regard as indispensable, e.g., tea, is a sufficient check on the animal drive. How strong a drive is that can be checked by such trivia, Senior did not stop to examine.

Say's Law is another by-product of the epistemology of the seventeenth century. Destined to remain the most powerful support of classical macroeconomics for over a century, this law, is, methodologically, an analogical fiction, the result of the state-of-nature type of argument upon which so much classical thought is based. In the world of the idea, production occurs either to satisfy personal consumption or for the purpose of exchange, which immediately leads to the consumption of the items exchanged. These "real" (imagined) relations evidently unveil the essence of capital-

17. Nassau William Senior, *An Outline of the Science of Political Economy*, p. 26.

istic transactions as well. The transference of a barter argument to a monetary, complex economy was doubtlessly suggested by the Lockean notion of the "neutrality" of money. The facile acceptance of this law by the whole classical school illustrates a few of the principles of the mind's working that we have noted. Thrown out as a passing observation by Adam Smith, less guarded and inferior minds first converted it into a law and then abstracted it from its true environment—the world of pure logical relations—and hypostatized it to apply to the world of men.

The hallmarks of a fiction are its usefulness, its contradiction of other important elements of the theoretical system of which it is part, and its denial of the very possibility of testing. Say's Law has all of these characteristics. Its political usefulness is only too obvious: it was no accident that the ideology of state intervention in economic matters emerging in the 1930s swept Say's Law away. Despite its usefulness and logical derivation, it is not clear that Say's Law is free from contradiction. It seems to undermine the fundamental postulate of economic theorizing, viz., that the accumulation of profits is the goal of the system. Profits take a *money* form so that it would seem that the cycle of production and spending is interrupted by the accumulation of businessmen. One can get around this difficulty by assuming that businessmen do not want profits as such, but the enjoyment of profits, that is, consumption. This, however, conflicts with the general aura of austerity conferred on the entrepreneur-accumulator by the whole classical school. Do businessmen accumulate or do they not? They must, for this is what drives production forward; they cannot, for if they did, the flow of spending would be interrupted and Say's Law would be suspended.

Once a fiction is created, the fact that it is not recognized to be a purely imaginative statement generally causes a tremendous theoretical effort to provide support for it. Fictions have their own constituency. Since such efforts follow the same methodology that created the original contrivance of thought, they succeed in convincing only those who accepted the original fiction. The classical quantity theory of money and the theory of the rate of interest are two props of Say's Law; both are instances of rationalistic, mechanistic constructs and both fell with Say's Law.

In recent years some economists, particularly Don Patinkin, found Say's Law to be "inconsistent" with the quantity theory of money.[18] This is exactly what we would expect. The inconsistency revolves around the fact that according to Say's Law the supply and demand of commodities depends on *relative* prices (a reflection of "real" economic reasoning); demand and supply are homogeneous of zero degree. This implies that the *total* demand for goods also depends on relative, not absolute, prices. But in fact a change in the general level of prices, leaving relative prices unchanged, will still change desired transaction balances, which in turn leads to opposite changes in quantity of commodity demanded and supplied, thus negating the "homogeneity postulate" of Say's Law. Thus it seems that the logicians committed a blunder, which was, typically, detected only after the fiction ceased to be useful and became an intellectual *curiosum*.

The theory of the interest rate in classical economics, another supporting pillar of Say's Law, was also found to entail a contradiction of the fundamental principle of all supply and demand thinking, viz., that the two functions be based on elements wholly independent of each other. Keynes argued that "the assumption that income is constant [following, say, a shift in savings] is inconsistent with the assumption that these two curves can shift independently of one another."[19] Rather, an increase in the savings propensity by lowering consumption reduces the marginal efficiency of capital and must shift the investment function, leaving the equilibrium rate of interest indeterminate. Classical economists were familiar with all the independent pieces of the above argument. They knew that an increase in savings entails a decrease in consumption and they themselves had created the marginal efficiency of capital concept as the "real" data on which investment floated. Nevertheless, they did not see the contradiction of which Keynes accuses them, just as the Mercantilists, although possessed with all the pieces of the specie-flow theorem, could not put them together in the "right" relation to each other. Mercantilist minds were too myopic in their practical concerns, classical ones too myopic in their abstractions.

J. S. Mill represents a step backward from Ricardo's abstractions. His *Principles* have been called "a halfway house" between Ricar-

18. A review of this controversy is found in S. Valavanis, "A Denial of Patinkin's Contradiction."
19. Keynes, *The General Theory*, p. 179.

dian and Marginalist economics. They are rather, as Mill himself was aware, an attempt to force economics to deal with ethical problems. To achieve this goal, Mill was forced to dilute the Cartesian qualities of Ricardo's economics. He tried to emphasize historical and customary factors in economic life. Too logical to be just a follower of Ricardo but not radical enough to found his own methodology or to join the rising historical school, Mill did not succeed in wedding history and theory or, which is the same thing on another plane, in joining the materialism of Ricardo's conclusions with the ethics of human nature. Only Marx, among economists, succeeded in accomplishing all this because his epistemology was non-Cartesian.

Mill's desire to widen the realm of reality by emphasizing the strength of customs, habits, policies, eventually led to the dualism of production theory, which alone he viewed as having scientific status, and distribution theory, where historical elements overshadow geometrical, eternal certainties. Man as a producer is in the grip of laws; as a receiver of national income, he can tamper with the divine order of things. Philosophically, Mill sensed that the materialism of economics denigrated man, deprived him of feelings, traditions, ideologies, and even of freedom.

The Benthamite calculus repelled and attracted him at the same time. Having learned the calculus from his father, J. S. Mill did not fully detect the avowed fictional nature of Bentham's positive contribution, but the mechanistic interpretation of man's behavior offered by Bentham's followers certainly offended him. By the same token, Mill's attitude toward the "iron law of wages" and toward the Malthusian population theory is ambivalent. He could not reject either without undermining the whole Ricardian system, so he reasserted their existence, appending pious hopes that labor unions and the laboring poor's "abstinence" may prevail over the "laws" in question.

The labor theory of value also commanded half-hearted support, perhaps because he detected the specious nature of Ricardo's arguments. We may note his dualism in his description of profits as, alternatively, the product of entrepreneurial "abstinence," or as deriving from the fact that "labour produces more than is required for its support,"[20] thus reconciling the ethics of classical and socialist economics!

20. Mill, *Principles of Political Economy,* Book 2, chap. 15, para. 5.

In the theory of money, too, Mill is less uncompromising than his orthodox predecessors. He reaffirms the neutrality of money and rejects the argument (a legacy of Mercantilist economics) that an increase in the money supply might stimulate physical output, an argument which was given a new lease on life by the gold discoveries of California and Australia with their attendant price rises in England. After having developed the theory of exchange in real (barter) terms, he finds that "the introduction of money does not interfere with the operation of any of the Laws of value laid down in the preceding chapters."[21] Money is a "veil." But he also discovers that an increase in the stock of money by raising prices affects the debtor-creditor relations, thus undercutting the whole dogma of the neutrality of money.[22]

Despite his antihypostatizing warnings, Mill could not resist the temptation of deriving a "stationary state" from the "tendency of profits to fall to a minimum."[23] There is no doubt that Mill viewed the stationary state as an emerging reality. He did not see, as Coleridge did, that "a secular trend of falling profits may well be a euphemism for a storm." Equilibrium analysis, the child of Cartesian idealistic and unhistorical premises, left no alternative but to deal in euphemisms.

Mill's work on economics is indeed a halfway house, not so much between Ricardian and marginalist economics, but rather between orthodox economics and the economics of the historical school, between rationalism and romanticism. He could not harmoniously amalgamate the two because he was hampered by an epistemology whose weakness he recognized but of which he could not free himself. Cognizant of the fact that Descartes' works are a "rich mine of almost every description of *à priori* fallacy,"[24] he did not or would not acknowledge that Descartes' way of reasoning had been copied throughout by economics.

21. Ibid., 3. iv. 3.
22. Ibid., 3. x. 5.
23. Ibid., 4. iv.
24. Mill, *A System of Logic, Ratiocinative and Inductive*, 2:342.

6

Hyperclassical Economics I

*What is abstract thought? It is thought without
a thinker. Abstract thought ignores everything
except the thought, and only the thought is, and
is in its own medium.*

              Kierkegaard

M OST HISTORIANS of economics find little to write about the economic thinking of the period 1870–1936. To the body of writings
between J. S. Mill and J. M. Keynes they devote only a fraction of
the space they grant classical economics. Roll's *History of Economic
Thought,* for instance, covers "Modern Economics" in thirty pages
—fewer than he devoted to Adam Smith alone. This, of course, is
no accident. For intellectual historians look for the meaning, the
ethical-political conclusions and implications of a system of thought.
And they realize that the whole body of marginalist writings has a
déjà vu quality. As Schopenhauer noticed, "When there is a great
deal of reflection and intellectual knowledge and very little experience, the result is like those books which have on each page two
lines of text to forty lines of commentary."[1] The "text" is still Adam
Smith. Hyperclassical economics is the "commentary."

    From our point of view, the hyperclassical period represents
the culmination of the logical tendencies of the Cartesian ego:

1. Arthur Schopenhauer, *The World as Will and Idea,* 2:254.

monism, symmetry, and elegance were very nearly attained by the creation of artificial concepts, which, when linked with each other mathematically, created an imposing and superficially consistent structure. But hyperclassicism also represents the culmination of the stresses that the Cartesian ego harbored within itself. These stresses came to the fore in the debates on "welfare economics" that arose during the same period. For the more introverted the economic mind became, the closer it came to recognizing its fundamental weakness—the fact that its truths were rooted not in the objective world but in the mind itself. The reaction to this realization was an extreme interest in the welfare (i.e., social and political) implications of the analysis, an interest that many economists found distasteful since it showed the hollowness of the scientific claim of the ego.

In this chapter we shall illustrate some of the discoveries of the economic mind in its ascetic withdrawal (value theory). The next will deal with the ego's return to earth, its passion and nemesis (welfare theory).

The fundamental Cartesian premise is that I know myself better than I know any other being because I am directly and immediately acquainted with my mind. Men, however, are identical in this respect: they each have a mind (reason) which is a something made of homogeneous stuff. Thus one who knows his own mind cannot help knowing all other minds, since reason is the same in all men. Cairnes, writing in 1888, asserts that economists have direct knowledge of economic matters "in [their] consciousness of what passes in [their] own minds." The economist, even before starting his research, is "already in possession of those ultimate principles governing the phenomena which form the subject of his study." Examining *himself,* the economist discovers that, when in the marketplace, he seeks to maximize his gains and minimize his losses.[2]

The fact that the source of economic theorems is the consciousness of the economist is also recognized by von Wieser: "The theory takes its point of departure from within, from the mind of the economic man"; "Certain acts are performed in the consciousness with the feeling of necessity. Why should [consciousness] first go to the trouble of deriving a law from a long chain of induction when

2. J. E. Cairnes, *The Character and Logical Method of Political Economy,* pp. 88 ff.

everyone hears the voice of the law within himself?"[3] Von Mises is just as clear. What we know about economic actions ("economizing, preferring, the relationship of means and ends," etc.) is not derived from experience. We know the answers to the problems raised by the mind by questioning the mind itself.[4]

The hyperclassical mind again considered the old question of the essence of value. Classical economics had rooted the phenomenon of relative price in exchange value—which implies social existence. The ego's self-analysis, instead, led to the discovery of use-value, which exists even in the absence of social intercourse. From the solitariness of thinking stemmed that inner, solitary judgment which economists call utility. Created by the ego, utility has the ego's very qualities: it is a quantifiable entity, it is universal (as is reason), and it is a fiction. Changes in utility have been historically illustrated with reference to a hypothetical person who is offered successive morsels of bread "without important intermission of time."[5] It is alleged that the utility of each successive morsel of bread is lower than that of the preceding unit. The reason for the time condition of the experiment is obvious: we must avoid that rebuilding of tastes and appetites that the sheer passage of time brings about. This is why, in effect, consumption is instantaneous. Furthermore, we must deal with "infinitesimally small" units of consumption and morsels are as close as we can get to satisfying this requirement.

We meet here with a clear case of the medium of analysis determining the nature of the "experiment." The calculus proceeds by infinitesimally small, continuous steps: so an experiment is conceived that enables us to illustrate certain qualities of the calculus. Once we have established the fact that marginal utility falls constantly, the physical units (morsels) are dropped and the conclusion of the experiment is transferred to actual units of purchase (pounds, gallons, kilos). At the basis of diminishing marginal utility is a false analogy between the "continuous" consumption of morsels of bread and the purchase of finite and large items, some of which (e.g., automobiles) are bought infrequently.

This passage from consuming morsels of bread to buying actual

3. Ludwig von Mises, *Epistemological Problems in Economics*, pp. 21–22, quoting von Wieser's *Social Economics*.

4. Von Mises, *Epistemological Problems*, pp. 13–14.

5. Jacob Viner, "The Utility Concept in Value Theory and Its Critics," in *The Long View and the Short*, p. 180.

goods might have been facilitated by the fact that in economic theory, categories have always had a certain serviceable flexibility, as all idealistic (i.e., contentless) terms generally have. Adam Smith, for instance, lumped cattle and workers together: "Not only his [the farmer's] labouring servants, but his labouring cattle are productive labourers."[6] James Mill, trying to reply to the argument that wine increases in value by the sheer passage of time (which undermines the labor theory), writes that "If the wine which is put in the cellar is increased in value one-tenth by being kept a year, one-tenth more labour may be correctly considered as having been expended on it."[7] John Stuart Mill, by an appropriate handling of the category "liberty," even succeeded in justifying labor unions. To outlaw such organizations means to deny a right obviously covered by freedom of contracts.[8]

This elastic quality of logical definitions was to become very useful in the hyperclassical phase. In connection with diminishing marginal utility, for instance, somebody alleged that the last coin or stamp collected has greater utility to a collector bent on completing a set than each of the previous acquisitions. Also, it was argued that the utility of a last yard of wallpaper or gallon of paint needed to complete the room is greater than that of the previous yards or gallons. An appropriate broadening of the category "good" solved the problem: in the case of the stamps or coins, it was argued that the "complete set" is the unit of study and in the case of wallpaper, the entire wall.[9] These arguments all neglect the fact that in the marketplace coins and stamps are not sold by the set, and that wallpaper and paint are not sold by the room. The mind, however, is not bound by the empirical.[10] Indeed, once it has en-

6. *The Wealth of Nations*, p. 344.

7. *Elements of Political Economy*, 1st ed. (1821), pp. 97–98. In the third edition (1844) Mill eliminates this statement, but his example of the machine shows the same desire to identify time with labor (pp. 100–101).

8. *Principles of Political Economy*, pp. 933–39.

9. Viner, *The Long View*, p. 185.

10. A meter, yard, or gallon has far greater degree of precision and objectivity than a "room" does. Since 1790 a meter has been one ten-millionth of the earth's quadrant passing through Paris, while rooms have always been very variable in size and hence in wall space. But the idealistic method can easily give the "room" the same objectivity that a meter has. For the ego does not consider the room as a real entity—this room or that room. Its empirical characteristics—among which is size—fall out. The room becomes a universal concept. As such, a room is a room is a room. The *idea* room partakes of the same objectivity that a meter has.

tered the aprioristic track of analysis, there is no way of surmounting intellectualistic obstacles but to rely on pure intellect itself. In production theory (as in utility theory) the mathematical ego demanded the same qualities of infinite divisibility and it led to the conclusion that inputs are substitutable at the margin. Pareto thought otherwise: more workers and less cocoa do not make the same amount of chocolate as before. Stigler, repeating what had been said countless times, asserts that "if two resources must be used together in some functional relationship, then the pair form a technical datum. As such they must be treated as a single factor of production."[11]

Passing from "utils" to a price-quantity relationship on which the powerful tools of the calculus could be applied also entailed innumerable difficulties. They were surmounted in the usual way by an appropriate handling of fictions. As Marshall clearly indicated, the equilibrium condition for the consumption of commodity x is $MU_x = P_x MU_e$, the latter term expressing the marginal utility of money income. Since MU_x falls constantly, the consumer can be induced to buy more units of x only if P_x falls. The equal sign in the equation does not guarantee this decline in P_x unless, of course, MU_e remains constant. By positing constancy of MU_e, more x will be bought at a lower P_x, and the whole relationship acquires the hallmarks of clearness and distinctness. Alas, useful as this postulated identity is, it conflicts with the very (imaginary) experiment of lowering P_x since a decrease in P_x clearly increases, ipso facto, MU_e. Now the mind is caught in a dilemma. It must uphold the stability of MU_e if it wants to derive a demand curve of unequivocal negative slope. Yet the very decline in P_x makes this stability of MU_e impossible. Marshall's way out was to argue that MU_e remains "effectively constant" when the commodity considered is "unimportant." To uphold the logic of this fiction, partial equilibrium analysis can thus deal with only "unimportant" goods, those on which a very small fraction of one's income is spent. It would appear that the high standards of Cartesian truth have severely limited the relevance of the analysis. This is not so, however, for a double standard exists in the realm of theory and in that of practical applications. The restrictive assumptions of the theory perform their function of meeting the mind's standards; henceforth, they are ignored. Mill thought this shedding of restrictive premises to

11. *Production and Distribution Theories: 1870 to 1895*, p. 367.

be an error of logic. We rather think it is inevitable, given the impossible demands the mind makes on itself: to be coldly logical *and* to be relevant. Textbooks illustrate Marshallian demand curves with reference to such "unimportant" commodities as automobiles, agricultural goods in general, durable goods, public goods.

Moreover, Marshall's fiction of "effective constancy of real income" makes a mockery of the claim of logical precision which is the mainstay of Cartesian clearness and distinctness. For a negligible error is, logically, still an error. In its unrestrained flight, the mind often reaches a point when it can no longer bend the laws of logic to its purpose. Then the claim of strict logical correctness is overcome and an open appeal to expediency takes its place. The Keynesian short run in which the size of the capital stock does not change (by definition) while capital accumulation (investment) does occur is another example of this device of ignoring something because it is quantitatively small. It is presumed that the annual addition to the existing capital stock is so "negligible" that it can be ignored. But at the same time investment is so important as to be the main element generating booms and depressions! In fictive thinking, logic is not a set of rules aiding the attainment of truth; it is rather like a taxi to be entered into or alighted from at will, for fictive thinking is expedient thinking.

Marshall's illogical attempt to retain real income constancy in the face of a price change did not please every economist. Pareto, for instance, was unimpressed and openly acknowledged the possibility of some demand curves being positively sloped.[12] Fresh problems were caused by the substitution effect, which also may give positively sloped demand curves. The way out of this new difficulty was, generally, to broaden the meaning of the commodity (just as before a yard of wallpaper became a roomful) so as to eliminate the postulated possibility of substitution! Thus, while it is not only conceivable, but possible, that margarine be an "inferior good," it is highly improbable that "food in general" is. This broadening of category, of course, conflicts with Marshall's requirement of the constancy of MU_e. But expedient thought is myopic, all focused on the narrow problem at hand, devising techniques for *its* solution but inevitably creating contradictions with other aspects of the theory.

So contradictory were the problems of utility, so specious their

12. George J. Stigler, *Essays in the History of Economics*, p. 136, quoting Pareto's *Cours*, 2:338.

solutions, that Cassel and Barone preferred to avoid basing their demand curves on utility. But the vast majority of economists lent themselves to playing this coy mental game of hide and seek. When problems arose, the fictions that caused them were never boldly attacked. Real life cannot be faced courageously for it is not amenable to systematic treatment. The obstacle must be overcome, a way out of the blind alley must be found, but only within the established methodology. So other fictions are contrived that often prove serviceable for the problem at hand but are themselves illogical and come into conflict with other aspects of the theoretical status quo.

In the end, despite the principle of diminishing marginal utility, the right of positively sloped demand curves to exist had to be granted. Laws have a very ambiguous status in an idealistic system. Thought aspires to discover *the* law, the clear-cut relationship (if a, then b and b only). But idealistic thinking also craves after generality and thus desires to cover the *whole* range of possibilities, real or imagined. Then the presumed law becomes "if a then b, or c, or d, etc." This is why, as Ralph Turvey has noted, "The theory [of public finance] is not used because it is useless. There are very few definite propositions: an income tax may raise or lower the supply of effort, the substitution of death duties for a tax on investment income may raise or lower savings, replacing a direct by an indirect tax may or may not improve resource allocation— and so forth."[13] The customary way out of this situation is to select that relationship that proves more serviceable than any other *in practice.* For instance, classical macroeconomics (a practical branch of economics) has never been troubled by the fact that a wage cut might increase labor supply, as is the case in Robbins' well-known article.[14] In this way, monism, elegance, and certainty are attained while the "exceptions" (the footnotes) give a halo of becoming intellectualism to the analysis.

Giving expression to the drive toward generality, Edgeworth was one of the first economists to introduce so-called generalized utility functions in which the utility of commodity x was made a function not only of its price but also of the price of other goods.

13. See Ralph Turvey's book review of *Public Finance in Theory and Practice* by A. R. Prest.
14. Lionel Robbins, "On the Elasticity of Demand for Income in Terms of Effort."

It is not surprising that "economists adhered to the additive utility function with considerable tenacity," as Stigler writes, for Edgeworth's generalization creates more problems than it solves. It was now less certain than ever that demand curves are negatively sloped. The various editions of Marshall's *Principles* illustrate the travail of a mind torn between the conflicting desires of obtaining as much generality as possible without giving up the Cartesian ideal of certainty.

The indifference curve approach is sometimes hailed as having dispensed with measurable utility. An individual faced with two commodities, x and y, whose prices he does not know, is asked to rank combinations of these goods such that he is indifferent to any such combinations. The continuity of the indifference curve clearly betrays the divine attributes of the consumer since he has to detect that infinitesimally small increment in x that will just compensate him for an infinitesimally small decrease in y. In substance, there is just as much measurement in weighing a commodity against another commodity as there is in weighing a commodity against utility. All that indifference curve analysis accomplishes is the purely formal substitution of the concept of marginal rate of substitution for that of marginal utility. Neither does the revealed preference approach represent a methodological change.[15] Indeed, the more complex the mathematics, the more obvious it is that the source of economic laws is the economic mind following what it believes to be universal principles of reason: today the "logic of ordering," yesterday the logic of the state of nature or of the popular Bentham.

Rationality is indeed pushed to extremes in consumer theory. Having deduced how much to buy at various hypothetical prices from the self-knowledge of utility schedules, the economist goes on to estimate "the excess of price which the consumer would be willing to pay rather than go without the commodity over what he actually pays" (consumer surplus). Asking this question is comparable to asking oneself, "What would be the set-up of Europe if Hitler had never existed?" Those who assume that the raw material of economic theorizing is human experience cannot explain how such "problems" arise.

After utility was discovered to be the real factor behind demand, the standards of elegance and symmetry naturally led to the dis-

15. H. S. Houthakker, "Revealed Preference and the Utility Function."

covery of "disutility" (sacrifice) as the real factor behind supply.
To treat supply empirically as mere costs of production would have
created an imbalance in the theory: something "real" had to be balanced by something just as "real." Though the wisdom that work
is painful is very ancient, the fact that capital does not have a
nervous system and hence can hardly suffer pain seemed to wreck
the whole conception. Not so, however, for the *provider* of capital
feels pain by "abstaining" from one guinea's worth of pleasure
(consumption) today. At the outset, we are confronted with a basic
contradiction: while economic phenomena are timeless, here is a
phenomenon, interest, that owes its very existence to time. Socialist
writers beholding the abstinence view of interest have added another problem by accusing economics of being especially propagandistic and sycophantic: they never understood the notion of the
abstemious millionaire. The attempt to squeeze from under these
problems makes capital theory one of the most fertile fields of
study from the standpoint of the ego, but one which we shall not
pursue here.

In any case, the turning of all productive factors into a homogeneous mass (disutility or sacrifice) clearly represented a step
forward toward monism. And this step was inevitable once the categories labor, capital, etc., attained full-fledged spiritual status. While
these categories did have some historical-sociological content in the
classical school, now, having been drained of all coarse matter, they
came to partake of a common substance, i.e., nothingness. Logically,
therefore, these factors could be considered as one and the same:
hence the conclusion that at the margin they are perfectly substitutable. Wickstead, one of the founders of the marginal theory of
distribution, wrote, "Within limits the most apparently unlike of
these factors of production can be substituted for each other at
the margin, and so brought to a common measure of marginal
serviceableness in a product. Thus though no amount of intelligence or industry can make bricks without straw, yet intelligence
may economize straw, and one man with more intelligence and
less straw may produce as good bricks as another with more straw
and less intelligence." And later he adds, "even managing ability
may, at the margin, be a substitute for skills and intelligence in the
hands, and vice-versa."[16] Mind and matter thus melt into one:

16. Stigler, *Production and Distribution Theories*, p. 333, quoting P.
H. Wickstead's *The Common Sense of Political Economy*, pp. 361, 363.

mental skills and digital skills are one and the same, having been spiritualized in the laboratory of Wickstead's own mind.

Things that are different in reality become identical by their common paternity—the economic mind. Flux' observation that the linear homogeneous production function (which needs all factors to be substitutable) "can easily be extended to an indefinite number of factors of production"[17] confirms our point as to the emptiness of economic categories. For Flux suggests that hyperclassical economic theory considers only three (four?) factors by the historical accident of having inherited the classificatory scheme of the classical school. In reality, the mathematical method allows us to deal with an "indefinite" number of factors. To say this is to acknowledge the totally subjective nature of the whole classification. In the alchemy of the mind, first all factors are made into one; then, having thus been made homogeneous, they are divided into an indefinite number. Wickstead, for instance, preferred to assume only two factors, land and "capital-and-labor." With the nonchalance of one who knows he will not be called to task, he refers to the latter category as "an idealized amalgam," a "very vague factor." It contains "we know not what."[18]

One of the merits of an iron methodology like the mathematical one is that the temperament of the scholar plays little role in the creation of the system. Man-the-scholar (existential man) is nothing; the ego-medium is all. It is largely the latter which, following its own rules, imposes the direction of the analysis, as Kierkegaard recognizes in the quotation at the beginning of this chapter. But there are limits to the fictions that even a mathematician can absorb. Edgeworth, another eminent founder of marginalism but evidently not wholly possessed with the right Cartesian temper, was apparently amused by the linear homogeneous production function. He ridiculed it as "a remarkable discovery; for the relation between product and factors is to be considered to hold good irrespective of the play of the market: 'An analytical and synthetic law of composition and resolution of industrial factors and products [Edgeworth is here quoting Wickstead] which would hold equally in Robinson Crusoe's island, in an American religious commune, in an Indian village ruled by custom and in

17. Stigler, *Production and Distribution Theories*, p. 335.
18. Ibid., p. 330, quoting Wickstead's *Coordination of the Laws of Distribution*, p. 20.

the competitive centers of the typical modern industries.' There is a magnificence in this generalization which recalls the youth of philosophy. Justice is a perfect cube, said the ancient sage; and rational conduct is a homogeneous function, adds the modern savant."[19]

Wickstead's rhetoric follows logically from the timeless quality of economics which is another aspect of the timelessness of abstract reason. And Edgeworth seems to have detected the normative nature of the marginal productivity theory: it consists of portraying symbolically one of the loftiest and most persistent ideals of mankind—the ideal of justice. For, under the theory, every productive factor is rewarded exactly in accordance with its own contribution to production. To receive no more and no less than we give is one of the aspirations of free men. Obviously, the justice portrayed by marginal productivity theory is of a purely formal type. It must be interpreted as platonic and contentless; the type of justice symbolized by the tautology "to give one his due." Economics accidentally hit upon the principle of justice by virtue of its rationalistic method. It is another case of reason discovering itself in its own psychic products. Reason gives birth to equity and justice—in fact, to reason. It is hardly surprising that, in a system where all actors follow the most rigid principles of reason, they all receive such "reasonable" remuneration as exactly their contribution to total output.

The linear homogeneous production function is a useful fiction. All fictions have this common characteristic: they do not simplify reality, they complicate it. The full divisibility and perfect substitutability of factors are complications of reality. Managers do not usually worry whether they should substitute *any* input for *any* other. Experience limits their degree of freedom. But there is more. A discovery of the mind, the linear homogeneous production function makes demands which conflict with other intellectual creations. Essential to the application of Euler's theorem is the assumption that the price of the output produced stays constant, or, in other words, that perfect competition prevails. But perfect competition and constant returns to scale (linear homogeneity) are not compatible with each other. It is argued that if long-run costs are above the price line, the firm will not even exist; if the cost line is below the price line, the industry will become a monopoly; and if cost

19. Stigler, *Production and Distribution Theories*, pp. 341–42, quoting Edgeworth's *Collected Papers*, 1:31.

and price line coincide, output will be indeterminate. In all cases, theoretical problems emerge.

The mind is now faced with the usual contradiction attendant on the use of fictions. In search of both generality, and clearness and distinctness, the mind must make a hard choice. But choice is impossible since both the fiction of perfect competition and that of the linear homogeneous production function are highly serviceable each in its own sphere. The mind has to call on its inventiveness to bridge the chasm. It does so by creating the fiction of entrepreneurial "perfect knowledge," a fiction which neglects the fact that if each entrepreneur knows how the others will respond to his moves, the industry will be, in effect, a monopoly. Stigler, on the other hand, suggested that the impasse may be overcome by assuming that "technological processes" are "fully divisible."[20] We readily confess that we do not know what is meant by this phrase. The Ariadne's thread that we have used to enter the labyrinthine paths and bypaths of the economic mind proves inadequate and we hasten to retrace our steps.

The real factors behind demand and supply (utility and disutility) are essentially the same, in the sense that negative numbers are the natural continuation of positive numbers. It was therefore easy to "marry" them to each other. At the margin they produced an offspring and they called it Equilibrium. The intellect discovered in the margin the true open sesame of reality. Through it, its ideal (e pluribus unum) became reality.

The margin determines everything: the marginal product of labor, the marginal product of land, the marginal product of capital, in conjunction with their respective marginal sacrifices, determine wages, rent, and interest. It is the marginal unit of a commodity bought that determines its value; the marginal consumer determines the price and the marginal producer gives us normal profits. It is marginal cost/marginal revenue considerations that determine the output of the firm, while the marginal irksomeness of labor in relation to wages determines the length of the working day. Marginal utility per dollar spent rules the optimum allocation of consumer income; marginal physical productivity per dollar of outlay determines efficient production. It is still customary for textbooks of public finance to assert that governments extend (or "should" ex-

20. *Production and Distribution Theories,* p. 381.

tend) their outlays to the point where marginal social costs equal marginal social benefits—a notion that recently has received a new lease on life in the cost-benefit budgeting principle.

The margin makes everything comprehensible. When the principle upon which marginalist thought is based is mastered, anybody can be a theory-builder. These are the steps. Reality is interpreted as a struggle between two "independent" forces, one labeled "good," the other "evil." While one strikes a blow, the other (by the ceteris paribus assumption) stays still. The forces of evil may have such labels as irksomeness, sacrifice, and costs; the forces of good may be utility, pleasure, and returns. We then postulate (as good Benthamite disciples must), first, measurability of good and evil and, second, a "negative slope" for good and a "positive" one for evil. These principles being fictional, they can easily be applied to anything, as they actually have been. For instance, the marginalist tools have even been used to determine the "optimum" population size of an underdeveloped country, which would strike us as no mean achievement if we were not acquainted with the wonderful qualities of the ego.

The margin succeeded in bringing varied phenomena under one heading: it is to be considered as the great (formal) hinge toward which all economic thinking has groped since Adam Smith.[21] And it would appear from what we have said that of the two principles of homogeneity ("something is a special case of something else") and specification ("everything is unique"), which Kant regards as two alternative and opposite regulative principles of reason, economic theory used the first. This, at least, is what is suggested by subsuming every phenomenon under the force of (positive or negative) utility. This is not so, however, for fictive thought is, above all else, expedient thought. When logic stands in the way, logic is ignored. The useful assumption of homogeneity of each factor of production within itself is sometimes dropped. Some workers are recognized to have certain "natural" skills so that their compensation is partly wages, partly rent.[22] Firms, too, may supplement their "normal" profits with quasi-rents because of peculiarities of location (is not every location different from every other?), managerial differences, etc. In one word, the differences among workers or

21. The substantive hinge remained Adam Smith's self-interest.
22. Why rent? Because workers are "like" Ricardo's land. Analogical reasoning is involved here.

firms which were first assumed to be zero so that laws could more easily be derived are later found to be positive: first not to exist, then to exist.

In the conclusion, the original fiction (homogeneity) is cast away and the economist reverts to the concept of heterogeneity embodied in Ricardian rent. This procedure can hardly be called (as it has mistakenly been called) the method of successive approximation, for two antithetical logical principles are used. Neither does this method lead to a greater degree of realism. It is only designed to allow for the possibility of profit and wages to vary from firm to firm and worker to worker. A reversion to the principle of heterogeneity may thus be interpreted as an acknowledgment of the failure of the principle of homogeneity. In any case it is alleged that, in the long run, these "rents" become "costs," and so homogeneity triumphs after all!

What can be said of the claim that hyperclassicism resolved the Smithian paradox of the relative value of diamonds and water, the first "useless" but high priced, the latter so useful but free? The solution is a purely formal one which throws no light on the problem. The economic mind draws out of itself a string of very high marginal utility figures for diamonds, very low ones for water, and hence deduces a high price for the former and a low one for the latter. Societies where diamonds are worthless and water high priced obviously present no problem. There the marginal utility of diamonds must be negligible, that of water very high. This type of reasoning is making the "economics of pollution" one of the most fictive branches of our discipline.

The greatest ambition of rationalistic mechanicism is to be able to ascertain the state and location of the various elements that comprise the "model" at any time. Economics is full of comparisons with astronomy, the science which, in possession of certain laws of planetary motion, can easily determine the location of any celestial body at any moment in the past, present, or future. Darwin's discoveries provided even headier spirits to a mind already inebriated by Descartes' wine. Bergson quotes Huxley as asserting that, given a knowledge of the original "cosmic vapour," a "sufficient intellect" contemplating that vapor billions of years ago "could . . . have predicted, say, the state of the Fauna of Great Britain in 1869, with as much certainty as one can say what will happen to the vapour

of the breath on a cold winter's day."[23] For Huxley all there was
to evolution was the primordial vapor and the laws of composition
and rearrangement of its molecules. Once these laws are discovered
we are in possession of the Eternal Timetable. Nothing can affect
it which was not in the sufficient intellect contemplating the original nebula.

More sedate thinkers would probably find Huxley's claims
hyperbolic. J. S. Mill, for instance, attacks them but, such being
the force of rationalism, provides in the process another mechanistic view of nature just as uncompromising as Huxley's. Nobody
can contend, he says, that it is possible, "setting out from the
principle of human nature and from the general circumstances of
the position of our species, to determine a priori the order in which
human development must take place, and to predict, consequently,
the general facts of history up to the present time."[24] Why not?
Because "after the first few terms of the series, the influence exercised over each generation by the generations which preceded it,
becomes . . . more and more preponderant over all other influences
until at length what we now are and do, is in a very small degree
the result of the universal circumstances of the human race . . .
but mainly of the qualities produced in us by the whole previous
history of humanity."[25] Mill's argument seems to be the opposite of
Huxley's but in reality belongs to the same species. If we stand as
"sufficient intellects" at the threshold, we cannot predict the future
because each generation adds something to the preceding generations. On the other hand, from the perspective of the present, the
freedom of the present and future generations is very narrow: the
past weighs like a leaden cap on us and on them. We are, so to
speak, chained by our past and become more and more enslaved to
it with the passage of time. Starting out with a healthy skepticism
about deductive, a priori mechanism ("the principles of human
nature"), Mill ends by embracing a kind of biological determinism. Once we have the original cosmic vapor or the past "steps"
of man's history, a blind mechanism takes over with such over-
powering force as to annihilate the new, the unexpected, the
chancy, the non-mathematical.

23. Bergson, Creative Evolution, p. 44.
24. Predicting the past may seem an idle occupation. But when empirical
knowledge (history) is denigrated, all that is left is giving a rational basis to a
past about which we are ignorant.
25. J. S. Mill, A System of Logic, Ratiocinative and Inductive, 2:513.

The Walrasian system is the flowering of the same form of reasoning in a static context. The original endowment of resources is the primordial cosmic vapor, the given "first steps." Whence they came is unknown but toward what they strive (optimum allocational efficiency) is known with certainty to the sufficient intellect of the economist who has discovered (we should say, created) the laws of composition and rearrangement in production and distribution.

The remarkable conclusions of Huxley, Mill, and economic theory are all offshoots of the rationalistic outlook. And to rationalism, despite its talk about fauna, generations, labor, capital, etc., the alleged actors of change are mere epiphenomena of the mind. Born of a morbid doubt and striving to repress it, rationalism has, quite simply, lost any sense of wonder toward the physical or social universe. Time, though mentioned, is actually a mere sound. Huxley even equates the billions of years of evolution with the few instants it takes for the vapor of the breath to condense on a cold day. Rationalism sees in true time an enemy. For time is the one element which makes everything truly unique and hence inimical to the goal of clearness and distinctness. Thus it does not regard time as an intrinsic quality of reality. In economics, time is a creation of the subject, a mode of perception, a discovery of inspectio. It should never be misconstrued as an entity related to the revolution of the earth. It is a purely subjective entity, a fiction that enables us to split the analysis into two parts and thus complicate, not simplify, reality. If the long- and short-run dichotomy were interpreted as experience and common sense dictate, it would lead to absurdities such as the long run is sometimes shorter than the short run. For example, once management has decided to increase output, it may well buy a machine and put it into operation in a week's time, while the hiring and training of extra labor may take much longer.

The meaning of time in economic theory is so peculiar and misunderstood that it will be useful to examine it at greater length. Time in economics is an independent variable, one that, when mentioned at all, is isolated from all the other variables. The movement from the short to the long run does not cause a change in what, if time were historical time, would inevitably have to change. Time in economics is not the time of real life, inextricably attached to, and accounting for, the uniqueness of the events being examined. It is merely a link between one state and another, a bridge between the beginning and the end products of theory; it is *t*. It may be an infinity or a very brief instant—past, present, or future. When economics starts from a state of equilibrium and then changes a variable, thus obtaining a new equilibrium state, there is nothing that prevents us from supposing that the universe vanishes from *t–1* to *t*, when it suddenly reappears. Marshall's dictum (*Natura non facit saltum*) is paradoxical in that the only element of nature that proceeds without jumps is time but the economist chops it up into finite, homogeneous elements (period 1, 2, 3 . . .) which are then abstracted from the object of analysis. The mathematical world, in which the state of a system is calculated at two points in time, *t–1* and *t*, is a world dead and reborn at every instant. It is dead when equilibrium is destroyed by a (hypothetical) parametric change and reborn when equilibrium is regained.

What happens between equilibrium states is beyond the scope of theory, clear indication that the "now . . . later," *t–1* and *t*, "weeks" and "periods" spoken of in economics have nothing to do with historical time. If we take away equilibrium states from economic theory, we find nothing, for nothing is exactly what is sandwiched between them. This is why when the theorist tries to convey a general explanation of events whereby equilibrium is reattained, he has to resort to false analogies like the *tâtonnement*, or he is forced to reason illogically from effect to cause: "this must be so because in equilibrium it is so."[26] The time spoken of by theorists is reversible: a given state, which by a change of a parameter was destroyed, now can be recaptured by the opposite parametric change. In the world of men it is beyond anybody's power to return today's Ford Motor Company to what it was ten years ago, or even yesterday.

Lately, the belief has arisen that economic theorizing has finally become "dynamic." "Dynamic economics" is supposed to give a "description of the actual path followed by a system going from one 'comparative static level' to another." This is accomplished by using the differential calculus. Whatever the calculus does, however, it certainly does not advance our understanding of the world outside the mind. "No complications of the mathematical order with itself . . . can introduce an atom of novelty in the world."[27] The economist simply uses certain properties of higher mathematics to artificially

26. For an example of this form of reasoning, see Gardiner Ackley, *Macroeconomic Theory*, p. 135.
27. Bergson, *Creative Evolution*, p. 238.

link "today" to "yesterday," t to $t+1$, etc. But t is only an abstraction, just another algebraic symbol: it can be a year, a century, or an instant, at will. This abstract time, of course, carries with itself abstract "events," modern versions of the state of nature. And just as the qualities and characteristics of the state of nature predetermined the conclusions of the argument, so the engine of mathematics is such as to admit of no occurrence which is not programed in the original model. Once the system has been set up, not revolution, war, or any of the innumerable subtle influences continuously at work in a society (which go undetected largely because we look at society with the calculus mentality) can influence the outcome. Dynamic Keynesian models are actually inferior to Keynes' own imaginative method as ways of understanding economic reality, as we shall indicate later. The abstract nature of t should be obvious by the fact that whenever an attempt is made to give exact dates to the t's of economic theory, the results are ludicrous. More than one "historical" econometric study has concluded that consumption was negative in the days of Cotton Mather.

The elimination of real time from economic thinking is another effect of the Cartesian epistemology. Descartes' consciousness is timeless. In respect to the treatment of time, Cartesian rationalism proves to be even more abstract than that theology from which it was trying to escape, for Christian theology takes as its point of departure an event which theologians regarded as a *fact* of history, God's incarnation and His actions in the world. The God of the Schoolmen was a God who had left His imprint on the world. But Descartes cared little about the world, for the world of the senses cannot be known with certainty and clearness. This is why his God is an abstraction whose only mark on the world is his creation of an abstraction: *mens*, consciousness, or the ego, whose transcendental expression Descartes called the soul. "The god of a philosopher and his world are correlated [writes a modern interpreter of Descartes]. Now Descartes' God, in contradistinction to most previous Gods, is not symbolized by the things He created; He does not express himself in them. There is no analogy between God and the world; no *imagines* and *vestigia Dei in mundo*; the only exception is our soul, that is, a pure mind, a being, a substance of which all essence consists in thought, a mind endowed with an intelligence able to grasp the idea of God. . . ."[28] This pure mind, this abstrac-

28. Koyré, *From the Closed World to the Infinite Universe*, p. 99.

tion, created an abstract God and an abstract universe of strictly uniform mathematical qualities: ". . . the world created by the Cartesian God, that is, the world of Descartes, is by no means the colorful multiform and qualitatively determined world of the Aristotelian, *the world of our daily life and experience*—that world is only a subjective world of unstable and inconsistent opinion based upon the untruthful testimony of confused and erroneous sense-perception—but a strictly uniform mathematical world, a world of geometry made real about which our clear and distinct ideas give us a certain and evident knowledge."[29] Mathematicians have no need for the concept of time and neither do the social scientists who rely on mathematics to express ideas clearly and distinctly. Walras' general equilibrium model—that Schumpeter admiringly called the "Magna Charta of exact economics"[30]— is the epitome of "timeless occurrences."

In one major respect, however, the economist-rationalists were unable to meet Descartes' exacting standards. He knew that teleological conceptions and explanations have no place and no meaning in mathematics. The economists knew it too, but most of them found themselves unable to meet this stoical requirement of the medium, as the positive-normative debates indicate.[31]

If the time involved in economic theory is in fact an independent variable isolated from, and independent of, the other variables, then the economist, when changing the variable time, must (by the ceteris paribus assumption) keep all other variables unchanged. However, this would lead to absurdities. A practical discipline like economics is not interested in time per se but in the different events that the passage of time carries along. A historical moment is necessarily associated to the events of that moment. Yet if we are correct in considering economic time as an independent variable, we must show that at least some economists logically change it without changing anything else.

This is admittedly difficult to prove: economics, after all, takes some liberties with logic. But Viner, one of the most clear-minded economists, came close to following the dictates of logic: he changed "time" without allowing it to perform its work of changing some-

29. Ibid., p. 100. Emphasis added.
30. *History of Economic Analysis,* p. 968.
31. See chap. 7.

thing else.[32] In his 1931 article "Cost Curves and Supply Curves," after having portrayed the usual short-run equilibrium situation ($mc = mr$), he went on to establish the link between short- and long-run adjustments. The long run is a period long enough to allow the businessman "to make such technologically possible changes in the scale of his plant as he desires, and thus to vary his output either by a more or less intensive utilization of existing plant, or by some combination of these methods."[33]

Thus, the unsophisticated student may be induced to believe that the long run is a period of time during which the firm expands in size by buying more modern machinery or by introducing more effective means of control within the firm—internal telephones where there were none before, duplicating machines to quickly transmit memos and orders, etc. As a matter of fact, expansion of plant that takes advantage of more advanced technology is specifically ruled out. As Viner wrote in his article, "The theoretical static long run, it should be noted, is a sort of 'timeless' long run throughout which nothing new happens except the full mutual adjustment to each other of the primary factors existing at the beginning of the long-run period" (p. 58).

Viner's "time" is only a subjective category because what generally occurs in objective time is not allowed to take place. Yet Viner is forced to adopt this paradoxical definition of time because he senses that the true bases of economic theory are ideal and unempirical. Viner knows that economic truths are *universally* true and logically concludes that these truths cannot possibly "carry" genuine events, historical facts which are by definition time bound, unique, peculiar to the circumstances—in a word, the very opposite of universal.

And yet, if in Viner's long run nothing really happened, then the concept would be undistinguishable from the short run. Evidently, something must be allowed to occur, and Viner dreams up "the full mutual adjustment to each other of the primary factors existing at the beginning of the long-run period." It is difficult to tell here precisely what Viner has in mind, but one thing is certain: his "mutual adjustment" (which lowers unit production costs) implies that the original (short run) plant ac was the result of an er-

32. Actually, we already met with this phenomenon in connection with the law of diminishing returns. See chap. 5.
33. Reprinted in *The Long View*, p. 57.

ror, of an unscientific input mix, or of some other irrationality which "time," experience, and "mutual adjustments" will solve. But this mode of reasoning contradicts everything on which short-run costs are based: isoquants, isocosts, perfect knowledge, rationality, entrepreneurial foresight, etc. The mathematical medium of analysis *demands* these ideal attributes, and they conflict sharply with the world of facts, experience, and "mutual adjustments." Viner's definition of long run is logical (in that it rules out most changes which occur in time) but only at the price of attributing *lack* of logic to the short run.

Viner's article provides us with yet another illustration of the medium of analysis prevailing over common sense. It will be recalled that Viner's instructions to the draftsman were "to draw the [long-run] *AC* curve so as never to be above any portion of any *ac* curve" (p. 66n16). Why this instruction? Exactly because Viner realized that it would be contradictory of the all-pervading assumption of rationality to assert that one and the same output Q can be produced at lower unit costs in the long run than in short-run equilibrium (where $ac = mc = mr$). Unfortunately the draftsman, who had his own mathematical conventions to serve, "saw some mathematical objection" to Viner's instructions, which is hardly surprising for Viner had asked him to perform something impossible, even within the realm of mathematics. Viner's way out was to let the draftsman impose his rules (reflecting the superiority of the medium) so that his *AC* cuts all *ac*'s lowest points from above when in the descending phase and from below while in the ascending. Realizing that this solution entails its own contradictions, Viner rose to truly speculative heights when he asserted that the *AC* curve has significance only at the points of intersection with the *ac*'s lowest points. Such are the contradictions to which a dedication to logic leads.

Other economists could not accept the fact that a line exists as a series of unconnected points. Mathematics, after all, does not make jumps or makes at most infinitesimally small ones. Viner yielded and the familiar "envelope" relationship arose. The *AC* is now interpreted as the locus of points of successively larger plants (*ac*'s). But we can explain how a given output is produced at lower costs in the long than in the short run only by acknowledging that the original plant *ac* was, in some sense, an error. The current formulation bought realism at the cost of logical consistency.

Consciousness, reason, timelessness, infinity, omniscience—in economic theorizing these qualities are all intertwined, being different aspects of the same methodological ego. Occasionally economists have tried to escape from the conclusions this methodology imposed, but without success. Wicksell's attempts are a good illustration. We already saw how Hume and Locke dealt with money and prices by laying down the axiom that a change in money supply leads to an equi-proportionate change in prices, leaving the "real" variables of the economy unchanged. This conclusion was reached by the method of reason and, of course, imputed rational behavior to all economic agents. Faced with occasional economic disorders (inflation, depressions, crises), economists had a ready-made explanation for them: they were clearly due to "irrational" behavior, either to money hoarding or to central bankers' ignorance (unwarranted money creation that artificially created a state of euphoria "eventually" leading to a collapse). Wicksell tried to weave those insights into his model. He attempted to graft the irrational factors of hoarding and unjustified money creation into the very model of his predecessors, a model based on the assumptions of utmost rationality and foresight. As a healthy body resents the intrusion of germs and fights them, so mathematics (rationality) rejected the irrational strains that Wicksell tried to introduce. Equilibrium, the offspring of reason, could not be restored, except by making both hoarding and money creation equal to zero. As Ackley puts it, Wicksell's " 'sophisticated' quantity theory of money gives the same result—in equilibrium—as the naïve one,"[34] that is, as the Humean one.

It is hardly surprising that Keynes pours his poetic scorn on a mental exercise similar to the one just reviewed: "At this point we are in deep water. 'The wild duck has dived down to the bottom—as deep as she can get—and bitten fast hold of the weed and tangle and all the rubbish that is down there, and it would take an extraordinarily clever dog to dive after and fish her up again.' "[35] As a characterization of the theoretical mind inextricably mired in the weeds, tangle, and rubbish of its own fiction-making, Keynes' metaphor can hardly be improved on. The pre-Keynesian macrosystem is the child of the idealistic ego. Orthodox texts, as is well known, first developed the analysis of "real" relations (dominated by Say's

34. *Macroeconomic Theory*, p. 161.
35. *The General Theory*, p. 183.

axiom, the homogeneous production function, the pleasure-pain calculus of the labor market) and on this they superimposed, generally in the last chapter, an analysis of the monetary economy. Certain important concepts—utility, consumer surplus, short- and long-run costs, quasi-rents, multiple equilibria, unstable equilibria, etc.—which are the scaffolding of the whole analysis dropped out of sight in the more policy-oriented macrosystem, where everything is so simple that even politicians can grasp the model.

Classical macroeconomics is not a theory of income fluctuations because fluctuations are a phenomenon of economic life, and economic science never had a method for understanding life. To say, as it has sometimes been asserted, that the hyperclassicists were unconcerned with fluctuations because these were unknown in their days is absurd. Industrial fluctuations have existed since the birth of industry. Jevons devoted much of his efforts to unlocking their secrets. His explanation is, in fact, a notorious application of mechanicism to social problems, in the course of which economics and astronomy became one,[36] just as in Smith's methodological essay philosophical inquiries are guided by the history of astronomy.[37] It is strange that those who ridicule his "sunspot" theory do not ridicule his value theory, for they are twins, the offspring of the same intellectual outlook.

The conclusion that an economy cannot produce unemployment forced itself upon economists by virtue of the apparently innocuous fiction of mistaking consciousness (the act of rational thinking) for human behavior. From epistemology's geometric reason ensued tautologically a social reason which produced the peace, harmony, world government (in economics, international comparative advantages), maximum happiness, and justice which were postulated at the outset.

36. Jevons' sunspot theory brings to mind another instance of analogical thinking by the same author. We refer to his studies on British coal supplies. Jevons took the Malthusian-Ricardian model, substituted "coal" for "corn," and just as the former economists saw mass starvation, so he foresaw the strangulation of British industry due to diminishing returns.

37. See pp. 74–75.

7

Hyperclassical Economics II

There is nothing more illogical than abstract logic:
it gives rise to unnatural phenomena, which finally
collapse.

Goethe

THE HALLMARK of rationalism is its tendency to create, unintentionally, purely intellectual problems and then to circumvent them
by resorting to specious "distinctions." By the middle of the nineteenth century, the abstractions of economic theory had led the
unaware mind into a serious contradiction from which the mind
tried to extricate itself by making a distinction. We are alluding to
the distinction between positive and normative economics or between economics as a science and economics as an art.

This dichotomy had the overt purpose of separating economic
theory proper (value theory) from practical policy recommendations. Only to the former were ascribed the Cartesian qualities of
certainty, clearness, and distinctness. Even when policy recommendations were nothing but the literary translation of economic
theories normally expressed symbolically (that is, in the language
of algebra), they were deemed to be uncertain, tentative, and incomplete. To uphold the purity of economic science, the economist
was enjoined to separate clearly the (positive) statements of economic theory from the normative and possibly value-laden prescrip-

tions of "practical economics," as Menger and others referred to the more policy-oriented areas of the discipline.[1] Discussions on this split of theoretical and normative economics have hitherto centered on whether a value-free economics is possible, and then on its limits. No attempt has been made to explain why the dichotomy arose at all. Fortunately, our interpretation of the nature and guiding principles of economics can shed some light. For the schism between a theoretical and a practical economics was an implicit acknowledgment of the weaknesses of the Cartesian epistemology on which the science was based. The separation itself was the child of this epistemology.

The opposition between the propositions of theoretical and those of practical economics was foreign to the founders of political economy. Adam Smith's work is consciously hortatory, designed to assist the birth of the "simple system of natural liberty." Bentham, another radical thinker, had no use for the distinction,[2] perhaps because he detected its fictive bases. Practical applications guided his thought from beginning to end. When he forged fictions, he did so with a practical (ethical) goal in mind, such as to advance certain reforms. Before Nassau Senior and J. S. Mill,[3] therefore, the distinction did not exist primarily because means and techniques had not yet freed themselves from the implications, goals, and purposes of the analysis. But a generation after Ricardo, economic abstractions had acquired a nearly total autonomy from practical results. Following their own dynamics, means had become independent from ends.

By Walras' time a grand contradiction had arisen, and attempts to get out of it gave rise to the science/art distinction. In strict logic, the discoveries of economic theory left no room for the making of policy suggestions. The analysis, paradoxically, undercut the very need for economics and for economists. Economists believed

1. Menger, *Problems of Economics and Sociology*, pp. 51, 68, 69, and passim.

2. Hutchison, *"Positive" Economics and Policy Objectives*, p. 27: "The distinction between 'art' and 'science' as Bentham draws it has no element of the positive-normative distinction, because for him the distinction did not exist. . . ."

3. The former introduced it in his *Outline of Political Economy*, the latter in his essay "On the Definition of Political Economy and on the Method of Investigation Proper to It," reprinted in *Essays on Some Unsettled Questions of Political Economy*, pp. 120–64.

that economic theory reflected reality. They further maintained that economic truths were eternal, forever true. Moreover, the truths of marginalist economics all portrayed a divinely arranged world: a world of optimum resource allocation; of distributive justice; of maximum output and highest consumer satisfaction. These conclusions, it must be noted, were never recognized for what they were —purely psychic creations having nothing to do with reality. An inadequate appreciation of the epistemological roots of economics forced economists to regard them as the intellectual reflection of the actual organization of economic activity. But now, if reality is so divinely arranged, what is the sense of making policy suggestions? What *can* the economist suggest if the scientific branch of the discipline (the one dealing with the "is-ness" of reality, with the indicative mood, as J. S. Mill put it) proves the inherent perfection of the economic order? The general equilibrium model, it must be understood, is no different from Marx' state of communism. It is Marx' communism in the present actuality. Marx, who was highly conscious of the fact that social theories bear the stamp of one's epistemological premises,[4] quite consistently concluded that in the communist social order there would be no social thinking. Social theories, policy-making, and their tools (the state, bureaucracies, parties, etc.) would all "wither away." But classical economists, although they portrayed a state of bliss as complete as Marx', did not clearly see that in this perfect state economics had no further role to play. The divorce of economic theory and policy recommendations is as close as the economists came to recognizing that in an economic society ruled by "forces" that produce a perfectly competitive optimum, economics and the economist lose their raison d'être (as completely as dentists would lose theirs if cavities and other odontological diseases were driven underground).

One may argue that some economists realized more or less imperfectly that economic theory only portrayed the way "we should like the economy to behave," as Keynes wrote. Let us grant this for the sake of argument. Then the economist's task would become that of drawing reality closer to the world of theory. This standpoint would have pitted the economist squarely against society: no business or labor organizations were to be tolerated. The state or some other organ was to enforce to the letter a competitive situation— which, of course, would have led to more "interferences" than even

4. See epigraph of chap. 2, and see chap. 10.

the Mercantilists would have tolerated. Realizing the impossibility of bringing reality into line with economic theory, the science/art dichotomy was invented as a way out. It had the purpose of protecting reality from the radicalism that always accompanies the setting up of an ideal world opposed to the imperfect empirical world.

In other words, throughout its development economic theory continued to harbor the contradiction contained in Adam Smith. We saw that his confidence in the Invisible Hand was severely qualified by the lively realization that businessmen like "to narrow the competition" through monopolistic practices. Adam Smith did not shirk his responsibility of inveighing against these activities. A century later, the list of "practices" that thwarted the Invisible Hand had grown immeasurably, partly because economics had turned more and more "inward," and partly because reality had deviated more and more from the competitive norm. What in Smith's days and in the light of his "loose" method were minor peccadilloes had become, in the framework of the austere and rigid methodology of the later classical economists, major crimes, the removal of which would have torn society to pieces.[5] The science/art dichotomy, by allowing the economist to deviate (in his political recommendations) from the *dictates* of the theory, introduced considerations of expediency in whatever practical recommendations he chose to make. The science/art dichotomy, we are saying, prevented economics from going down the road traveled by the political standard-bearers of rationality. This rationality took the form of a desire for liberty, fraternity, and equality, and the effort to implement these ideals led to the Terror. From this standpoint, then, the dichotomy represented a convenient way out of the radicalism immanent in the method of Descartes.

The fact remains, however, that expedient devices, born of a contradiction, can only be illogical and self-contradictory. The science/art device is no exception. It is argued that economics as a science "deals in facts," while economics as an art "deals in pre-

5. So-called British empiricism hardly mellowed that radicalism which Alexis de Tocqueville detected in the Physiocrats: "The past is an object of unbounded scorn for economists. . . . There is not one institution, however ancient and well-founded in our history, whose abolition they did not demand if it inconvenienced them or distorted the symmetry of their plans." Georges Sorel, *The Illusions of Progress*, pp. 60–61, quoting Alexis de Tocqueville, *L'Ancien Régime*, p. 159.

cepts," that the first is a "collection of truths," while the latter is "a body of rules, or directions for conduct."[6] Now, this distinction in social thought can only be made "in the mind." It represents, so to speak, a dualism of second degree. Having first split all reality into the psychic and the material, the economist now further splits the reality of economic thinking into a "scientific" and a "prescriptive" branch. It is clear, however, that positive economic theory itself is only a set of rules of conduct, indicating how labor, the entrepreneur, etc. behave when faced by certain occurrences (e.g., a change in wages, the imposition of a tax, a fall in profits). It is not merely normative economics that deals in what Mill calls the imperative mood ("do this; avoid that"). So also does positive economics. In the face of an increase in profits, for instance, the producer acts (in economic theory): he increases his output. As Machlup says in a recent article, the dramatis personae of economics are mere "puppets" ordered to respond in a certain way because they have been so "programmed" by the economist's own a prioris.[7] G. L. S. Shackle understood this when he wrote, "Conventional economics is not about choice, but about acting according to necessity. Economic man obeys the *dictates* of reason, follows the *logic of choice*. To call this conduct choice is surely a misuse of words, when we suppose that to him the ends amongst which he can select, and the criteria of selection, are given, and the means to each end are known. . . . Choice in such a theory is empty, and conventional economics should abandon the word."[8] The only distinction that can be made between positive and normative economics is purely formal and trivial: while in positive economics the power doing the ordering is abstract reason, in normative economics the creator of reason (the economist) comes out in the open. But since this creator is, of course, a real man (not an ego) he realizes that practical-political reality has different qualities from those possessed by geometry. Therefore, his practical recommendations have often very little to do with his scheme of theory. Keynes noticed this when he wrote, perhaps ironically, that "it is the distinction of Prof. Robbins that he, *almost alone*, continues to maintain a consistent scheme of thought, his practical recommendations

6. "On the Definition of Political Economy," p. 124.
7. "Theories of the Firm," pp. 1–33.
8. Quoted by Hutchison, *"Positive" Economics*, p. 163. Emphasis in the text.

belonging to the same system as his theory."[9] Walras, like Robbins, unhesitantly transferred the conclusions of economic theory to the world of men. He has been severely criticized for saying that a world of competitive firms maximizes social utility. The least that can be said about his conclusion is that it is at one with the theoretical scheme and conclusions of all conventional economics.

Although the positive/normative split is an attempt to overcome the weaknesses of the Cartesian epistemology, it is also the offspring of this same epistemology. It is therefore not surprising that the attempt was unsuccessful. Caught in the Cartesian vise, the economic mind could only try to circumvent the problem by exploiting the very methodology that had created the difficulty.

We know how Descartes' reconstruction of thinking began with doubting everything. Eventually, from doubt arose certainty. But two centuries later this certainty had given way to a deep philosophical skepticism once again. The positive/normative controversy represents economics' bowing to this current of skepticism. Descartes' fear of being deceived by the objective world reached almost morbid proportions. The philosopher dwells at length on a mystical crisis he experienced in November 1619, a crisis caused by a feeling of moral and epistemological emptiness.[10] The European intellectual house of the early seventeenth century was in shambles. As Descartes says repeatedly, each center of learning contradicted the other. To discover one's thoughts (scientific and moral) to be so aimless is to be seized by a sort of spiritual vertigo. "Quod vitae sectabor iter?" Descartes asked himself ("How shall I orientate myself in the world?"). His feeling of terror was so strong that he had a dream in which his room was filled with flakes of fire and shook with divine thunder. He overcame this trial. In the same night "there came to him the revelation that he alone was the man to complete the corpus of the science, including the science of human happiness, the definitive science of ethics."[11] Descartes had discovered the thaumaturgic properties of geometry. This trying intellectual pilgrimage from what we may call metaphysical

9. *General Theory*, p. 20n. Emphasis added.
10. The meaning and implications of this crisis are examined in detail by George Poulet, *Studies in Human Time*, in the essay "The Dream of Descartes."
11. Marthinus Versfeld, *An Essay on the Metaphysics of Descartes*, p. 168.

anomie to certainty we have traced in the progress of economics from the late Mercantilists to the hyperclassical economists.

Descartes died in 1650 but his philosophical outlook underwent change. By the beginning of the nineteenth century, Cartesianism had already done its historical work of shaping the world and was moribund.[12] The concept of reason, when it was used at all, was so broadened as to be antirationalistic. Social contract theories gave way to Carlyle's lectures on the Hero and Hero worship. Logical modes of thought came under suspicion. The circle was completed. Descartes' hyperbolic doubt, which had given birth to just as hyperbolic a feeling of certainty, caused first self-doubt and eventually a rejection of the social science applications of the Cartesian method. Geometrical thinking in the nineteenth century was deemed as untrustworthy a guide to understanding society as traditional authority had seemed to Descartes two centuries before. Now, educated men like J. S. Mill, Menger, and Edgeworth could not be blind to this current which was sweeping intellectual Europe. Within economics this change in outlook was given expression by the German historical school and the socialists. But conventional economics withstood the onslaught and the main tool of defense was the clear, though impossible, separation between the positive and normative elements of economics. The separation was natural to economists for the dichotomy is merely the sanctioning of the psychophysical dualism of the Cartesian epistemology. On one side we have the psychic world (pure theory, "real" economics); on the other, there is matter (the world of political actions, welfare suggestions, business cycle studies, etc.). The science/art dichotomy gave the methodological *imprimatur* to a split which had been more and more in evidence since Ricardo. Hence the two facets of the science/art dualism: it was a distinction to protect the right to exist of abstract, a priori, fictive thinking, and, at the same time, it was a natural product of the very methodology that intellectual Europe first questioned and then rejected.

As a device to maintain one's intellectual equipoise and trust in reason, the positive/normative dichotomy was admirable. As noted, it allowed the economist to bring to full flower the method of Ricardo, undeterred by the stormy philosophical skies of the nineteenth century. Self-doubt did not enter the economic main-

12. See chap. 11.

stream till 1936, when the science/art dichotomy was, incidentally, overthrown.[13] Yet economics purchased this intellectual equipoise at a high price, in fact, the highest intellectual price. For, in the process, economics had to give up its distinctive characteristics as the only social science founded on a view of man as a rational being. Both Robbins and von Mises, for instance, in their eagerness to reassert the value-free nature of economic theory, were compelled to regard any goal as rational by definition: Robbins emphasizes that "Economics is entirely neutral between ends. . . . Economics is not concerned with ends as such. . . . The ends may be noble or they may be base. . . ."[14] Von Mises is just as clear: "Modern economics makes no distinction among ends, *because it considers them all equally legitimate.*"[15] The economist who follows these methodological prescriptions has given up that redeeming quality of idealistic fictions to which Bentham and Kant called attention: their moral loftiness. Schacht's methods in Nazi international finance are as legitimate as any.

The *homo economicus* that emerges in Robbins' and von Mises' studies does not have that moral autonomy, that stoicism, which was one of the most endearing traits of his nineteenth-century predecessor. The economic man of J. S. Mill (which his author recognized to be fictive), being a creature of the enlightened philosophers, consulted the "moral law within" and acted in accordance with the dictates of reason. *His ends could not help being always noble.* The twentieth-century economic man created by Robbins and the "positivists" has lost this quality: his "ends may be noble or they may be base." He is no longer a rational "individualist." He may well choose to accept the ends of an "immoral society."

This redefinition of the psychology and philosophy animating the economic agents entails a redefinition of the ethical standpoint of the economist: while Smith's attitude toward the world was that of an angry prophet to whom many human actions seemed irrational and many institutions stupid, the attitude of "positivist" economists must, logically, be one of professional acquiescence and acceptance.

13. In the work of J. M. Keynes. Post-Keynesian economics re-enthroned it, along with much else that Keynes had repudiated.

14. Lionel Robbins, *An Essay on the Nature and Significance of Economic Science*, pp. 24–25.

15. *Epistemological Problems in Economics*, pp. 35, 60, 88, 180. Emphasis added.

Innumerable pages have been written on the ethical problem caused by this professional passivity possibly in the face of evil.[16] We, who are solely concerned with explaining historically and logically how a certain position came about, will limit ourselves to remarking that the dismissal of ends from economic theory is the last act of a drama which started with Descartes' *Discourse on Method*. The world created by Descartes is not the finite, hierarchically organized world of the Middle Ages when every value and every policy had its place *above* something and *below* something else and could be judged by its ability to advance or hinder the attainment of a universally agreed goal. In Descartes' world, instead, all component parts are on the same level of being. The finite became infinite; the vertical chain of being became a horizontal *catena*. "Better than" or "worse than" have no meaning and no value in the Cartesian universe of discourse. Goals, values, ends have no place in this world because they have no meaning and no place in mathematics.[17] Absolutes mean nothing. It is true that, by developing the idealistic side of Cartesianism, economics was led to use words like optimum—the best. But it was obvious to the most clear-minded economists that this word had no connotative meaning whatever. Such words "wormed" their way into economics, but it was only a matter of time before they would be detected and exposed as pseudoscientific. Much of the efforts of "positivist" economists has consisted of purging words like equilibrium, growth, sacrifice, etc., of their ethical-behavioral significance (recall, for instance, Robbins' "equilibrium is just equilibrium").

Once again we are then faced with another case of the medium imposing its standards and biases on the science and markedly narrowing its interests. The medium—mathematics—is value free because it is totally contentless: *a* is *a*, a mere scribble on a page. Certainly, mathematics does not concern itself with good and evil. When the medium, in the hyperclassical phase, was recognized

16. The traditional abdication of a concern with ends does reflect a predicament of modern civilization to which we think Nietzsche was one of the first philosophers to call attention, in his Parable of the Madman (from *The Gay Science*). A modern interpreter of the German philosopher summarizes it thus: "We have destroyed our faith in God. There remains only the void. We are falling. Our dignity is gone. *Our values are lost. Who is to say what is up and what is down?*" (Walter Kaufmann, *Nietzsche*, p. 97. Emphasis added). It is frankly unrealistic to expect economists to solve this problem.

17. Koyré, *From the Closed World to the Infinite Universe*, pp. 99–100.

to be nine-tenths of economic theory, then the time was ripe to disclaim a concern with the ends of economic actions.

Economic theory was striving to liberate itself from the strictures of life since its Cartesianization began in the works of Hume and Locke. Aims, values, goals, ends are the language of life which is inherently flux and purpose. But the same words are not to be found in the lexicon of mathematics which is unteleological and purposeless.[18] Thus the science/art hierarchy sanctioned that gulf between life and theory whose historical origins we traced back to Descartes' psychophysical dualism. The devalorization of life implicit in Cartesianism eventually influenced economics, causing a widespread scientific disinterest in goals.

Nothing in the positivist dichotomy naturally prevented the economist as a man from making policy recommendations. No matter how fictive theoretical thought is, it strives to point to its "implications" for policy. But policy suggestions continued to be vitiated by a methodological flaw. The point of departure of economic theory was the *isolated* individual who was "nearer to himself than to any other person." But practical suggestions in the area of policy have to take society as the focal point; hence the dilemma. If the solipsism of the isolated man is bridged by assuming at the outset (as in the popularized versions of Adam Smith) a "natural harmony" of interests, then there is no need for making policy suggestions. If, however, the premise of harmony is temporarily suspended, the economist has no means whereby to bridge the gap between the individual and society. By virtue of its atomistic methodology, economics had to recognize that the individual was, logically, the ultimate, indeed, the sole judge of the effects of a policy. This led to the paralyzing conclusion that if a million persons felt themselves to be better off but there was one person who felt he was worse off as a result of a policy or economic occurrence, then the economist was compelled to suspend judgment as to the desirability of that change. As H. Liebenstein puts it, "Where universal consent does not exist, then welfare economists simply are unable to declare whether there has been an increase in welfare in the cases in which some people feel better off and others feel worse off." This is an-

18. It may be worthwhile to recall that the first Cartesian theorem of economics (the specie-flow mechanism) conveyed the very clear message that to work toward a certain end (in this case, the national accumulation of gold) is futile. As Smith was translated into Cartesian symbols, doing anything became a futile interference with "laws."

other way of saying that the "Pareto optimum" grants a "veto power" to anyone opposed to change.[19]

Despite these unpromising elements, economic thinking on welfare matters valiantly fought to burst through its own methodology. Hypostatizing the conclusions of economic theory was tried (by Walras and others) but did not pass the exacting standards of the strict methodologists. Other devices have been tried with varying degrees of acceptability. Since these devices are the same ones that had been tested in the development of value theory, we shall review them very briefly.

1. We asserted that mature idealistic rationalism is monistic. This monism impelled economists to view that which "ought to be" attained as a monistic single and simple goal. Likewise, a policy is judged in terms of its effects on this simple goal. The One Goal, as it may be called, underwent many name changes. Edgeworth and others called it Social or Universal Utility by analogy with the individual utility of value theory. Having discovered the One Goal, monism allied itself to idealism; Universal Utility became U or W (welfare) or, later, Y/P (per capita income), and thus expressed, this symbol could link itself mathematically with other similar familiar symbols standing for resources, investment, capital, etc.

2. The ceteris paribus assumption on which economic theory proper is based also turned out to be serviceable. Arthur Pigou, for instance, presumed a "stable general culture" (such as one he felt existed in the Western Europe of his days) as the necessary sociological premise which was to make welfare analysis meaningful.[20]

3. The same Pigou devised a way out of the simple fact that there is no such a thing as a "strictly economic" policy or effect since everything is interrelated in the world. He merely assumed a "complementarity" between "economic" and "other aspects of welfare." An inherent harmony exists, that is, between maximizing profits in a freely competitive environment and, say, the flourishing of the arts and letters in that environment.[21]

4. The habit of dealing with the future as if it will be like the present (a habit that Keynes was to criticize) induced some econ-

19. "Notes on Welfare Economics and the Theory of Democracy," esp. pp. 310–11.

20. *Economics of Welfare*, p. 21.

21. Ibid., chap. 1.

omists to suppose that whatever monistic goal they currently assumed would continue for all eternity. In reality, every generation
of economists has made up different goals. Concern for allocational
efficiency has waned in recent decades, but it was the concern of
pre–World War I days.

In recent years the positive-normative dichotomy has been
given a new twist by Milton Friedman. He argues that the hallmark
of a positive science is its predictive value: *"the only relevant test*
of the validity of a hypothesis is comparison of its predictions with
experience."* As if this were not clear enough, Friedman proceeds
to give an example of what he means in his well-known illustration
of the leaves: "I suggest the hypothesis that the leaves are posi-
tioned as if each leaf deliberately sought to maximize the amount
of sunlight it receives, given the position of its neighbors, as if it
knew the physical laws determining the amount of sunlight that
would be received in various positions and could move rapidly or
instantaneously from any one position to any other desired and
unoccupied position."[22] Friedman has thus cut loose the assumptions
of a theory from the facts to be explained. The whole construct
may be apparently false, even absurd, but if it succeeds in explaining observed behavior, then we have "positive" science. It apparently does not occur to Friedman that mythology and even fables
would pass his standards of truth for they invariably "explain"
some aspect of life, often with the help of animistic constructs such
as the one he instances.

But the important thing is that Friedman's botanical example
is wholly in the tradition not of science but of seventeenth-century
social thought. If we recall the authors whose works we reviewed
in chapter 2, we find at work the same methodology that gave rise
to Friedman's leaf example. Namely, out of their imagination they
draw a "hypothesis" which eventually "accounts" for some fact of
contemporary life (the rise of civilization, the need for laws, the
acquisitiveness of men, etc.). With his well-known acumen, Friedman has detected the fact that economic theorems have always
been based on fictions (Benthamism, propensities, etc.) and he
encourages us to face this quality of economics without being self-
conscious about it for, he mistakenly says, this is the method of
"positive science"! His remarks on methodology show the vitality

22. "The Methodology of Positive Economics," in *Essays in Positive Economics*, p. 19.

of the Cartesian outlook in economics three centuries after it first made its appearance.

Friedman refers to the need for testing. Testing is the last citadel into which the economic ego has withdrawn. But even here it cannot escape from itself, for the hallmark of its creations (fictions) is that they can be so handled as to "prove" anything. An adept handling of elasticities can "explain" (retrospectively, of course) why, as a result of a specific tax, the price of the article did or did not go up by the full amount of the tax. A skilled handling of elasticities can "prove" why a wage cut leads to less employment offered, or more. An adept handling of elasticities can "explain" why a devaluing country receives more foreign exchange, or less.

Elasticities are not the only fictions that prove serviceable to a "positivist." So does psychology. The last word on psychological "explanations" has been spoken by Fetyukovitch, Dimitri Karamazoff's defense counsel. Commenting on the prosecutor's reconstruction of the crime on the basis of fragmentary evidence (a reconstruction steeped in "psychological insights"), he notes that "psychology lures even most serious people into romancing, and quite unconsciously." He then proceeds to use this "knife that cuts both ways" to interpret the same facts differently in the light of just as valid "psychological insights." Economics handles psychology to the same purpose. Currently, for instance, the traditional impact of tight money policies has been reversed by an appropriate handling of psychology. It is alleged that these policies lead to lower, not higher, interest rates because they throw businesses into a "pessimistic mood," thus undercutting the demand for loans (presumably, by more than the supply). Higher demand in the face of higher prices is also "explained" psychologically ("inflation psychosis"). Anybody who has opened a textbook on business fluctuations knows how easy it is to account for "turning points" by pulling out of the sleeve the ace of psychological moods at the appropriate time.

Economic theories have no verifiability. They are weighted with fictions. And fictions, to paraphrase Bergson, are like those roly-polys with sand at the bottom. You can stand them on the head; you can lay them on the side; you can toss them in the air. They will always spring upright.[23] In economics, reality will always "con-

23. This characteristic behavior of roly-polys is also due to their having empty heads.

firm" the hypothesis because the controlling element of both the hypothesis and the test is not objective reality, but our way of perceiving it. Economic theory is possessed of a dialectic as powerful as Hegel's.

Friedman's dubbing this methodology "positive" is a little baffling. Newton is often called the first great positivist,[24] and we saw that he had an absolute terror of exactly that unbridled fabrication of "hypotheses" that Friedman actually encourages.

Friedman's methodological stand springs from the same ego that, for two centuries now, has created economic hypotheses. With classical methodologists (Robbins, J. S. Mill, etc.), method was, at least partly, the guardian of the discipline much as ethics is the guardian of behavior. With Friedman, methodology abdicates this task. It joins the fiction-creating ego and puts its methodological imprimatur on it.

This way of conceiving the method of economics and the function of methodology leads to contradictions (as fictions always do). It is well known that Friedman claims to be politically "conservative." But economic theorizing along the lines suggested by him (without reality exercising any restraint on thought) must result in a plethora of contradictory hypothesizing ideally designed to create that intellectual chaos that is generally the first step toward social chaos.

To sum up we wish to call attention to another odd phenomenon, which, so far as we know, has never been detected, let alone explained. We refer to the clash between the peaceful, harmonious, delicately balanced view of the economic universe embodied in economic theory, and the violence and acrimony that characterizes some of the greatest methodological writings. Reason hovers above theoretical economics; unreason prevails in methodological writings. Such writings arise not out of a desire to understand the nature, evolution, and problems of economic thinking, but out of a "battle." They are *Methodenstreiten*, in the course of which the economist (whose personality was pushed into the background in the theoretical work) betrays himself to be all too human. Thus, we find one well-known theorist lashing out against the "champions of Unified Science": they are "driven by the dictatorial complex. . . . They see

24. Burtt, *The Metaphysical Foundations of Modern Physical Science*, p. 223.

themselves in the role of the dictator—the duce, the Führer, the production czar, in whose hands all other specimens of mankind are merely pawns." As for "social engineers" (whoever they are), they are actually prepared to "liquidate all those who did not fit into [their] plan for the arrangement of human affairs."[25] The economist sees the disagreements of intellectuals as symptomatic of a general malaise of civilization caused by a "resentment against life," and by the thinker's desire to live "in the shadow of a great man."[26] The same author devotes a whole chapter to an exploration of the "Psychological Bases of the Opposition to Economic Theory."[27]

Another methodologist, referring to the intellectual stirrings for a modicum of planning in the 1930s, writes, "scratch a would-be planner and you usually find a would-be dictator."[28] The same methodological work closes in an emotional crescendo ending in apocalyptic vision: There have arisen in the western world some who have betrayed the "Cult of Rationality." They try to "escape from the tragic necessities of choice."[29] But the Eumenides are pursuing them: "in love with death, their love will overtake them."[30]

The fact that these embarrassing utterances could be multiplied calls for an explanation transcending the individual thinker's idiosyncrasies. And, in fact, such despondency is the inevitable result of the very method of rationalism. This method, we repeatedly emphasized, is totally powerless in grasping reality. Rather, it strains itself to portray life as it "ought to" be: orderly, beautiful, and harmonious. Faced with a phenomenon of life (the clash of social theories) that is the negation of harmony, it cannot understand it. Just as the theory cannot explain the historical existence of unemployment, so the theorist is baffled by criticism of his method. These attacks are not answered: they can only be exorcised by resorting to vituperation.

25. Von Mises, *Ultimate Foundations of Economic Science*, pp. 40–41, 94.

26. Von Mises, *Epistemological Problems*, pp. 91–92.

27. Ibid., pp. 183–203.

28. Robbins, *Essay*, p. 113n.

29. One would imagine that escaping from *painful* choices is exactly what a good Benthamite would do. But Robbins rightly senses that when men begin to feel themselves as free (free even from economic laws), they are likely to revolt against the "laws" of social scientists.

30. Robbins, *Essay* (1st ed., 1932), p. 141. It must be noted that the revised second edition (1935) is purged of such utterances.

In his early essay "On Christianity," Hegel chides Enlightened philosophers for thinking that they had explained Christianity by calling it "superstition." They, too, were compelled to resort to epithets by their rational method. That people believe in miracles is unintelligible to the Cartesian mind: hence, this belief must be a perversion of the mind.[31] Hegel, who was to widen the meaning of reason to include all that happens in time, observes that the motto of the rationalist is *Fiat justitia, pereat mundus* (let justice be done even at the cost of destroying the world).

An uncompromising dogmatic opposition to wide areas of life is inevitable when we attempt to understand life by means of the categories of rationalism. This is why, paradoxically, rational thinking shows itself to be a prey to passions exactly when true reason and fairness and intellectual understanding are most called for, i.e., in scholarly debates. Supporters of true theories need not succumb to this spirit: with them facts are supreme. It is only when appeal to facts is precluded that all that is left is the uncovering of the "psychological bases" of the opposing viewpoint.

31. Just as a "miser" is a "psychological monstrosity" (Robbins). Clearly, the mathematical *forma mentis* does not foster tolerance. Divergent opinions in mathematics are simply indicative of ignorance on someone's part.

8

The Meaning of Economics

There are three different methods of viewing and presenting the objects of our thought, and among them, the phenomena of human life. The first is the ascertainment and recording of 'facts'; the second is the elucidation, through a comparative study of the facts ascertained, of general 'laws'; the third is the artistic recreation of the facts in the form of 'fiction.'

Arnold Toynbee

KIERKEGAARD THUS commented on Hegel: "If Hegel had written the whole of his *Logic*, and then said . . . that it was merely an experiment in thought . . . then he would certainly have been the greatest thinker who had ever lived. As it is, he is merely comic."[1] It would be unfair to transfer this criticism from Hegel—at whose unabashed identification of his own thinking (the dialectic) with the movement of reality Kierkegaard leveled his criticism—to all hyperclassical economists. The strict constructionists of economic theory (Menger, Robbins, von Mises, Machlup), like the philosophers (Bacon, Kant, Bentham, J. S. Mill), are certainly full of warnings against giving material reality to psychic creations. They saw more or less imperfectly that the ego, not reality, was the con-

1. Cited by Walter Kaufmann, *Nietzsche: Philosopher, Psychologist, Antichrist*, p. 85.

trolling factor, creating the concepts of economic science and relating them to one another. But the strict constructionists were few:
their outlook is really a footnote in the history of economics. They
intuitively sensed that between economic theory and economic
reality there was a wide gulf, but they never showed historically and
logically why this was so.

By calling attention to the epistemological soil on which economics grew and by stressing certain tendencies of the rationalistic
mind, our work has provided a confirmation for what was only an
intuition of the ablest and most clear-minded economists. The epistemology of economics is founded on Plato's dictum that "to know
a thing is to know its essence." The Cartesian ego created essences
that had basically geometric properties and which could therefore
be linked with each other according to mathematical rules. Psychologically, the economist inherited from Descartes what Nietzsche
called the "will to a system" (a fact already obvious in Smith's
essay on astronomy): the desire to produce a "well-rounded,"
"harmonious," systematic model. It is perhaps this "will" that Leontief and Hahn criticize as "scandalous," in the quotation presented
in the first chapter. If so, they have the encouragement of Nietzsche
himself: "The will to a *system*: in a philosopher, morally speaking,
a subtle corruption, a disease of the character; amorally speaking,
his will to appear more stupid than he is. . . ." And further on, the
philosopher flings the ultimate insult to the intellectual: "building
systems is childishness."[2]

This is perhaps too extreme. But Nietzsche has a point. Despite
the complications of the analysis, the system-builder lays himself
open to the charge of being superficial, for within the framework
of the system he cannot question his premises. And the thinker does
appear childish because, once the premises are accepted, the conclusions are predetermined. In fact, they are identical with the
premises themselves.

The disinterest in the truth-content of axioms—openly acknowledged by economists from J. S. Mill to Friedman—is the surest
indication that economic theory is avowedly fictive. It is in works
of fiction, in art and in literature, that criticism never attacks the
realism of the assumptions that the artist chooses to make. Nobody
in his right mind would reject *King Lear* on the grounds that the
fundamental arrangement which set the tragedy in motion is spe-

2. Ibid., p. 80. Emphasis in the text.

cious, unrealistic, and in fact, self-contradictory.[3] The value of fictive creations is esthetic and ethical, and these characteristics economic theory, too, possesses.

Before returning to this point, we wish to consider a case not of uncritical acceptance of the fictive premises of economic rationalism, but of their actual rejection by an economist bent on explaining a social fact. J. A. Schumpeter, himself a gifted fiction-maker in economic theory, in his essay "The Sociology of Imperialisms," openly denies that men are rational.[4] Reason, which economic theory alleges to guide the decisions of consumers, businessmen, statesmen (in their marginal social costs/marginal social benefits computations), is not to be found in an important historical fact: the colonial expansion of Western peoples in the late nineteenth century. On the contrary, Schumpeter decides that this phenomenon is rooted in an "atavistic" remnant of bygone centuries (p. 84). Imperialism is nothing more than the "objectless disposition [another "propensity" of human nature?] on the part of a state to unlimited forcible expansion" (p. 7). It has no purpose but itself. It is "expansion for the sake of expanding, war for the sake of fighting . . ." (p. 6). Moreover, Schumpeter adds, " 'objectless' tendencies toward forcible expansion, without definite, utilitarian limit—that is, *non-rational and irrational, purely instinctual inclinations* toward war and conquest—play a very large role in the history of mankind." And again, "it may sound paradoxical, but numberless wars—perhaps the majority of all wars—have been waged without adequate [utilitarian] 'reason' " (p. 83; emphasis added).

This is not at all paradoxical. What is paradoxical is that Schumpeter, when analyzing the social phenomena of the marketplace (in economic theory), finds the utmost rationality, but when analyzing such comprehensive social phenomenon as expansion, he

3. King Lear, feeling himself old, decided to bequeath his kingdom to those daughters who loved him most. We can accept as not totally unrealistic (though misguided) the trial to which he subjected his daughters, but his arrangements with the inheritors of his kingdom defies common sense and even logic. For Lear did not keep a castle for himself and his servants but planned to live (with one hundred knights) with the two daughters, one month with one, one month with the other, for the rest of his life. The hardship of traveling twelve times a year from one corner of the kingdom to the other on the part of a man who felt the weight of his years adds self-contradiction to unrealism.

4. This essay has been reprinted and translated in Joseph A. Schumpeter, *Imperialism and Social Classes.*

finds collective folly. Man is possessed with godlike qualities in the marketplace, but as a citizen of the state (and Schumpeter believes that "objectless expansion" has been a mass, popular phenomenon whose evolution he learnedly traces through the history of the Egyptian, Assyrian, Persian, Roman, Arabic, and Frankish empires, through the absolute dynasties of the seventeenth and eighteenth centuries, and through the democracies of the nineteenth century), man is an insane megalomaniac, a Cecil Rhodes, who fell into despair when he contemplated the sky, regretting "these vast worlds which we can never reach. I would annex the planets if I could."[5]

Just as the natural law philosophers posited now a brutish, now a bucolic, state of nature, just as Adam Smith started now with the axiom of sympathy, now with that of self-interest, so Schumpeter assumes now rationality, now irrationality, at will. This is sufficient proof of the volatility and precarious status of axioms in a fictive methodology.[6]

In his essay on imperialism, Schumpeter turns his back on his mentor (Descartes) and shares, instead, the epistemological doubts of another brilliant mathematician who had detected the weakness of the geometrical ego when dealing with human events. We refer to Pascal, ironically a contemporary of Descartes. After writing, at age sixteen, a treatise on conic sections, Pascal became absorbed in the problem of the extent and limits of geometrical knowledge. And he made a fruitful distinction between the "geometrical spirit" and the "acute or subtle spirit." The geometrical spirit excels in all those subjects that are capable of being reduced to their first elements. Then, once this element is isolated intellectually and nailed down as an axiom, deductions can be made yielding absolute truth. But, Pascal notes, not all reality is capable of being analyzed by

5. Hannah Arendt, *The Origins of Totalitarianism*, p. 124, quoting S. Gertrude Millin, *Rhodes*.

6. Schumpeter's essay on imperialism, although starting with a premise about human behavior which is the antithesis of the one used in conventional economic theorizing, is itself a fine example of the idealist-fictive method. For what Schumpeter does, literally, is to manipulate definitions to fit his purpose. He *defines* the spirit of imperialism in a narrow and peculiar way. He likewise *defines* the spirit of capitalism in as narrow and peculiar a way and, lo, shows that imperialism is not a capitalist phenomenon since the qualities and characteristics of capitalism are diametrically opposed to those of imperialism (both terms as defined by him). Rather, as noted, imperialism is an atavistic leftover of a less enlightened past. The whole essay is "a play on words," as Murray Greene had no difficulty detecting. See his article "Schumpeter's Imperialism —A Critical Note."

the mathematical method. There are things that display not a geometrical but a "subtle" spirit, and pre-eminent among them are the mind of man and the behavior of man. "It is ridiculous to speak of man as if he were a geometrical proposition. A moral philosophy in terms of a system of geometry . . . is to the mind of Pascal an absurdity, a philosophical dream." And this is so because "contradiction is the very element of human existence" and of human institutions.[7]

The derivation of logical conclusions from arbitrary premises, although of no value to attain truth, is often of great ethical value. We illustrated this with reference to the contract theories of eighteenth-century philosophers, and we can do so again by recalling that typical natural law document, the American Declaration of Independence: "We hold these truths to be self-evident, that all men are created equal; that they are endowed by their Creator with certain inalienable rights. . . . ." Jefferson lays down an axiom and logically derives a clear prescription: that to fight for the creation of a good government is not only desirable but it is a duty. The fact remains that the truths of which Jefferson speaks are self-evident only within his Cartesian epistemology. In fact, from the empirical-descriptive point of view (*which is blind to the realm of the spirit*), it is simply false that all men are created (that is, born) equal. Even in Jefferson's days, some men were born in poverty, others in wealth, some healthy, others sickly, and others dead. The justification and the nobility of Jefferson's axiom does not rest on its being a "picture" of reality. It rather rests on the implicit promise his document makes: to restore to man his ethical dignity. A state, Jefferson clearly implies, should treat its citizens as the equals of those whom necessity casts in the role of administrators, trustees of society. Citizens should be granted knowledge of what is best for them and should be entrusted with the responsibility to carry out their own decisions. It is now everybody's duty to help achieve this ideal by overthrowing tyrannical government.

7. On Pascal's distinction see Ernst Cassirer, *An Essay on Man: An Introduction to a Philosophy of Human Culture,* pp. 10–11. The estrangement into which mathematical social thinking leads was also noted by Pascal: "I have spent a long time studying the abstract sciences. . . . When I began to study man, I saw that the abstract sciences are not suited to him and that I was more estranged from my human condition than others who remained ignorant of these sciences." Quoted by Sorel, *The Illusions of Progress,* p. 16, from Pascal, *Pensées,* fragment 144.

Not all deductive systems display the lofty ethics derived from Jefferson's a priori. In chapter 3 we remarked that systems based on false premises often lead to successful action and that this fact does not thereby prove that the system of thought is true. We illustrated this point with reference to nineteenth-century racial theory which supported the highly successful imperialist expansion of the period. We now wish to emphasize that these theories, too, follow "an absolutely logical procedure which starts from an *axiomatically accepted premise*, deducing everything from it." Like economic theory, racial theories, too, proceed "with a consistency that exists nowhere in the realm of reality."[8] They are fables, but their method is rigorously logical within their postulated premises.

We call attention to this formal similarity between the *method* of classical economics and that of racial theories because in reading many of the traditional methodological works one gets the impression that the economist believes that deductive systems *as such* (regardless of content) are somehow not only more "true" but also more uplifting than inductive ones. This notion is itself the off-shoot of an idealist epistemology. A deductive system does not allow itself to be "contaminated" by reality: it is "pure" by definition. By a sleight of hand, methodological purity becomes moral purity as well. This is not necessarily so. It all depends on the basic axioms. The deductive system of Ricardo, for instance, was rapidly building evil onto falsehood. A generation after Ricardo the system was clearly turning into an ideology with a marked tendency to encourage immoral political and social behavior. This quality of Ricardianism was detected by many thinkers, including J. S. Mill, Marx, and Keynes. Keynes, for instance, wrote that Ricardo's teaching "translated into practice, was austere and often unpalatable. . . . That it could explain much social injustice and apparently cruelty as an inevitable incident in the scheme of progress. . . ."[9] A few decades after Ricardo's death, Darwin's speculations in natural history, by an easy and unavoidable analogy, allied themselves with Ricardian economics and were applied to the world of men. Animals, men, and cultures were thrown into one big bag. And the ability of Standard Oil to prosper thereby proved the moral superiority of its directors.

It was fortunate for the future development of economic theory

8. Arendt, *Origins*, p. 471. Emphasis added.
9. Keynes, *General Theory*, p. 33.

that, at about this time, the relentless march of means toward perfection led to the discovery of the concept of the margin and opened up new intellectual horizons. Economists learned to divorce theoretical speculations from practical suggestions and eventually tended to ignore the latter altogether. Above all, they discovered that in the drawer "data" one could file away and forget the whole world outside the reasoning ego. Economics thus turned as pure ethically (except for Robbins' regrettable dictum that all ends are equally legitimate, so far as economic theory is concerned) as it had always been epistemologically. Ricardo became a "faux pas," an unnecessary "detour" (Schumpeter), and social Darwinism was left by default to pamphleteers, propagandists, a few sociologists, and many sycophants.

Although the margin did not enable economics to explain reality any better, at least it made the discipline more ethically and esthetically pleasing. Economic science began to yield those "thousand agreeable [intellectual] effects" which Adam Smith foresaw would derive from looking at society "in a certain . . . philosophical light." Economics came to describe not the actual but *one possible* arrangement of things. And this possible world was eminently satisfying to the sense of beauty and, although less so, to the moral sense. When that mixture of chicanery, deceit, blackmail, and downright crime which is existential competition entered the machinery of marginalism, it emerged as the loftiness of optimum allocational efficiency and distributive justice.

There was a tyrant in Greek mythology who devised a way to receive genuine enjoyment from the shrieks of people in pain. He built a bronze ox (Philaris' ox) inside which he placed the unfortunate man. Under the ox a slow fire burned. The mouth of the bronze ox was so formed that the cries of the victim came out as sweet music. What the tyrant did consciously, the method of Cartesianism applied to economics attained unconsciously. Not only is (theoretical) competition a thing of beauty, but the international struggle for markets—that some historians insist on considering a cause of the Great War and indeed of many wars—becomes the wine/cloth exchange, the quintessence of "elegance" and reasonableness. The frequently "irrational" decisions of politicians as to how much to tax and on what to spend the revenues becomes the delicate pas de deux of marginal social benefits and marginal social costs.

Though avoiding the immorality of imperialist racial theories (which, we trust, is more than a value judgment) and of social Darwinism, economic theory could not very well fulfill its promise to arrange the world under the aegis of Reason (Justice): "from each according to his ability, to each according to his contribution" (marginal theory of distribution). The idealism, dogmatism, and extremism inherent in the method of rationalism were singularly unfit to allow the economist to participate in a dialogue with the rest of society. The very normative/positive distinction that enabled economics to escape the immorality of social Darwinism now stood in the way of working for the implementation of its own uplifting ethical vision. Purity, once achieved, demanded to be defended, and this could be done only by keeping reality at arm's length. The economist vis-à-vis the world took the attitude of Archimedes in the last moments of his life (as portrayed by many biographers and paintings). The great geometer was so absorbed in drawing circles that he was unaware that his city had just fallen to the Romans. Disturbed by a soldier who will slay him, Archimedes waved him away with the now famous remark "*Noli turbare circulos meos* [Do not disturb my circles]."

Just as the propagandistic and morally reprehensible implications of early classical theory were left to the social Darwinists to develop, so the reformist mantle did not fit economists either. Marx inherited it.

9

Hegel

Muss es Sein? Es muss sein.
Beethoven

W E SAW that throughout the seventeenth and eighteenth centuries the prevalent metaphysics believed that the world could be grasped by the thinking ego drawing deductions from "instinctively" clear axioms. In social thought this way of proceeding led the mind away from the empirical world as we have illustrated in connection with political philosophy and economic theory. The natural delusion that whatever is spoken of exists prevented a recognition of the weakness of the conventional mode of thinking. Exactly because it was possessed of a feeble grasp of reality, the Cartesian ego succeeded in creating something perhaps higher than truth: namely a world ruled by justice and reason. Accordingly, one may say that Enlightenment modes of thought substituted the godlike in man (his reason) for the traditional all-wise God.

One great economist stands outside the stream of orthodoxy going from Adam Smith to Marshall and Pigou: Karl Marx. Our thesis—that the development of political economy reflected the epistemological premises of the times—would be weakened if we were forced to regard Marx as an "exception," if we could not find a link between his method and a metaphysics and way of reasoning as opposed to that of the Enlightenment as Marx' thought and method were opposed to the classical school. But such a link exists: Marx' thought differs in methodology and substance from that of the orthodox school of economics because he was influenced by the metaphysics of Hegel, which displays important differences from that of the Enlightenment.

In this chapter we will briefly summarize Hegel's opposition to the fundamental conceptions of the *philosophes,* and especially his definition of reason. In the chapter on Marx we will show how, by tinkering with Hegel's novel viewpoint, Marx produced a system radically opposed to the idealism and rationalism of conventional economic theory.

We already had occasion to mention Hegel's early criticism of the Enlightened tendency to dismiss religion as "stupidity." With veiled irony Hegel asks, "How is it possible to explain the construction of a fabric (religion) that is so repugnant to human reason and so erroneous through and through?"[1] How can Enlightened thought, whose essence is clarity, explain what the philosophers themselves regarded as muddled and superstitious? How can reason even detect the irrational and judge it to be so? How is it possible to apply the tools of mathematics to explain such phenomena as miracles, the incarnation, and people's obvious belief in such phenomena?

What Hegel really questions is the subservience in which substance is held by form, the latter being synonymous with the method of the ego whose fundamental expression is the syllogism. The inability to deal with certain aspects of reality on the part of any discipline that prizes systematization (form) is well known. The most brilliant explorations of "states of mind," for instance, are not to be found in psychology texts but in novels. The reason is obvious. Psychology tries to explain taxonomically what is not amenable to be so explained. The novelist is free from such a delusion.

Hegel suggests that the Enlightenment does not even have the categories necessary to understand the historical existence of religion as an institution and as a set of feelings. It viewed religion as an abstract set of dogmas divorced from the social milieu, the

1. Quoted by Bruce Mazlish, *The Riddle of History,* p. 136, from *Hegels theologische Judendscriften;* the English translation, *On Christianity: Early Theological Writings,* is incomplete.

epochs, the countries, and the peoples where it arose. And it consequently dealt with social reality fictionally, not historically. Hegel's advance over his Enlightened predecessors consists mainly of his assertion that understanding should let itself be guided by history rather than by mathematics, that the categories of correct thinking are rooted in factors like customs (*Sitten*), the spirit of the age, and the like. They are more useful than natural law axioms and neat classifications to explain the real. And it is this outlook that gives an inkling of the fact that the nineteenth century would become the century of historical and evolutionary studies, just as the eighteenth had been that of mathematics and mechanics.

Once this shift of outlook away from thinking via axioms to thinking historically was discovered, all the rest of Hegel represents the reductio ad absurdum of Enlightened ways of thinking. We saw that the Cartesian tradition meant by ideas mental pictures, things "in the mind"; and by matter it meant the world "outside" the mind. Correct ideas were identified with reason, the process or mode of thinking characteristic of logic and mathematics. Further, many of them naïvely concluded that the ways of the geometrical mind reflected the ways of reality. Hegel's metaphysics is not too different: having recognized that Reality[2] is flux, he first conceived a mode of thinking (an engine for pushing ideas forward, so to speak) that would reflect such a flux (the dialectic) and then, just as the most naïve Cartesians had asserted that *their* logic and differential calculus reflected the world outside, so did he dogmatically assert that the dialectical mind (*its* laws of thinking) reflected the movement of the world in perfect congruence. The dialectic cannot but reflect the Real: it only has "to let itself go." The world "has no power within it capable of withstanding the courage of man's knowledge: it must give before him, and lay bare before his eyes for his enjoyment, its riches and depths."[3] With these brave words, the doubts of Hume, Locke, Bentham, and Kant were set to rest and the epistemological problem disappeared. After two centuries of debate whether ideas "in the mind" were trustworthy reflections of the world, the mind gave up the struggle

2. In this chapter the capitalized words Reality, Real, and Reason shall be used in a Hegelian sense, to distinguish them from similar Cartesian terms which shall not be capitalized.

3. G. W. F. Hegel, *The Phenomenology of Mind*, p. 40. Quoted from an address by Hegel to his students in Berlin, October 22, 1818.

and "let itself go." And just as naïve Cartesianism had identified reason (as geometrical thinking) with reality, so did Hegel effortlessly identify dialectical Reason with the Real.

There is, however, one important difference between the Cartesians and Hegel. Given the narrowness of axiomatic thinking, the Cartesians' ego built a world ruled by reason in a narrow sense: a reasonable world. This is why their thinking took on a radical character. Hegel, instead, defines Reason as practically everything which is found in the real world. His metaphysics, therefore, acquired a conservative hue.

In an early exercise of his historical method,[4] Hegel traced the emergence of the narrow and ethical concept of reason to the religious outlook itself. Christianity, he alleged, found itself in opposition to the world and accustomed men to look at reality ethically as a struggle between good and evil. It also stressed the inherent moral autonomy of the individual, his spiritual divorce from the community and its laws and customs. Not society, but the "moral law within man" became the beacon light of behavior and hence of thought. This principle of moral autonomy, of which Socrates was an early exponent, destroyed the balance between public and private life which existed in antiquity and led to the tendency of the mind to interpret events by means of the inner moral categories of consciousness, rather than by means of the categories of Reality.

Having thus diagnosed the error of his predecessors genetically and logically (as the result of a historical fact and as thinking on the basis of a narrow definition of reason), Hegel maintains that Reason (his own brand) is not to be discovered in the ego or in the "moral law *within* man" but *in the world itself*. And this landed him effortlessly in the second half of his own dialectical movement. Previously he had asserted that whatever is thought of dialectically exists; now he asserts that whatever exists is Reasonable—indeed the highest embodiment of Reason. His aphorism "whatever is rational is real, whatever is real is rational" is well known. And it means exactly what it says. It is, of course, the second half of the aphorism—the identification of the apparent cruelties, stupidities, and evil of the world with the work of Reason—that pleased those in power (e.g., the Prussian state) as much as it repelled and exasperated those thinkers who conceived of at least the possibility of

4. Hegel, "The Positivity of the Christian Religion," in *On Christianity: Early Theological Writings*.

a reasonable (i.e., just and humane) world emerging in the future.[5]

But Hegel's view should be seen in its proper perspective. The Hegelian system is the logical outcome of Descartes' metaphysics. One may say that it is Descartes' metaphysics minus its error, i.e., thinking geometrically. For a century this metaphysics had been obscured by soul-searching doubts of the ability of the mind to grasp reality. Once these doubts were removed by the substitution of historical for geometrical thinking, the "sanctioning of the existent as such" naturally followed. The Cartesian mind itself had identified the ways of *thinking* with the ways of the world although it had defined right thinking as geometrical thinking. Hegel was hardly the first one to identify the ways of the world with history; indeed this is so by definition. And since the greatest ambition of the intellect is to reflect the world, nothing was left but to acknowledge boldly that truth resides in man's deeds, that is, in history. It is history that embodies all that is Rational, and Reason can be seen at work in history. What Hegel did, in other words, was to bring about the rapprochement between nature and thinking, the object and subject, which was the greatest aim of Cartesians and thinkers in general. That in the process Hegel "justified" the ways of reality followed as a matter of course since now Reality was, by definition, historical reality. To put it differently, once we admit that reality seldom conforms to our ideas (once we notice, for instance, that laws do not emanate from a constitution but from lobbying interests, greed, and the like) *and* once we acknowledge that the task of the intellect is to explain reality, then the way is opened to doubting not reality but our ways of perceiving it. And this is exactly what Hegel did: he criticized not reality but the conventional way of perceiving it. In a true Copernican revolution of social thought, he then concluded that reality is as it "should be." This last step was demanded by the very claim of "positivism" and freedom from value judgment that social thinkers themselves have always made. Hegel recognized his philosophy to be "positive" and called his idealism "objective" to distinguish it from the "subjective idealism" of Kant, who, according to him, only gave us a "philosophy of reflection," not of Reality.

This inherent kinship between Cartesianism and Hegelianism is illustrated by a slip of some economic theorists. Aspiring to ex-

5. Among Hegel's severest modern critics is Karl R. Popper. See *The Open Society and Its Enemies*, vol. 2, chap. 12.

plain economic life, economics first identified the laws of the logical mind with the laws of reality. But later, realizing that the prescriptions of economics (reason) were actually *radical,* but wishing, like Hegelianism, to be value-free, many theorists (e.g., Robbins) were compelled to say that *any* act is, by definition, a rational one. Thus, just as Hegel is alleged to justify Bismarck and Hitler, so classical economics has been accused of justifying the Robber Barons, the use of child labor, imperialism, poverty, and much else as examples of the Providential Order of Things (in Hegel, the Divine Idea). This affinity can be seen in the fact that whenever economics abandoned its static technique and turned "philosophical" (which, fortunately, occurred only in popularizations of economics), it generally ended in a kind of naïve evolutionism and Social Darwinism, as teleological as the progress of Hegel's Idea.

The only difference between Robbins' amoralism and Hegel's is that, while the broadening of the concept reason in economics was a thoughtless expedient to get out of the accusations that it (economics) was value-laden, and while the evolutionary outlook is largely a footnote in economics, both broad Reason and the evolutionary viewpoint are intrinsic elements of Hegel's metaphysics. But more than one road leads to Rome. Hegel arrived there directly and logically. Economics stumbled there by way of equivocations and in the attempt to avoid contradictions (only to fall into greater contradictions).

The comparison between economics and Hegel is strengthened if we note that both systems are optimistic in their conclusions: "The insight . . . to which . . . philosophy is to lead us is, that the real world is as it ought to be—that the truly good—the universal divine reason—is not a mere abstraction, but a vital principle capable of realizing itself. . . . Philosophy wishes to discover the substantial purport, the real side of the divine ideal, and to justify the so much despised Reality of things."[6] Thus wrote Hegel. Read economics in lieu of philosophy and the above would not be a false rendition of the ultimate meaning of economics, *if we allow ourselves to hypostatize the concepts of economics.* In classical economics, the "truly good" can easily be recognized in the workings of supply and demand, in the various Pareto optima, in the absence of unemployment, in the kingdom of justice that the marginal theory of distribution portrays, and in the Invisible Hand.

6. Hegel, *The Philosophy of History,* p. 36.

We started this chapter by proposing to show the opposition between Hegel and Descartes and ended up by showing the similarity
between Hegel and the brainchild of Cartesianism, economic theory.
The similarity is not in the mode of analysis but only in the ethics.
And it is a similarity solely caused by the two errors of economics:
first, the identification of economic thought with economic reality;
second, the illogical broadening of the meaning of reasonable in
(positive) economics.

To return to Hegel, his Reason, being writ large in history,
manifests itself in anything that moves men, not excluding egoism,
narrow-mindedness, and ambition. Hegel has no delusion that the
great figures of history were moved by praiseworthy motives. Despite this, the dialectic always proves that whatever happens, happens for the best. The ambition of Caesar became the vehicle
whereby the ancient world was unified under Roman Law, a fact
that eventually facilitated the spread of Christianity. Napoleon,
similarly motivated by ambition, was the instrument of the Idea
(Reason) in extending the declaration of the rights of man from
France to the rest of Europe. This is the Hegelian optimism to
which we have referred. When events are looked at from the perspective of the present, they always seem to have caused the best
and most desirable results possible under the circumstances.
Reason advances by bending to its will men's thoughts (often rational plans) and their passions: "the one the warp, the other the
woof of the vast arras-web of Universal History." And it is upon
passions rather than upon well-laid-out rational balancing of pleasure and pains that the Idea relies to unfold itself. This Idea evidences a "cunning" of its own, bending to its will and using for its
purposes the most unlikely motives. To find it at work you only
have to read accurately this "cunning" with the assistance of
dialectical thinking. The final cause, the teleological denouement
toward which the development of the essence of things (and therefore of events themselves, for the former are only the latter apprehended in thought) strives, Hegel calls the Idea, the Absolute Idea,
the Highest Good, the Scientifically Comprehended Universe, the
Ultimate Cognition of the Spirit, the Universal Divine Reason, all
terms which one can interpret as either understanding as such or
events not excluding such ethical desiderata as Freedom, Happiness,
the Heavenly City on earth, or Socialism, but definitely not Utopia.

It is even possible to read in Hegel a certain becoming humility toward events. For the restoration of human passions to their rightful place in human affairs and the recognition of the inherent "cunning" of human events leads Hegel to restrict the power and ability of the mind to an understanding of the past alone. After all, in the face of a present-day massacre, it may be callous to see the Absolute at work, but in the perspective of a few decades or centuries the massacre may well be discovered to have caused something desirable.[7] The Terror, for instance, caused Napoleon (nothing particularly good about him), but in turn Napoleon caused many populations to revolt and demand freedom and constitutions. Now we are trapped, for we must acknowledge that freedom and constitutions are desirable things, if for no other reason than they are possessions of the present age. And thus, whether through profound wisdom or a cunning of his own, Hegel maintains that wisdom is at best retrospective: "When philosophy paints its grey in grey, then has a shape of life grown old. By philosophy's grey in grey it cannot be rejuvenated but only understood. The owl of Minerva [philosophical knowledge] spreads its wings only with the falling of dusk."[8] Further, just as all events occur in a time continuum, from an examination of which thought cannot exempt itself, so Hegel was aware that any theoretical system, including his own, is the product of the age: "Philosophy is its time apprehended in thoughts. It is, therefore, just as foolish to fancy that any philosophy can transcend its present world, as that any individual could leap out of his time and jump over Rhodes."

This conception, if applied to Hegel's own brew, presents serious problems. For if his own ideas are to be understood as the peculiar product of the times, then the absoluteness claimed for the dialectic seems to go to pieces. We can solve this contradiction by proposing the following solution. The past and the present do not stand, in Hegel's mind, on the same footing. The past is viewed through the present. Now there is a kind of "temporal ego-centrism" in man (similar to the spatial ego-centrism of Ptolemaic man). Just as we regard ourselves the "most advanced" product of evolution, so we are drawn to judge the present (merely because we live in it) as superior to the past. We view past ages as steppingstones to our own epoch. And the moment we define our epoch as, in

7. Few people are, in fact, particularly distressed by reading history textbooks.

8. Hegel, *Philosophy of Right*, introduction.

some sense, superior to the previous ones, we are forced to admit that whatever happened in the past has a positive value and purpose, to wit, to make possible the present order of things. Hegel's optimism relies, in other words, on a psychological trick. The appeal of this form of reasoning is so great that even Marx succumbed to it. Much as he despised capitalism and its institutions he was forced to regard them as a "necessary" step in the attainment of socialism. Thus, capitalism had its redeeming quality! In any case, Hegel's conception of the temporality of everything— including his own philosophy—is a pole apart from the claims of eternity of Cartesianism. Also inimical to it is Hegel's notion of the "cunning" of reason. It suggests that Reason proceeds not with the unilinear directness of Descartes' geometry but with the deviousness of history, full of labyrinthine turns, blind alleys, and occasional setbacks.

A great realist who aspired to show the way politics really works, not by studying constitutions but by observing the behavior of rulers, was eventually forced to acknowledge that element of mystery in human affairs which, we think, is what Hegel intends to stress when he refers to the "cunning" of Reason. Machiavelli's goal, like that of so many thinkers of his age, was to create a "science of politics." His program is similar to Galileo's.[9] But what distinguishes him from natural law thinkers is that historical knowledge and personal experience, not axioms, provided the raw material for this theorizing. Eventually, his ambition to be "scientific"— which calls for precision—and his methodology—observation and induction—clashed. But Machiavelli's commitment to the truth won out. He recognized that even the most artful scheme carried out by the most determined and knowing leader is liable to failure. Events may at any time take an unexpected turn. Briefly, history and the leader are partly under the influence of Fortuna. To an examination of Fortuna, Machiavelli devoted a long chapter in The Prince:[10] it is an obscure chapter full of apparent contradictions. No sooner has the author hammered down a thought or shown a relationship than he denies it and asserts the opposite. It reminds one of some of the pages in the General Theory where Keynes was faced with the same problem, to be lucid while dealing with vague concepts like "uncertainty" and "ignorance." Fortuna and the "cunning" of

9. Ernst Cassirer, The Myth of the State, p. 156.
10. Niccolò Machiavelli, The Prince, chap. 25.

Reason are possibly two different names for that element of imponderability in man's history that the Enlightenment ignored exactly because conventional logic and mechanicism cannot trap it. The paradoxical and the unexpected, of course, were discovered neither by Hegel nor Machiavelli. They were recognized by the Greek playwrights and by Christian thinkers. But in rationalist thought they played no role.

A twentieth-century thinker compares the goals and results of World War I thus: "Our one agreed aim [writes H. N. Fieldhouse, referring to the Allies' goals in World War I] was to break up German militarism. It was not part of our original intention to break up the Hapsburg and Ottoman Empires, to create Czechoslovakia, or resurrect Poland, to make a Russian Revolution, to treble the size of Serbia and double that of Rumania, to create Iraq and Estonia, and Lithuania, and a Jewish National Home, or to give the keys of the Brenner and the Adriatic to Italy. Yet, in the outcome all these—and much else—sprang from the war . . . while the one thing we promised ourselves, the destruction of German militarism, we failed to achieve."[11] Hegel would have read in all this the "cunning" of Reason and, undoubtedly, he would have been able to show the finger of the Absolute at work, perhaps in the attainment of independence on the part of so many nationalities previously held in fetters, or perhaps in the hastening of America's hegemony. But if we survey the ruins of the war rationally, we are compelled to admit that the war was caused by blindness and stupidity.

Stripped of its mystical halo, the concept of the cunning of Reason is not a bad antidote to the unwittingly materialistic and dogmatic attitude of the Cartesian ego. For it cautions us against being too sure of our mental constructs. It warns us that today's triumphs may be labeled blunders tomorrow, and that the by-products of actions may be more important than the intended results. But Hegel's construct also tells us that triumphs *and* blunders are the stuff of life. Thus this peculiar invention of Hegel is harnessed to accomplish the task toward which all of his philosophy strains: to reconcile man the observer with observed facts.

Reason develops dialectically: history walks like a crab, proceeding via antinomies and contradictions. It cannot be otherwise,

11. Quoted by Bertram D. Wolfe, *Three Who Made a Revolution*, p. 607.

one supposes, for the Idea wastes so much time to harness passions which are rather blind and unpredictable and subject to no time-table. Truth (the synthesis) is attained via a conflict of actions and beliefs. The historical synthesis is a period when the dialectic is held in abeyance. Normally, a thesis causes its own negation and in time produces a new synthesis. Just as conventional logic is so intimately tied to the ways of geometry, so Hegel's dialectic is related to the ways of politics where compromises of opposing views are the way legislation comes into being. The law of contradiction is superseded by this method which often gives Hegel license to court paradoxes and, in the opinion of many, to twist common sense into nonsense and vice versa.

We noted before that Hegel regarded the dialectic as, at the same time, the way of proceeding of *reality* and the way of proceeding of correct *thought*. It follows that the raw material of a dialectical exercise can be either a historical epoch (or history as a whole) or the mind itself. In giving an illustration of the dialectic at work, we shall choose as an example thought itself, that is, we shall present the closest thing to epistemology to be found in Hegel.

The reconciliation of interpretative philosophy with life is the central theme of Hegel's political writings. And the reconciliation of the subject with the object, of the mind with matter, is the theme of his *Logic*.

Hegel calls conventional logic the method of the "understanding." According to him this method is continually met with an either/or: either A or *non-A*, as epitomized by the law of contradiction. It does not realize that the truth lies in neither of the two views but in their dynamic synthesis. Understanding, or raisonnement, must be superseded by the true method of Reason, the dialectical method. Reason à la Hegel joins what the understanding severs, the ego and objective reality and, moreover, it claims to impart a dynamism to thinking that reflects the movement of life. Being, nothing, and becoming are the foundation stones of Hegel's logic. The first concept is the abstraction that we behold when we deprive anything of its qualities. Thus, if we say, "the book is brown," and then eliminate the predicate "brown," we are left with the bare fact of the book's is-ness, its existence. This is-ness is the book's *being*. But something that exists without any material qualities (color, shape, etc.) hardly exists. It is empty, indeterminate, featureless—in fact, nothing. *Nothing*, then, is the second category arising from, and contained in, being. The very process of the birth of nothing out of being gives us the third category, *becoming*. And since the process is reversible we have two forms of becoming: coming into being and passing away. The rhythmic movement of this Hegelian triad is carried on throughout his work, which has been called "an analysis of the life history of the human spirit" conceived as "a reaction against the ingenious manipulations of principles *in abstracto* which characterized the theories of his immediate predecessors."[12] Others, we must aver, saw this movement as the most extreme example of such vacuous manipulations.

The process of transcending mere raisonnement is a step forward toward thinking dialectically, for it entails the unification of opposites. Thought is "a function of the subject and the controlling center in the reality of the object." That thought and object appear separate is due solely to the erroneous metaphysics and epistemology of the past. In the higher reaches of reason we cannot say that the subject dominates the object any more than that the object dominates the activity of the subject. They are inseparable elements and develop pari passu.[13] The subject becomes aware of itself in the object and the object adapts itself to the function of the subject. Thus, according to Hegel, reason is free from the one-sided idealism of Berkeley and from the dualism of British empiricism. "There is no need for distrust or hesitation on the part of reason in dealing with the world; it has but to let itself go" and reality will yield its secrets. Dialectical thinking is, so to speak, natural to man. The psychophysical dualism of the most critical Enlightened philosophers was a false problem.

This amalgam of the object and subject is the essence of Hegel's negation of dualism; thus, we must deal with it at greater length. At the most superficial stage of mere apprehension or sensuous consciousness, the object is apprehended immediately as "here" without any intermediate links between it and the subject, and as pure abstract "is-ness," devoid of any characteristics. But abstractness as such is inadequate and untrue. It, therefore, negates the previous step, sensuous consciousness (the awareness of the object with its characteristics) and leads to sense perception as the syn-

12. J. B. Baillie's introduction to Hegel's *Phenomenology of Mind*, pp. 13, 14.
    13. Ibid., p. 39.

thesis.[14] Sensuous consciousness, that is, displays inner contradictions. It claims to be aware of the "this-ness," but, however the
"this-ness" is defined, being a mere abstraction, it turns out to be a
universal, that is, the opposite of the particular, which "this" alleges to be.

Sense perception, the synthesis of the process of affirmation
and negation of the particular, seems to eliminate this clash since
through it the object is apprehended as one of a class. But this too
is self-contradictory, for we are asked to view the object as unique
and as a member of a group at the same time. Neither does it help
to regard the object as one "from one point of view" and many
"from another point of view," for to do so would be to lapse into
the dualism Hegel was at pains to refute.[15] This self-contradiction
in sense perception as such creates a synthesis between it and the
previously noted sensuous consciousness. The latter, as we saw,
gave us "bare singleness," the former both singleness and universality. The synthesis Hegel calls one of pure universality: the object
ceases to contain traces of individuality and becomes a pure universal.

As a pure universal, it loses its sensuality: law, gravitation,
unity, force, are examples of such universals. When consciousness
attains this level of reason, it has become intellect, the highest step
of Enlightenment raisonnement.[16]

Intellect views objects as "a kingdom of laws": behind the immediate phenomena of falling bodies it sees the "law of gravity,"
just as behind the innumerable acts of hiring labor lies the law of
marginal product, or behind buying commodities, the law of diminishing marginal utility. Thought that reaches this stage believes
that the universal (the "law") is the reality, while the individual
phenomena to which it refers are only instances or forms of the law.
Further reflection, however, shows that such laws are only a manifestation of consciousness (ego). Through them, the subject has
so overcome the object that thought which stops at this stage is
purely idealistic thought. As thought realizes that the object is a
pure universal, something of the same nature as the thinking subject—its projection on the world, so to speak—it reaches the state

14. Ibid., chaps 1, 2.
15. It would be relapsing into dualism by reason of regarding the object
as merely dependent upon the observer's way of looking at it.
16. Ibid., chap. 3.

of *self-consciousness*. In it the subject realizes that what is real in the object is simply his ego.[17]

The progress from intellect to self-consciousness is a step forward in philosophical insight. Thought frozen at the level of intellect (Enlightenment raisonnement) never realizes that it only attains tautological explanations: to say that lightning (the phenomenon) is "caused" by electricity (the "law") is to say nothing since lightning *is* electricity; to explain the fall of bodies by the "law of gravity" or allocational efficiency by the "profit motive" is likewise tautological. In such explanations the mind only rediscovers itself, its premises and axioms.

The stage of self-consciousness entailing the realization that the object is identical with the subject contradicts sense perception which realizes that the object has independent existence. And this is the stage that *critical* Enlightened thought (Hume, Kant) reached but could not transcend. In Hegel, however, the contradiction generates a new onward movement as the subject tries to overcome the tension by abolishing and destroying the object, as in desire. The simplest instance of desire is hunger, the object of which, through consumption, is destroyed. According to Hegel, any desire involves the drive to eliminate its object. This drive involves a contradiction since the very fact that the ego can attain its satisfaction through the destruction of the object shows that it is dependent on the object for its self-satisfaction. Hence, since the self cannot logically negate the object, the object must negate itself: it must be viewed as another ego and thus the stage of self-consciousness recognitive is reached.[18]

This transition of the object into another self that the subject can recognize is extremely obscure and subject to various interpretations. We choose one which has economic significance. A laborer (at least one steeped in Hegelian metaphysics) who contemplates a machine and recognizes it not merely as an object (toward which he may be antagonistic) but as the embodiment of the labor of other workers has reached the stage of self-consciousness recognitive. Marx himself made use of this logical stage in his view of machinery as "congealed labor." At any rate, the existence of the

17. We may note that rationalistic thinking in economics never attains this realization; the mechanics of hypostatization unjustifiably re-establishes the connection between consciousness ("laws") and the world of phenomena.

18. *Ibid.*, chap. 4.

two egos face to face does not yet entail acceptance of one by the other. The relation of lord to bondsman is illustrative of this situation: the lord attempts to subjugate the slave, but he can hardly destroy him without destroying himself as lord in the process. The slave must be granted independent existence and self-consciousness. A mutual acceptance of all egos by each other ensues in what Hegel calls *universal self-consciousness*—which might have given Marx the clue for his socialist brotherhood.

The ego now recognizes the independence of all other egos: one's self-consciousness is identical to another's self-consciousness. Therefore, by contemplating it, the ego contemplates itself. The subject sees the original distinction between itself and the object as a distinction within itself. This is the viewpoint of Reason, the ultimate in philosophic understanding. "From the fact that self-consciousness is Reason, its hitherto negative attitude toward otherness turns into a positive attitude. *Qua* reason, assured of itself, it is at peace . . . for it is certain of itself as reality, certain that all concrete actuality is nothing else but it. Its thought is itself *eo ipso* concrete reality."[19] Just as Hegel's philosophy of history leads to a reconciliation of our outlook with history, so his logic entails the reconciliation of subject and object. Reason is the "certainty of being all reality,"[20] the synthesis of consciousness and self-consciousness. In consciousness the object is independent of, in self-consciousness it is identical with, the subject. Only in Reason is the object both distinct from, and identical with, the subject. As in his political writings, Hegel restores dignity to "despised reality" and sets the mind at peace with its environment.

Hegel views these considerations as ending the secular travail of consciousness. Through the centuries before him, man only attained a shadow of true consciousness, imperfect and ephemeral because one-sided. The historical lord-slave relationship symbolizes this state of affairs. In it the bondsman attains a self-consciousness consisting of the *thought* that he is identical to the master. It is inner freedom only, of the type stressed by the Stoics. Persisting in this attitude leads to contradictions and finally to skepticism: a point is soon reached when we can no longer listen with patience to the priests asking the slave to tolerate his lot since he possesses paradise in his soul. Neither, we may add, is society

19. Ibid., p. 173.
20. Ibid., p. 276.

willing to tolerate indefinitely political economists teaching that laborers' wages are determined by their Malthusian behavior, or that full employment is the norm. Inner freedom demands to be actualized. Consciousness that has reached a purely formal definition of freedom is in continuous danger of breaking down. As long as it persists, it causes the "unhappy consciousness" or the "alienated soul" to come into being. The self is conscious of its divided nature, of its being and not being.[21]

Hegel finds its symbol in Abraham's wandering over the world, alone and free but divorced from life. The learned Faust at odds with his own knowledge and his fellow men may be a more poignant and modern symbol:

> I have studied, alas! Philosophy,
> And Jurisprudence, and Medicine too,
> And saddest of all, Theology,
> With ardent Labour, through and through!
> And here I stick, as wise, poor fool,
> As when my steps first turned to school.
> Master they style me, nay, Doctor, forsooth,
> And nigh ten years, o'er rough and smooth,
> And up and down, and acrook and across,
> I lead my pupils by the nose,
> And know that in truth we can know—naught!
> My heart is turned to coal at the thought.[22]

21. Ibid., p. 251.
22. Goethe, *Faust*, First Part.

10

Marx

The subjective thinker possesses fantasy, emotion. . . . But first, last, and always passion, for it is impossible to contemplate existence existentially without becoming passionate, because existence is a monstrous contradiction.

Kierkegaard

M ARX' LATE economic writings—the only ones that have attracted the attention of economists—were the fruition of decades of wrestling with the thought of Hegel and Hegel's admirers and critics. The true foundations of Marx' economics are found in this vast amount of philosophical and polemical works. What we call the Marxian system is the final outcome of an intense effort which left the Hegelian method unscathed but was anti-Hegelian in its conclusions. Hegel's grand synthesis of all human history, political and intellectual, has invited comparisons with Aquinas'. Marx, who spent many years studying, attacking, and modifying Hegel, also accomplished as complete a synthesis as the Angelic Doctor's.

From Hegel, Marx took the conviction that truth is historical truth and that reality develops dialectically, aiming toward some Higher Good. But while Hegel's outlook is contemplative and the Ideal emerges independently of men's conscious will, Marx' is activistic and the Ideal must clearly be recognized and fought for.

And this activism clearly distinguishes Marx not only from Hegel but also from orthodox economists. The latters' analyses and prescriptions bore little relation to each other. As Keynes puts it, "they live in two worlds," a necessary result of thinking in isolation from reality, and of wishing, nevertheless, to make policy recommendations. Marx' system, instead, is harmonious, his prescriptions following logically from his analyses exactly because his theory was rooted in historical reality and was to be implemented by acting on reality. Marx' own life was hardly an instance of retired scholarship. He was the editor of radical newspapers, the contributor to other papers like the *New York Tribune*, the drafter of pamphlets, and the promoter of labor organizations. Hegel wrote of thought reflecting practice; Marx instanced such union of intellect and action in his own life. Cognizant of the limitations of both narrow rationalism and of pure passion and romanticism, he succeeded in harmonizing the two, thus overcoming the limitations of each.

Thinkers in the conventional philosophical tradition have been dismayed by his discovery of the "ideological" roots of social thought, just as orthodox clergymen, at about the same time, were dismayed by Darwin's suggestion of evolution, or by Freud's discovery of the determinants of behavior. Actually, Marx' theory of ideology (or false consciousness) is, intellectually, an eminently conservative discovery when placed in juxtaposition with the disintegration of idealistic thought after the breakdown of the religious world view. For Marx simply says that people think *as they must*.

Marx, like Bentham, Hume, and Kant, was unfavorably impressed by the discordance of sociophilosophical ideas. And instead of adding another idealistic ego-spun world view to the plethora of existing ones, he first set himself the task of explaining the existing cacophony of thought. What factors actually shape men's consciousness? What determines, *in reality,* men's views on social matters? Having absorbed Hegel's historical outlook, Marx sought the answer in the world of history. He removed the epistemological question from the studio of the philosopher and placed it in the social environment. Epistemology thus ceased to be another product of the philosophers' consciousness and came to share the main characteristic of science: empiricism and hence ability to be undermined by facts. Having found the key to how men actually think, Marx then reconstructed history, and discovered the underlying thread behind such intellectual products as economics, religion, ethics, and jurisprudence. In particular, he criticized those who regarded these spheres of human endeavor as the embodiment of some ideal like wisdom (e.g., the wisdom of legal minds or of Founding Fathers), abstract intelligence, or the Absolute.

Broadly, then, these are the logical steps in the formation of Marx' thought (logical, not temporal, for Marx' works generally addressed themselves to facts and to epistemology, history, economics, ethics, at one and the same time): first, an understanding of the ultimate roots of social thought; second, the drawing of historical meaning and implications from this understanding; third, the analysis of capitalism. These elements are naturally interwoven for they are held together by an ethical vision, by an all-enveloping philosophy *consciously* held. In fact, perhaps the greatest difference between conventional economists and Marx is this: that the former, writing after the Cartesian method had established its sway on the Western intellect, were not conscious of their underlying philosophy and methodology, while Marx, who viewed his work as the dawn of a new social science, was perfectly conscious of the ultimate epistemological foundations on which it rested. The quotation from Engels introducing chapter 2 suggests that the fathers of scientific socialism were aware that one's epistemology determines the nature of one's thought-contrivances and of one's relation to life.

Before Marx, the history of modern European philosophy had been idealistic in method. In its most extreme formulation, ideas were innate and owed nothing to the surrounding material. Marx soon detected that Hegel's philosophy was exactly in this Cartesian tradition. "To Hegel [he wrote] . . . the process of thinking, which under the name of 'the Idea,' he even transforms into an independent subject, is the demiurgos of the real world, and the real world is only the external, phenomenal form of 'the Idea.' "[1] This epistemological idealism seemed to Marx a huge hypostatization, as other philosophers writing at about the same time also detected. And it led to erroneous judgments and to a total inability to influence reality. The experience of E. Bauer, a radical Young Hegelian, is an illustration of this: sentenced by the Prussian State for his radicalism, he replied loftily but irrelevantly that the judgment meant nothing to him since his philosophy denied the existence of the

1. *Capital: A Critique of Political Economy,* 1:19.

state. His dialectic, Marx noted, was as flawless as it was impotent in keeping him out of prison. Inability to affect reality is not so much the result of willful choice but of a theory of knowledge that regards thought as arising mystically from the self-consciousness of the individual.

The tool for the expression of the idealistic world view Marx recognized to be the universal, a concept transcending empirical reality. Feuerbach had already criticized Hegel's concept of being for its abstractness. From it, empty words like Reason and the Idea naturally follow. Marx carried the criticism further and linked the rise of abstractions to the emergence of a division of labor between manual and intellectual occupations. The fact that thinkers are removed from active life deludes them into the belief that life is the reflection of their ideas. Political economy has been ruined by universals: it speaks of wealth and poverty when it should speak of rich men and poor men, says Marx,[2] in a language hardly different from Bentham's. "Fictitious" constructs like the "primordial state of nature" allow political economy to assert as a fact what it should prove (e.g., that egoism leads to the highest good), just as religion "explains" the existence of evil by the myth of the fall of man.[3]

The abstraction par excellence in political economy is the market: there "men" enter "freely" into contractual relations. The market becomes "a very Eden of the innate rights of man. There alone rule Freedom, Equality, Property, and Bentham. Freedom, because both buyer and seller . . . of labor-power, are constrained only by their own free will. . . . Equality, because each enters into relation with the other . . . and they exchange equivalent for equivalent. Property, because each disposes only of what is his own. And Bentham, because each looks only to himself. The only force which brings them together and puts them into relations with each other, is the selfishness, the gain and the private interest of each. Each looks to himself only, and no one troubles himself about the rest, and just because they do so, do they all, in accordance with the pre-established harmony of things . . . work together to their mutual advantage."[4]

This web of "essences" beclouds the understanding of reality. It prevents an appreciation of the *historical* change through which

2. *Economic and Philosophic Manuscripts of 1844*, pp. 143–44.
3. Ibid., p. 107.
4. *Capital*, 1:176.

labor, as real men, passed from slavery to serfdom to modern factory work. A realistic analysis of society is out of the question when we think through universals. The fact that "Ideas and categories are . . . historical and transitory products"[5] is necessarily ignored. Thus it is that the so-called radical Young Hegelians, in spite of their " 'world-shattering' statements," are the "staunchest conservatives." They oppose "phrases with phrases," since they too share the idealistic viewpoint of the thinker (Hegel) they claim to fight.[6]

Marx' rejection of the idealistic standpoint does not, however, imply acceptance of materialism—the belief, that is, that the mind merely "reflects" objective reality. Marx is aware that materialism involves itself in even more serious contradictions than idealism. Associating the process of thinking with the brain and rejecting anything that the senses do not perceive, materialism has always been hard put to explain the nature of thought, which is obviously not a material thing, or the very existence and development of those disciplines like mathematics that owe little or nothing to matter. All formulae of a "correspondence" of thought with the material object break down against the obvious fact that between ideas and material reality there is no common quality. This is why a consistently materialistic standpoint is impossible. Sooner or later, it lapses into idealism, because it itself is unempirical: it ignores the process of the actual formation of ideas. The thinking of Feuerbach, Marx alleges, displays this shortcoming. Against him, Marx directed his so-called Third Thesis on Feuerbach: "The naturalistic doctrine concerning the changing of circumstances and education forgets that circumstances are changed by men and that the educator himself must be educated."[7] That is, an explanation of the origin of ideas wholly in terms of environmental conditions ignores that the social environment itself is shaped by men.

Materialism, like idealism, logically leads to inaction. For if thought mirrors reality, it must forever trail reality—never lead it, as Hegel, the idealist, had observed in his famous simile of the "owl of Minerva." And, as in Hegel, this materialistic thought turns reactionary. One need only recall, for instance, the approval given by American Socialists to the formation of trusts on the belief that, after the trusts, Communism would emerge; or the approval given

5. Marx, *The Poverty of Philosophy*, p. 119.
6. Karl Marx and Friedrick Engels, *The German Ideology*, p. 6.
7. Ibid., pp. 197–98.

by some German "Marxists" to Hitler on the ground that "Nach Hitler, Ans" (after Hitler, us).

When wishing to avoid these reactionary conclusions, the materialist recurs to a glorification of the "leaders," thinkers, ideologists, statesmen, and prophets, who apparently "rise above" matter and ultimately move history. This reversion to an idealistic conception, this having to call on an "exception" to explain history, betrays the contradictions of materialism as a philosophical and practical standpoint.

By basing thought only on what the senses perceive, consistent materialism is far too narrow. The passage from sensuous perception to the production of full-blown philosophical systems is left unexplored. Moreover, if thought were passive, we should all see the same thing. Instead we are continually faced with different interpretations and reactions to events. The materialist unwittingly ignores social things and is forced to postulate an abstract, isolated ego[8] just as Descartes did. Marx called this materialism "contemplative" because it did not comprehend that even sense perception is the result of practical activity.[9] It, too, leads to the glorification of individualism and self-interest. Bentham, whom Marx evidently knew only through the writings of classical economists, is the chief architect of this atomistic materialistic viewpoint. Because of him, political economy has become an apologia for the existing order, a proof that under given conditions the present relations of men to men represent the best and most useful relations possible.

Marx also illustrated this metamorphosis of an allegedly materialist viewpoint into a de facto idealistic one with reference to Feuerbach's characterization of his own philosophy (Feuerbach's) as being that of "man," of "communal man," "communist." Thus, Marx says, in Feuerbach's mind, what is, in practice, a specific political organization with definite beliefs becomes a "mere category," so that any man who lives in society is a communist.[10] Feuerbach's major work, The Essence of Christianity, is tainted with the same error. In this book he asserts that anybody who has an aim, an aim which is in itself true and essential, has, eo ipso, a religion. This conception, Marx notes, turns the convinced atheist into a believer. An adroit manipulation of definitions, guided by the

8. Ibid., pp. 198–99; "Sixth Thesis on Feuerbach."
9. Ibid., p. 199; "Ninth Thesis on Feuerbach."
10. Ibid., p. 33.

generalizing drive, can turn white into black and black into white.

Marx provided a positive theory of knowledge which avoids the defects of both idealism and "contemplative materialism." It entails one of those shifts of focus which led to innumerable re-interpretations of the totality of human life in its practical (historical) and intellectual (theoretical) aspects.

Realizing that the fault of both idealism and materialism lay in their taking as a starting point a fixed non-historical element (consciousness or matter, respectively), Marx' contribution to the theory of knowledge emerged by centering attention on empirical men (in the plural), that is, on men living in a social setting which is in the process of continuous transformation. The flux and movement that orthodox economists from Smith to von Mises feared and regretted, Marx not only acknowledged but actually courted. Ideas reflect certain realities and in turn influence them, so that Marx' theory of knowledge, like Hegel's *Logic*, explains both the formation of ideas and the phenomenon of historical change simultaneously.

It is largely social ideas pertaining to religion, politics, ethics, economics, and jurisprudence that interested Marx. And they arise from men's social life. Even self-consciousness, which Descartes conceived as arising from the solitary act of doubting, emerges as a result of social interaction: "Peter only establishes his own identity as man by first comparing himself with Paul as being of like kind. And thereby Paul, just as he stands in his Pauline personality, becomes to Peter the type of *genus homo*."[11] While previous thinkers had either ignored society or conceived of it as superior and prior to the individual, Marx warns against treating individual and society as separate entities. To do so would lead to the abstractions exemplified by classical economics on one side and by Hegel on the other.[12]

Thus, consciousness is neither a mystical gift from the gods nor a mere "copy" of external matter. It arises rather from the relations of men with other men. Of all the reasons for these relations the economic reason is by far the most important, so consciousness, social ideas, and theories are formed by, and in, this economic

11. *Capital*, 1:52n.
12. Marx, *Manuscripts*, pp. 137–38.

setting. They must be in harmony with the realities of arrangements entered into in the process of producing and exchanging
goods. In a definite historical milieu characterized by certain productive relations, ideas are born which support and perpetuate
these relations. Social thought can thus be called the theoretical
expression of social relations. "The same men who establish social
relations conformably with their material productivity, produce also
the principles, the ideas, the categories conformably with their
social relations."[13] Moral, philosophical, and political thought arise,
broadly speaking, from the "economic sub-structure." Social thought
is anchored on the ultimate rock of the social arrangements which
stem from the need to satisfy material wants. "In the social production of their life [Marx wrote] men enter into definite relations
that are indispensable and independent of their will, relations of
production which correspond to a definite stage of development of
their material productive forces. The sum total of these relations
of production constitutes the economic structure of society, the
real foundation, on which arise the legal and political superstruc-
tures, and to which correspond definite forms of social consciousness. It is not the consciousness of men that determines their social
being, but, on the contrary, their social being that determines their
consciousness."[14] Marx thus turned Descartes' "I think, therefore I
exist" into "I exist in economic society, therefore I think." And he
opposed the psychologism of Enlightened thinkers who were forced
to imagine a "natural man" or a "social contract" as starting points
of their theorizing with his own evolutionary view of the movement of social ideas centering on changes in the modes of production broadly conceived. In "turning Hegel right side up again"
(Marx' own characterization of his work), he also did the same with
regard to Descartes and all the idealistic theorizing, including economic theorizing, stemming from Descartes. Social ideas and systems
are the verbal expression of the struggle against nature and against
other men for the satisfaction of wants. Just as Hegel considered it
impossible to study religion in abstraction from the history of a
people, so Marx thinks it is incorrect to study the development of
ideas in abstraction from their economic environment. "It is only
where speculation ends—in real life—[that] real, positive science

13. Marx, *The Poverty of Philosophy*, p. 119.
14. *A Contribution to the Critique of Political Economy*, pp. 11–12
(preface).

begins. . . . Empty talk about consciousness ceases, and real knowledge has to take its place."[15]

We can illustrate briefly the implication of these ideas with respect to Marx' treatment of communism, which to Feuerbach was a "mere category." Since social ideas are a reflection of the economic substructure, Marx' theory of knowledge quickly leads out of the strictly intellectual into the realm of historical reality. Communism is not an abstraction. It is not a condition that is to be established nor an ideal to which reality must adjust itself. Communism "is the *actual* phase necessary for the next stage of historical development."[16] It is reality in the process of maturing. Dialectical thought is only the medium for understanding and explaining its historical emergence. The very premises of communist theory are *not arbitrary* dogmas (as natural law conceptions were for liberalism) "but real premises from which abstraction can be made in imagination. They are the real individuals, their activity and the material conditions under which they live. . . . These premises can thus be verified in purely empirical ways."[17] Evidently, Marx wanted to separate clearly his own ideas from those figments of the idealistic imagination which found expression in Utopian socialism.

We have stressed the dependence of social ideas on their material substratum. But if ideas stem solely from men's social arrangements, what causes a change in the social arrangements themselves? From a strictly materialistic position, one would be incapable of answering this question since most human sources of change (as opposed to changes due to natural causes, e.g., the erosion of the coastline by the sea) would be eliminated by turning the mind into a passive mirror. Marx avoided this impasse by calling attention to "human needs" as the bridge between the present and the future, the subject and the object, and the source of men's ingenuity and drive to change. The need to free industry location from water power led to Watt's invention of the steam engine; the need to restore the balance in the productive cycle between spinning and weaving led to the inventions of Crompton, Cartwright, and others; the need to overcome the atavistic remnants of medieval regulations caused the emergence of Smith's and Bentham's ideas. The whole

15. Marx and Engels, *German Ideology,* p. 15.
16. Marx, *Manuscripts,* p. 146.
17. Marx and Engels, *German Ideology,* pp. 6–7. See also Karl Mannheim, *Ideology and Utopia: An Introduction to the Sociology of Knowledge,* pp. 112 ff.

laissez-faire philosophy (its concepts of right, freedom, property) reflects the need of the bourgeoisie for ideas more consonant with its new role in the economic process. Since need has two dimensions, material and psychic, the traditional dualism of object and subject is avoided. The mind emerges as an active element, but not so active as to be totally free from the strictures of existence. No amount of ingenuity could cause economic society to "jump" from the windmill to the atomic plant.[18]

Cartesian intellectuals defined truth as consisting of propositions that "carry their proofs within themselves": propositions that would be true even in a dream. In harmony with his social and activistic epistemology, Marx lets practice (*praxis*) set the standards of what is true and what is false. If an inventor creates a contrivance which fails to gain acceptance, Marx would say that his ideas were incongruent with objective reality: he misjudged the need. Practice, the real market, refused the product of his head and, therefore, in his assessment of a social need, he must have ignored some vital factor. It is likewise with social thought. The theories of the "true Socialists," of Proudhon, of Robert Owen and the Utopians, were also false since action based on them led only to failure. "The question whether objective truth is an attribute of human thought —is not a theoretical but a *practical* question. Man must prove the truth, i.e., the reality and power, the *this*-sidedness of his thinking in practice. The dispute over the reality or unreality of thinking that is isolated from practice is a purely scholastic question."[19]

Just as Marx places epistemology within the broader canvas of man's history, so he finds the test of truth there. Thought that abstracted from material reality had created standards of truth like clearness and distinctness *of ideas*. Marx, who viewed correct thought as the resultant of an interaction of thought with material forces, found *in* material factors the test of truth. Successful action implies that the theory on which the action is based is correct; unsuccessful action betrays the falseness of theory. Action, political and social (and hence history), is the laboratory of the social scientist. It is here that ideas are tested. Through the link of action the importance of ideas is vindicated. History is moved by ideas, not by any ideas but only by those that are consonant with emerging reality, that ride on the antithesis which will produce a new syn-

18. See, however, below, pp. 197–98.
19. Marx and Engels, *German Ideology*, p. 197. Emphasis in the text.

thesis. This is why Marx views men as "simultaneously the authors and actors of their own history." Clearly addressing himself to Hegel, he says, "It is rather man, real living man, who does everything. . . . It is not history that uses men as means to carry out its ends as if it were a separate person, for it is nothing else but the activity of man in pursuit of his ends."[20] In the pursuits of such ends men test the truth of their ideas.

From this conception of the formation of social ideas and of their truth it follows that "pure thought" does not exist. Every theory ceases to be "pure" and becomes a material power once it is absorbed into social or class consciousness. The thinker may yet delude himself that he is only speculating in the abstract and that he is free from "value judgments." But if his theorizing survives and becomes a social force, it must be because it has social importance. This very social importance makes a mockery of his "scientific" claims. The Hegelian warp-woof theme is repeated by Marx: ideas cannot give reality to anything at all. For the realization of ideas, men are needed who provide power.[21] Hegel's "idea plus passion" becomes Marx' "idea plus power."

Just as ideas arise from the social context, so does society pass judgment on them. Marx' theory of knowledge is empirical and historical from beginning to end. The reason for this remarkable ability of his theory to live in the same narrow world of facts is that Marx limited his epistemology to only those ideas that "count" historically. He would conclude, for instance, that Adam Smith's first major work, *The Theory of Moral Sentiments*, does not exist. Society rejected it and it lives only as a curiosity. It was not attuned to the needs of the bourgeoisie, but reflected rather a religious outlook which had ceased to be a social force long before. Something more in congruence with the needs of late-eighteenth-century British conditions—characterized by an explosion of productive effort—was needed, and Smith finally provided it with the *Wealth of Nations*. Practice judged one work, found it incongruous, and ignored it; it judged the other and found it the expression of a social need. The one is a relic, the other still lives. And Marx is interested only in the living.

Ideas can be fought by other ideas, but the battle of ideas as

20. Karl Marx and Friedrick Engels, *The Holy Family*, pp. 139–40. See also p. 160.
21. Ibid., introduction.

such leads nowhere. For the abolition of the idea of private property, the idea of communism, its *logic*, is perfectly adequate. The idea of private property was justified by natural law fictions and axioms. It is, in theory, fully destroyed by Proudhon's counter-axiom, "Property is theft." But the *practice* of private property is supported by facts, laws, judges, and actions. Thus, "It takes *actual communist* action to abolish actual private property. History will come to it, and this movement which in *theory* we already know to be a self-transcending movement, will constitute *in actual fact* a very severe and protracted process."[22] Notice how, here as elsewhere, Marx feels the need to italicize certain words that stand for historical events, not for hypostatized empty ideas.

Thus the philosophic issue of the primacy of ideas and reality is solved by the interaction of the two. In correct thought, ideas and reality merge into each other and the very question of primacy becomes a purely scholastic question. The oft-quoted substructure-superstructure simile, with its suggestion that the material factor is the basis on which the "superstructure" of ideas rests, is actually misleading: it does not reflect Marx' more thoughtful judgments. In reality, the substructure and the superstructure are the same thing in different forms, just as in Hegel ideas and reality are one and the same. This does not deny the obvious fact that there are periods when thought is more "passive" than usual, as, for instance, when a new synthesis has just been attained and the dialectic is temporarily held in abeyance. It is, indeed, only in this phase (one of stability) that the superstructure of ideas "reflects" the substructure of the modes of production. At other times, thought, though still checked by material conditions, runs ahead of changes in the latter. Indeed the goal of philosophy is exactly this: to press forward ideas that affect the (as yet) unclear shape of things to come. "Philosophers have only interpreted the world differently—the point is to change it,"[23] Marx says, in opposition to Hegel's contemplative stand.

But there is another point that deserves attention, for it, too, is a source of serious misunderstanding. Marx' insight has been alleged to denigrate originality and genius. This interpretation stems from mistaking his sociological and historical method as a psycho-

---

22. Marx, *Manuscripts*, p. 154. Emphasis in the text.
23. Marx and Engels, *German Ideology*, p. 199; "Eleventh Thesis on Feuerbach."

analytic one. Marx did not deal with individual men as such, nor
with the factors that "give us" a Da Vinci, a Beethoven, or a Ricardo. Whenever he refers to individuals he does so because he
regards them as "ideal types," their thoughts being identical with
what he was really interested in: the consciousness of the age, the
clichés (as we may call them) that move people. Marx' epistemology is a social one. It is not fit, it does not claim, and should
not be used to explain the origin of, say, Spencer's ideas, but only
the reasons for their social acceptance, only the fact that they became fashionable, that they percolated down to the level of journalistic and propagandistic writings. In sum, Marx' theory of ideas
really deals with what academicians regard as the most superficial
instances of "collective thinking" in society: the thinking of Chambers of Commerce, of politicians, of newspaper editorials, of the
popularizers of economics, and of salons and political clubs. Such
thought *is* superficial, but it so happens that it is also a great moving force. The idealistic mentality was not concerned with it because it saw history as moved by *lofty* ideas. As a scholar Marx
knew that to quote the newspaper or Miss Martineau, or to conceive questionnaire surveys, would have hardly been worth the
trouble. Thus he traced social ideas, the social consciousness of the
time, back to its early exponents and quoted them. Placed in this
context, a statement like "Adam Smith was a product of the industrial revolution" is un-Marxian nonsense. The *origin* of Smith's vision
is beyond the bounds of intellectual speculation and certainly beyond the grasp of Marx' theory. Casual conversations, haphazard
readings, "hunches," and countless chancy events may give a writer
the nucleus which, labored over for many years, eventually develops into a system. Marx himself was not possessed with the concept of the unconscious which was later to become the open sesame
of the inherently unknowable, the (retrospective) key to unlock all
psychic creations. What Marx' theory of ideas helps in explaining
is the eventual acceptance and popularization of Smith's view by
nineteenth-century liberal thought. It follows from this that the so-
called Marxist method of "relating" *a man's* ideas to the economic
substratum is a modern vice of which Marx was not guilty. His
love for great literature must have given him an appreciation of
the element of originality in man's thought—an element which can
hardly be related to the economic or any other factor. What can be
so related is only pedestrian thought, the "modal" thought of the

bourgeoisie as a class, which, Marx well knew, moves history and which he endeavored to oppose with another mass creed.

This interpretation must be correct, for otherwise Marx' very life and thought would contradict his own theory. How, for instance, explain the fact that he, the son of a member of the German *haute bourgeoisie*, married to the daughter of a Prussian aristocrat, took up the cause of common laborers? The man who "forged the intellectual weapons of the proletariat" was actually an aristocrat by birth, upbringing, education, and taste. As for Engels, he managed his father's mills! By any interpretation of the "link" between each of them and the "substratum," they should have been apologists of capitalism. Marx' very existence and thought stand as clear rebuttal to those who turned him into a "determinist."

If we wish to understand the phenomenon of the origins of the ideas of Marx the man, the well-known bromide that the Germans have no sense of humor goes further than determinism. Marx took Hebrew-Christian ideals and the ideals of 1789 seriously. He searched for them in life and did not find them. What he found were charlatans like J. Townsend, a priest of the Church of England, from whose works Marx quotes at length: "Hunger is not only a peaceful, silent, unremitted pressure but, as the most natural motive of industry and labour, it calls forth the most powerful exertions." That the poor are such, the priest goes on to say, is another manifestation of the farsightedness of God. "It seems to be a law of Nature that the poor should be to a certain degree improvident [the reason for their poverty], that there may always be some to fulfill the most servile, the most sordid, the most ignoble offices in the community. The stock of human happiness is thereby much increased, whilst the most delicate are not only relieved from drudgery . . . but are left at liberty without interruption to pursue those callings which are suited to their various dispositions."[24] As Marx notes, this is the "delicate parson" Townsend from whom Malthus quotes whole pages. The reason why Townsend is worth quoting, in fact, is exactly that his platitudes were repeated by large numbers of people and were, thus, typical of a class' social outlook.

In his attack on society's hypocrisy, incidentally, Marx shows himself to be typical of the most advanced thinkers of his days. Nietzsche, Kierkegaard, and Schopenhauer, among others, found

24. Marx, *Capital*, 1:646–47, quoting the Reverend J. Townsend, *A Dissertation on the Poor Laws* (1817).

evidence of it in sizable areas of Western life: in religion, in the universities, in politics. We stressed the social aspects and interests of Marx' theory of ideology because many sociologists, historians, and economists have imputed to Marx much of the guilt for a certain habit of the contemporary mind: the habit of ignoring an argument and concentrating instead on "unearthing" its alleged "hidden foundations," its "subconscious" (economic) motives. This peculiar method generally ends up by proving what it assumes, to wit, that man is incapable of attaining truth. This way of argumentation bears no relation to Marx'. Rather what happened to him happened to many other geniuses: his ideas were popularized and propagandized; they were dragged into the political marketplace where they were mixed with other motives, with a different outlook and a different ethics, or with no ethics at all. Above all, his ideas were uprooted from their empirical soil and transformed into axioms. Thus, they became a straitjacket of the understanding as rigid as Cartesian geometrizing and certainly more dangerous to the truth. Marx always provided arguments and documentation for every allegation he made. The modern habit to which we are referring shuns documentation. Toynbee concludes his analysis of Marxism with the suggestion that the founder of scientific socialism may yet be responsible for a "re-awakening of the Christian social conscience."[25] Whether the latter consists of charity, justice, or reason, there is exactly the reverse of it in vulgar Marxism, for vulgar Marxism is not interested in the truth but uses the mere form (the jargon) of Marx to attain its own ends.

We noted before that what imparts movement to social thought and to reality is need, for need gives rise to thought often "running ahead" of matter and, if it is true and "scientific," eventually causes matter to conform itself to the idea. But there is another engine of change in Marx, namely, the fact that reality includes two classes, the exploiters and the exploited, who, being differently situated in relation to the modes of production of a given epoch, perceive of needs in often diametrically opposed ways. On the surface, the class basis of consciousness seems to complicate the problem of knowledge: if truth is relative to the class that expounds it, how can Marx claim superior truth-content for his (or the proletariat's) views? Marx solved this problem by defining true (unbiased)

25. Arnold J. Toynbee, A Study of History, 5:587.

thinking as the one possessed by the emerging class and by further believing that the upcoming struggle (between the bourgeoisie and the workers) would be the last one. The expected victors of this struggle are consequently possessed with absolute, not relative, truth for they are the last of the social classes. With the disappearance of exploitation, there will no longer be "class-truths" but only objective truth.

We saw that the test of correct thinking, as the test of right, is provided by successful action. The test is then removed from the regions of ideas and drawn closer to where it has always been politically—to real life. Marx' solution does not imply that "might makes right," but it does suggest that a right which is not supported by force or by a threat does not exist. Of this, Bentham himself was aware. Should any class employ violence (or its milder versions) to prove the correctness of its world view? Practice again solves the issue. An unsuccessful application of force (e.g., an abortive revolution) betrays a false assessment of the situation. Action was perhaps born out of an idealistic outlook. Successful action, instead, suggests that the theory that led to it was true. Force is, in the last analysis, only of secondary importance in promoting change. Blind, chiliastic, suicidal revolutions that have little chance of succeeding were hardly to Marx' liking. "Force is the midwife of every old society pregnant with a new one."[26] As the midwife is a relatively unimportant and dispensable accessory in the phenomenon of birth,[27] so is force. It becomes necessary solely because the declining class clings to its privileges and, blinded by a "false consciousness," an inability to see movement, is unwilling to concede defeat and pass away graciously, making room for those better located in relation to the new modes of production.

Since all history is becoming, the "now" does not exist in isolation from the "tomorrow." Those ideas are therefore most nearly correct that, based on an empirical study of history, are congruent not with the reality of today, but with the "becoming" of society, with the new social arrangements towards which history is groping and which Marxism helps to interpret correctly. For Marx' historical studies convinced him that just as the medieval lord had given way to the industrial and financial capitalist, so will the latter

26. *Capital*, 1:751.
27. By "phenomenon of birth" we mean all of the events from conception to parturition.

succumb in front of the proletariat. After all, had not the Mercantilists referred to labor as "our most precious commodity"? Therefore, the categories of the labor class, its ideas and theories, are the
true ones, for they are in the process of becoming. And these categories have little in common with the traditional Cartesian ones.
The latter were *static*, politically reflecting the self-satisfaction with
the status quo of the capitalist class that adopted them. Marx' are
dynamic, yearnings toward the morrow of socialism. Conventional
political thought was axiomatic, as befitting a class able to *dictate*;
socialist thought must be empirical, for the workers have to "make
a case": they are (as yet) in no position to dictate, to be axiomatic
and dogmatic.

Marx' concept of false consciousness is an integral part of his theory
of knowledge. It is perverted knowledge naturally following from
his division of the world into two classes, one interested in protecting its position and privileges, the other in acquiring them. His
false consciousness is an explanation of "distorted" social thought,
thought that, being static, finds itself overtaken by reality and
perennially looking backward, not forward. In this respect his
analysis has precedents in Bentham's, Hume's, and Bacon's works,
all thinkers who studied the pathology of thought.[28] A state of mind
is characterized by false consciousness when it is not consonant with
the reality of the situation in the process of becoming. Inability to
see the obvious fact that history has been, is, and will be development is the ultimate source of false consciousness. It causes thinkers
to employ categories of thought that reflect the false presupposition
of stability and tranquility. Accordingly they ignore history, which
is change, flux, and upheaval. A false conception of man arises
from this outlook: man as unchanging in his essential characteristics as an abstract entity. "Analysis" takes flight into formalism,
and myth-making supplants historiography. Bourgeois economists,
for instance, instead of relating the real history of "brutal force"
and "enslavement" that marked the beginning and growth of capitalism, invent fables akin to original sin in theology: "In times long
gone by there were two sorts of people: one, the diligent, intelligent and above all, frugal elite; the other, lazy rascals, spending
their substance, and more, in riotous living. . . . Thus it came to pass

28. Mannheim, *Ideology and Utopia*, pp. 55 ff.

that the former sort accumulated wealth, and the latter sort had at last nothing to sell except their own skins. And from this original sin dates the poverty of the great majority that, despite all its labour has up to now nothing to sell but itself, and the wealth of the few that increases constantly although they have long ceased to work."[29]

There is no doubt that, if economic theory is understood as referring to real men living in a real historical context, Marx' mocking rendition of its philosophy is justified. On the history of capital accumulation the classical view of the abstemious saver throws an immaculate veil. The true history is history of the expropriation of the yeomanry and of cottagers, of the pillaging of Bengal and India, of the slave trade, of the monopolization of the instrument of production, of the enslavement of the South American natives abroad and of children, women, and paupers at home. It is the history documented by the parliamentary investigations of the factories which Marx quotes. To refer to all this as "abstinence" and to "explain" it by "sacrifice" and by stories about the rude state of nature must have seemed to Marx as odd as hearing that the center of the earth is made of jam. Such an "explanation" offered by serious thinkers calls for analysis and Marx provided exactly an analysis of the mass madness that he calls "false consciousness."

The culprit is the habit of viewing reality in terms of abstractions: it enabled bourgeois thinkers to build up a web of relations among things, not among men. They tended to reify economic relations. Rationalistically, they saw a "purpose" in the economic process (producing material goods), hence they concluded that the laborer exists only to satisfy this purpose instead of, on the contrary, wealth existing to satisfy the needs of men. "As in religion man is governed by the product of his own brain, so in capitalist production he is governed by the products of his own hands."[30] The notion of the "reification" of human relations and of the consequent transvaluation of social into material relations Marx had first developed at length in his *Economic and Philosophic Manuscripts* of 1844. There he provided an analysis of capitalist production and of the intellectual attitudes it engenders.

Marx calls attention to a fact occasionally recognized even by orthodox economists like J. S. Mill, that workers become poorer

29. Marx, *Capital*, 1:713.
30. Ibid., p. 621.

the more wealth they produce. They become an ever cheaper commodity in inverse relation to their contribution to output.[31] With the increasing abundance of material things there proceeds, in direct proportion, the devaluation of men. The more objects the worker produces the more he becomes a "thing" of the marketplace, losing his human characteristics. Eventually, the objects which labor produces confront him as something alien, as a power independent of him. Far from being a creative act, capitalist production makes man the slave of his own creation.[32]

This notion of the opposition between labor-the-subject and the matter created by labor (the object) is typically Hegelian. In Hegel, it was the source of the "unhappy consciousness" that stunted true understanding. In Marx the antithesis of man-labor and matter-labor (as we may call it) leads to a distortion of man's "existential activity," of his "free conscious life."[33] His intellectual and esthetic powers, his humanity, are crushed and he feels alienated not only from the object (i.e., his work) but also from his fellow men. In fact, he "feels himself freely active only in his animal functions— eating, drinking, procreating . . . in his human functions he no longer feels himself to be anything but an animal. What is animal becomes human and what is human becomes animal."[34] Work, far from representing self-fulfillment, turns man into a "crippled monstrosity," intellectually and physically "deformed."[35]

Conventional economics would reject this analysis of the labor process as "philosophical" and hence unscientific. Marx would retort that the very distinction between philosophy and science results from the unnatural divorce of theory from practice, of thought from action, which turns even social science into idealistic philosophical thinking. The very distinction between philosophy and science is the product of false consciousness. Because of this fictional schism, political economy is part of the drama of labor. It shuns a philosophic-scientific consideration of the process of "estrangement" of labor, thus "concealing the truth."[36] From the natural sciences, political economy absorbs its materialistic outlook.

31. Marx, *Manuscripts*, p. 107.
32. Ibid., pp. 108–9.
33. Ibid., p. 113.
34. Ibid., p. 11.
35. Ibid., p. 109. See *Capital*, vol. 1, chap. 15 and passim for the documentation of this denigration of man by capital.
36. *Manuscripts*, pp. 109–10.

It describes relations among men as if they were relations among things. And just as the economic analysis is crude, so the ethics it embodies is vulgar. It is the ethics of "acquisition, work, thrift, sobriety."[37] Private property emerges as sacrosanct and eternal, rather than as the cause and effect of alienated labor.

Victims of "false consciousness," political economists, too, become alienated beings: without knowing it, they merely camouflage the selfish interests of the bourgeoisie by cloaking them in the dignity of "universal" concepts. It is not that bourgeois thinkers are the hirelings of the upper class, as vulgar Marxism often asserts. Their false consciousness lies in their inability to see that "each new class which puts itself in the place of one before it is compelled merely in order to carry through its aim, to represent its interest as the common interest of all the members of society."[38] The Invisible Hand myth is not the result of malevolence: it is the offspring of an uncritical attitude. Only an empirical, historical analysis of *real* society can destroy false consciousness. For despised history teaches that ideas that were once regarded as "natural," innate, and universally true later appear as ignorance. Intellectuals have abandoned their very calling by rejecting the study of the past. Thus, they end by making up illusions and myth for the benefit of others. To put it differently, so-called independent thinkers accept, without being aware of it, ideas, concepts, and theories forged as class weapons during a fight against the old order. Just as men, by their very birth, "enter into definite social relationships that are independent of their wills," so do thinkers inherit the concepts and modes of thought which once assisted the transition from the old to the new order, but which, in time, turn reactionary. The notion of the "state of nature," which was politically useful to fight monarchical and ecclesiastical despotism, when used later by economists had the effect of throwing a cloak over reality.

So strong is the grip of false consciousness that, instead of recognizing the transformation of what was once held in respect into what is now held to be false as a clue to reach, empirically, for the *reason* for the flux of ideas, thinkers dogmatically assume that past beliefs were mistaken ones and that those they now hold are the correct and forever true ones.[39] Conventional thinkers are like

37. Ibid., pp. 152, 117.
38. Marx and Engels, *German Ideology*, pp. 40–41.
39. Ibid., pp. 42–43.

worms imprisoned in a cocoon of their own making, whose breaking therefore must be left to others.

Marx' concept of "reification" is the traditional error of hypostatization on a social scale: the products of the idealistic mind
are viewed as material things. For both philosophy and Marx, reification represents erroneous thinking. But for Marx the error
is much more than just logical: it is an error of distorted perspective and it has social consequences. It is not an error of form but
one of substance. And this error has such deep historical roots in
the class split that, in a sense, one can say that by explaining it
Marx nearly legitimized it. Nietzsche was later to take this step
when he asserted that erroneous ideas, by existing and facilitating
action, establish their raisons d'être independently of their truth-
content.

A wide literature has sprung up around the question of whether
the bourgeois thinker can overcome false consciousness and attain
truth. This problem transcends Marx' theory of knowledge if we
interpret him rightly as being concerned not with the individual's
thought but with the thought of social classes. Of course it must
be possible for isolated individuals to reach a true perspective of
things. Marx' very intellectual labors prove this. He himself paid
a tribute to the humble factory inspectors of England and Scotland
who drew up the Blue Books. It is doubtful, he says in the preface
of *Das Kapital*, whether men as competent, as free from partisan-
ship and respect of persons, can be found anywhere in Europe.[40]
It is true that these people had an advantage over thinkers: they
looked at reality as reporters, their minds uncluttered by any desire to build a system or to unearth "the logic" of the market. Marx
would acknowledge that bourgeois individuals and even small
groups may see the truth; but he would stress that their truth
never enters the social consciousness of the dominant class until
the old class relationship is overturned.

Not only economics, but philosophy, too, has for centuries per-
petuated one grave error: that of believing that consciousness, ideas,
and social theories exist in isolation from the material activities and
the material intercourse of men. From Plato on, the tendency has
been to view thinking as independent of existence (this was also
the allegation of some of Marx' great contemporaries, Schopenhauer,
Nietzsche, Kierkegaard), and this gave men an "inverted" view of

40. Preface to the first German edition.

reality. They saw reality as through a *camera oscura*. Marx broke through habitual modes of thought by, first, concentrating attention on social thinking (letting natural and scientific thought alone) and then by reasserting the primacy of the institutional constraints within which thought operates.

The above treatment of Marx' social epistemology shows that it is not deterministic any more than it is idealistic. Man is free—within limits. In his doctoral dissertation (1841) Marx favorably compared Epicurus' "determinism with freedom" with Democritus' strict determinism. And in later life he wrote in the introduction to the *Critique of Political Economy* that "certain periods of highest development of art stand in no direct connection with the general development of society, nor with the material basis and the skeleton structure of its organization. Witness the example of the Greeks . . . or even Shakespeare."[41] Not only are artistic trends (let alone individual artists) so fully free, but even the law—in its aim for consistency—progressively loses the characteristic of reflecting the "material bases" of society. And the same freedom is conceded to some aspects of religious and philosophical speculation. It is not improbable that Marx would have granted that hyperclassical economics, in its aim to attain generality, logical consistency, etc., shed much of the apologetic overtones of the preceding decades and popularizations.

The concept of alienation is the foundation stone not only of Marx' philosophy but also of his economics, a distinction which, we must add, is foreign to Marx, for his thought—like reality—refused to be bound by academic confines.[42] Surplus value is the economic translation of the more philosophical term "alienation."

Alienation is the negation of freedom. In Hegel it arose when the subject became aware of the objective world and hence of the limits of his freedom and power. Hegel's therapy to overcome alienation is philosophical understanding of the ways of reality. The act of understanding the process of the Idea has the effect of destroying the object *qua* object: from a something opposed to consciousness it becomes absorbed into consciousness, enriching it. By it, hostility toward the world disappears and the dualism of subject and object ceases. Hegel's solution did not call for changing the

41. Sec. 4.
42. His chosen intellectual motto was *Nihil humani a me alienum puto.*

world but for changing our philosophy. His program, accordingly, is intended for an intellectual elite: it cannot even be forced on anybody, lest his system lose its "positive" qualities and become normative. Neither does it entail a psychological manipulation of one's mind: it is only an individualistic stoic act of conquest, "a voyage into the open, where nothing is below us or above us, and we stand in solitude with ourselves alone."[43] It is a purely personal experience. And this is probably the reason why Hegel's prescriptions for the regaining of the happy consciousness pleased neither the right nor the left, groups that, being political and activistic, were animated by goals other than the desire "to stand in solitude."

Marx accomplished what is probably the best known transformation of both the reason for alienation and the prescription for overcoming it. Schematically, the metamorphosis consisted of no more than this. The metaphysical opposition between subject and object became a *social* opposition between labor and capital. The "inhuman power" of the latter is the source of the masses' alienation. The process of conquering this alienation calls not for philosophical understanding, but, quite obviously, for action to redress wrongs—not *any* action, but action based on an understanding of the "laws" of history. By 1844 Marx had already worked out the general outline of his concept of alienation: his voluminous treatises on political economy are the "scientific" proof of the existence of alienation under capitalism (labor theory of value) and of its disappearance under the forces of a declining rate of profit, capitalist crises, monopolization of production, and possible revolution. Eventually communism is born and alienation is overcome.

Hegel saw alienation as a problem of the intellectual who expects the world to be rational (in a strict sense) but does not find it so. It is a problem affecting thinkers and it is caused by their being "bad philosophers," by their inability to grasp the process of the Idea. Marx turned it into a social problem affecting nearly all mankind. For different reasons laborers and capitalists and bourgeois intellectuals are its victims. Hegel's solution was purely intellectual (love history for what it is, for it is *Reason*); and it centered on the overthrowing of the narrow Enlightened definition of reason. Marx' solution was a material-historical one, entailing action on *matter*, not on our *outlook*. This is why, while to Hegel philosophy

43. *The Logic of Hegel*, p. 66.

has the task to teach the truth that history is *Reason*, to Marx it has the task to teach that history has hitherto been *unreason* (exploitation) but that it need not continue to be so. "Philosophy [Marx writes in the introduction to *The Holy Family*] cannot realize itself without the abolition of the [alienated] proletariat; the proletariat cannot abolish itself without the realization of philosophy." For both Marx and Hegel, philosophy has the same role to play: overcoming alienation. But for Hegel philosophy is an end in itself; in its Hegelian form, it is the overcoming of alienation and it survives this conquest. For Marx philosophy is a means for the attainment of true freedom; it disappears when this goal is realized.

Since Marx' days, psychiatry, sociology, journalism, and everyday language have appropriated the word "alienation." It was therefore inevitable that some thinkers compared the idea of alienation as conceived by Marx and by psychiatrists. Professor Tucker does exactly this and concludes that Marx' description of the alienated worker is "clinically accurate." His description of how an alienated worker feels can hardly be improved by an experienced psychiatrist. Like Marx, psychiatry asserts that an alienated individual feels "he is driven instead of being the driver."[44] But, Tucker adds, psychiatry says that the sources of the "neuroses" are in the individual himself. Thus, he triumphantly concludes, Marx was in error when he turned this psychiatric phenomenon into a social one by saying it was caused by the objective world of economic relations. Marx created a "myth" when he posited a "demon" (capital) outside the laborer. The real cause of alienation is purely internal, psychiatric. What a simpleton Marx was! He believed what the patient himself asserted. Instead of seeing that the worker is "alienated from himself," Marx splits the alienated man into two, the worker and the capitalist, and he finds the latter guilty of labor's own fears. In brief, the worker is really paranoid. He has a "persecution complex." This criticism claims that it goes to the heart of the Marxist system, and alienation is, in fact, central to both Marx' economics and his concept of history. If Marx completely misunderstood the nature of alienation, then the whole structure comes down (intellectually speaking, of course, for historical Marxism can well withstand the weapons of scholarly criticism). Tucker's claim that Marx transformed an "as though" into an "is" is particularly interesting to us since it implies that Marx' alienation is a fiction, a fig-

44. Robert C. Tucker, *Philosophy and Myth in Karl Marx*, p. 145.

ment of the workers' sick minds, which Marx swallowed "hook, line, and sinker."

To prove that Marx mistook man's alienated relationship to himself as an alienated social relationship of "man to man," Tucker alleges not only the evidence of modern psychiatry but also Marx' own words. Much is made of the following statement of Marx in 1856: "At the same pace that mankind masters nature, man seems to become enslaved to other men or *to his own infamy*."[45] This "slip" proves that Marx had a "dim realization that he was dealing with a servitude within man and a conflict of the alienated self with itself." This interpretation seems improbable. More likely Marx meant that man *qua* worker becomes enslaved "to other men" (the capitalists); and that man *qua* capitalist becomes enslaved "to his infamy" (his greed). That Marx' capitalists, too, are alienated is abundantly obvious: the "worshippers of money" who live by the first commandment of political economy—abstinence—are themselves unhappy beings, driven by the satanic urge to "accumulate, accumulate." They abide by the prescriptions of political economy: "The less you eat, drink and buy books; the less you go to the theatre, the dance hall, the public house; the less you think, love, theorize, sing, paint, fence, etc., the more you *have*—the greater becomes your treasure which neither moths nor dust will devour —your *capital*. The less you *are*, the less you express your own life, the greater is your *alienated* life: the more you *have*, the greater is the store of your alienated being."[46] Any possible doubt as to the power of the capitalist's greed to cause "his own infamy" and his estrangement from his own true nature, Marx removes when he quotes a capitalist landowner who, having expropriated his neighbors from their land with the help of the enclosure laws, remorsefully remarks to those who complimented him on his newly acquired property: "It is a melancholy thing to stand alone in one's country: I look around and not a house can be seen but mine. I am the giant of Giant Castle, *and have eaten up all my neighbors*."[47]

There then remains the evidence of psychiatry. Modern psychiatry, says Tucker, asserts that alienation arises because of man's conflict with himself, which the alienated man, in an effort to "escape," projects on some outer force. Professor Tucker evidently

45. Ibid., p. 215. Emphasis in the text.
46. Marx, *Manuscripts*, p. 150. Emphasis in the text.
47. *Capital*, 1:692n. Emphasis added.

views psychiatry as Descartes viewed geometry, the source, and the only source, of "clear and distinct" conclusions. Psychiatrists, we suspect, know better. They may even recognize that their understanding of mental illnesses is deeply influenced by their goal which is that of transforming unhappy into tolerably "well-adjusted" individuals. Adjusted to what? Adjusted to the world, we would guess. Psychiatrists take the environment as a datum, not as something to be manipulated. Dealing with people on a one-to-one relationship, they cannot possibly advise their patients to gang together and "fight the system." They must take social reality as is and try as best as they can to convince the patient that the fault lies neither in the stars nor in society but in himself. The presuppositions, the purposes, the universe of discourse of psychiatry and of Marx' activistic philosophy are simply different and it is vain to oppose one with the tools of the other. The superiority of one explanation over the other cannot be determined outside the goals of each. All we can say is this: that, given Marx' desire to free the proletariat (a *class*) from its bondage, his exploration of the causes of alienation is consistent with the rest of his system and is, in fact, one of its most powerful pillars. And this is so even though, as we strongly suspect, Marx never wasted any time exploring the psyches of a single worker.[48] He did not have to ask the patient to stretch on his couch for he could use sources of information apparently regarded too lowly by the idealistic method, namely parliamentary investigations of factories, the press, and pamphlets. He could have read the issue of Carlyle's *The Lion* from which Paul Mantoux, the historian, quotes the "well known catalogue of the sufferings of the factory apprentice, Robert Blincoe":

> At Lowdham (near Nottingham), whither he was sent in 1799 with a batch of about eighty other boys and girls, they were only whipped. It is true that the whip was in use from morning till night, not only as a punishment for the slightest fault, but

48. Tucker's motto on the title page of his *Philosophy and Myth* quotes Marx as saying, "The *philosopher*, himself an abstract form of alienated man, sets himself up as the *measure* of the alienated world." Tucker may, of course, suggest that Marx himself is one of the alienated philosophers, but Marx thought otherwise. He did not regard himself "alienated" for the simple reason that he possessed truth, and he possessed the truth because he did not deal with abstractions, but with life. The "philosopher" to which *Marx* refers is the *bourgeois* philosopher and the bourgeois social thinker, both victims of false consciousness.

also to stimulate industry and to keep them awake when they were dropping with weariness. But at the factory at Litton matters were very different. There, the employer, one Ellice Needham, hit the children with his fists and with a riding whip, he kicked them, and one of his little attentions was to pinch their ears until his nails met through the flesh. The foremen were even worse, and one of them, Robert Woodward, used to devise the most ingenious tortures. It was he who was responsible for such inventions as hanging Blincoe up by his wrists over a machine at work, so that he was obliged to keep his knees bent up, making him work almost naked in the winter, with heavy weights on his shoulders, and filing down his teeth. The wretched child had been so knocked about that his scalp was one sore all over. By way of curing him, his hair was torn out by means of a cap of pitch. If the victims of these horrors tried to escape, their feet were put in irons. Many tried to commit suicide, and one girl, who took advantage of a moment when the supervision relaxed and threw herself into the river, thus regained her freedom: she was sent away, as her employer 'was afraid the example might be contagious.'

At Litton Mill the apprentices used to struggle with the pigs fattening in the yard, in order to get some of their food in their troughs. . . . Overcrowding in unventilated rooms . . . favored the spreading of a contagious disorder resembling prison fever. . . . The promiscuity of both workshops and dormitories gave scope for immorality, and this was, unfortunately, encouraged by the bad behaviour of some of the employers and foremen, who took advantage of it to satisfy their low instincts.[49]

And so it goes on, the catalogue of "crooked backs, and limbs deformed by rickets, or mutilated by accidents with machinery." These facts are well known. It takes extraordinary cleverness to convert them into just another case of what the English dubbed "spleen" and the French, *ennui.*

Just as Marx' alienation has its roots in economic relations, so its overcoming entails a total transformation of these relations, their evolving into communism. As we indicated, Marx did not regard communism as a Utopian blueprint, the product of the thinking head, a *deus ex machina,* a fiction, or even an ideal to be imposed

49. Quoted by Paul Mantoux, *The Industrial Revolution in the Eighteenth Century,* pp. 424–26.

on a recalcitrant reality. Communism he viewed rather as the developing reality of nineteenth-century Europe, dialectically linked to man's past. Capitalism contains within itself the seeds for its own negation and for the slow emergence of communism. Marx never tired of stressing this point which, in fact, separates his socialism from all other brands which he denigrated as idealistic preaching. It is worth noting that Marx was hardly dogmatic about the precise outline of communist society. Unlike epiphenomenalism and natural law thinking, Marx' teleology does not claim to be able to calculate a priori the state of the whole social system of the future. It can only forecast the broad outlines of the becoming and it hopes to influence only the general trend of the process of transformation. This unwillingness to commit himself shows above all else one thing: that Marx was aware of the reciprocal interrelations of matter and mind and left some room for passions, chance, and the unexpected to exert their influence. It is certain, however, that communism entails the abolition of private property and the overcoming of alienation. It represents the genuine resolution of the conflict between man and nature, and between man and man, "the true resolution of the strife between existence and essence, between the individual and the species."[50] These schisms, with which philosophy has dealt idealistically since time immemorial, are seen as *real* problems of existence. Under communism the contradictions in theoretical thought (subjectivism and objectivism, idealism and materialism, action and contemplation, science and philosophy, freedom and determinism, man and society) cease to exist. They are already partly overcome by Marxist philosophy exactly because this philosophy is the shadow cast by the present order presaging a new future.

Capitalism's negation stems from two sources: From its irrationality (greed, surplus value, economic crises, "immiserization" of the masses, progressive monopolization of industry, etc.) and from its *potential* rationality. For Marx acknowledges that capitalism (as a "machine process") is capable of abolishing poverty (Marx is, after all, one of the originators of the phrase "industrial revolution"). But the economic system is not allowed to develop according to its potential by deep-rooted (though not ineradicable) passions. It is exactly because Marx sees both the forces of irrationality and rationality at work in capitalism that he cannot make

50. *Manuscripts,* p. 135.

up his mind as to whether revolution is inevitable. For, quite possibly, the positive forces of increasing output may keep revolution at bay by just satisfying the masses. Toward the end of his life Engels gave vent to the same feelings when he remarked that "we communists prosper better by democratic than by revolutionary means."

Communism is freedom, hence it lies beyond the sphere of material production in the strict meaning of the term, and beyond economics. It entails the ability of each individual to do what he pleases, "to do one thing today and another tomorrow, to hunt in the morning, fish in the afternoon, rear cattle in the evening, criticize after dinner, just as I have a mind, without ever becoming a hunter, fisherman, shepherd or critic."[51] The idealism that Marx kept well bottled up in his historical analyses of the past and present and in his polemics with friends and foes is evidently allowed to run loose in this early vision of the future. It is an eminently un-Smithian future, characterized by the negation of the sources of the wealth of nations (specialization and division of labor) which to Marx are the sources of alienation. Work, hitherto dehumanizing, turns into a creative artistic act. Communism is the ethical and esthetic stage of mankind. Where classical and hyperclassical thinkers created the beautiful and the just without knowing it, Marx did the same *consciously*, and he placed it in the future. That is why he needed no fictional support for his theorizing. He did not have to smuggle in ethical and esthetic concepts, for they bathed his whole outlook; and their conquest in the future was his overt goal. The most broad-minded person who deemed economics worthy of his interests, he devoted himself to economic matters exactly because he realized that such matters do not deserve to absorb our whole lives.

A brief review of the evolution of society toward communism will emphasize the fact that for Marx both material and spiritual factors are important. Communism is the final movement of a three-stage transformation: following the demise of capitalism, the "dictatorship of the proletariat" will emerge first, succeeded by socialism and then by communism proper. The first stage—which in the 1844 manuscripts is referred to as a "crude" or "raw" communism—is, in effect, a democratic republic characterized by the abolition of land property and inheritance, a severely progressive income tax, state

51. Marx and Engels, *German Ideology*, p. 22.

control of credit, equal liability of all to labor. The state retains its nature as the tool of the expression of the will and power of the upper class, but now this class is labor.

This stage is not the negation of private property, but its generalization. "Greed" and "envy" and the "urge to reduce things to a common level" are actually universalized at this stage.[52] The path toward communism is not without its own dialectic contradictions. Socialism is expected to consolidate the achievements of the previous stage, giving time for new values and for new outlooks to imprint themselves on the minds of the people. For the stage of communism a new breed of men is required. The first generation, tainted by possible violence and by the dead hand of the past, must perish in order to make room for men who have been reared in the new ethics. Freedom is finally attained, not as an empty category but as real behavior and feeling. In the well-known conservative phrase, a "change of hearts and minds" is necessary.

Many social scientists who regard predictive ability as the ultimate test of a theory, impressed by the fact that Western society today hardly conforms to the Marxist vision, are inclined to dismiss Marx as a myth-maker. There is something pathetically Don Quixotic in the attacks against a philosophy that has deeply affected our ways of thinking and that has inspired millions of people to shape history. To dare to apply our "critical tools" to Marxism when such "tools" cannot even explain the immediate reasons for an economic recession strikes us as another example of man's megalomania. The truth of the matter is that it is idle to look at reality for either confirmation or denial of Marx' vision of emerging communism, just as it is idle to appeal to psychiatry to discover the "true" cause of alienation. Many of the trends that have occurred during the past century could be brought within the molds of Marx' prophecies. We have witnessed an increase in the power of labor, "cradle to grave" welfare, a broadening of suffrage and education, the nationalization of credit, and a progressive income tax. Recently, there have emerged purely esthetic interests and concerns (pleasant parks, clean highways, and the like) while wars on poverty vie with conventional wars for attention and funding. "Guaranteed income" schemes have been framed and the opinion is prevalent in some quarters that we must begin thinking not in terms of scarcity but in terms of plenty.

52. *Manuscripts*, p. 133.

Large classes of the population (e.g., college students) are already freed from the burden of work. The average work week has been cut nearly in half in a century. Many people "work" solely because our language is slow to create new words to describe new activities. In reality they pass their time attending committee and board meetings, an activity which God hardly had in mind when he cursed Adam out of Eden. Fishing, golfing, boating, barbecuing, criticizing, and writing books take more time than real work (in God's sense and Marx') for vast masses of people. On the spiritual side, the ideals of parsimony and love of money reached their zenith some time ago. The "rags to riches" philosophy and Benjamin Franklin's maxims strike us as crude relics of a crude past. Even Schumpeter, an admirer of capitalism, has detected a flagging interest in the traditional capitalist values. All of these elements and many more may be alleged to suggest that contemporary society is the shadow of a new order not unlike Marx' communism.

Nonetheless, we are of the opinion that the common standards of scientific hypotheses—adherence of forecasts with facts—breaks down when used to assess the truth-content of Marxism. For a basic postulate of scientific testing is that the scientist should not influence the outcome of the experiment. Our notions of "testing" have been shaped by the astronomers. Having formed a hypothesis about the behavior of mice in a crowded cage, the scientist-observer takes pains to make himself inconspicuous so as not to disturb the mice's behavior. Now, Marxism was definitely not an inconspicuous experience in the history of the West during the past century. Since detached observation was not Marx' goal (for his was an ethics of action), the normal scientific testing is not the standard by which Marx would like his work to be judged. Influence in the affairs of men was his aim. This influence nobody would deny, although it has not caused, and probably never will cause, the emergence of the society he envisaged. Social theories with a negative content (forecasting "doom") should be judged correct if they do *not* bring about the prophesied result. For this may mean that the vision or theory awakened men from their complacent slumbers and induced them to take some action to avert the catastrophe. It is, for instance, idle to say that the "stagnation thesis" of the thirties has been proved false by events. The theory implicitly assumed the impotence of the theory itself (and hence government inaction). But once the theory percolated down to the social and governmental consciousness, it induced certain actions that changed the whole social equation and rendered the theory's forecast incorrect.

Marxism has taught innumerable people that history is the sum total of their actions. People then took certain actions (largely of a revolutionary nature) that destroyed Marx' forecasts. The system has not collapsed because it has adapted itself to demands inspired by Marx himself. For the same reason, it is idle to point at the Russian or Chinese experience as evidence that Marx' evolutionary view of history is wrong. The current communist countries have indeed passed from a "medieval stage" to communism's preliminary stage, the "dictatorship of the proletariat." They thus skipped the stage of capitalism. They had no bourgeoisie when the revolution swept away the old order. Does this mean that Marx' "stage" view of history was falsified by later events? Not if we agree that Marx (plus the material conditions of czarist Russia and early-twentieth-century China) inspired the very events that allowed these countries to dispense with the capitalist stage and excesses.

It is true that when we look at the so-called communist countries, we realize that, especially in the sphere of spiritual values (personal freedom, etc.), they fall seriously short of Marx' ideals. Perhaps this is the inevitable result of their having forced the hand of history much more so than socialism did in the West.

Marx' economics is an offshoot of his philosophy of history. It represents the detailed working out of the historical phase of capitalism written at a time when conventional economics was moving away from whatever history is to be found in Smith's and J. S. Mill's writings and was turning toward greater and greater technical perfection. Having already little in common with the classical method of the logico-fictional a priori, Marx' writings found an even less receptive soil in hyperclassicism, the full flowering of this method. Thus the Marxist analysis lived in the "underground of economics," as Keynes puts it.

We remarked that the essence of hyperclassicism is the supremacy of form over content: rules and techniques prevail over subject matter. The style becomes "flowery" and imagery is used for its own sake. In architecture this style is sometimes called rococo. There is a certain rococo quality in hyperclassical economics. This quality is absent in Marx' works. *Capital*, the book, is a great drama, and Marx' capital, the emasculated category of classical economics, is the counterpart of Schopenhauer's Will. Capital is not an abstraction, it is not an aggregate of machines. It is a passion. Just as Greek mythology portrayed human passions by certain symbols (lust by the satyrs, greed by Plutus, etc.), Marx conveys his meaning of capital by symbolic analogies. It is, alternatively, a "vampire," a "werewolf," a "monster which controls the living labor power and sucks it dry"; it is "an unbridled passion for self-expression," the embodiment of a satanic "drive," the sordid avarice, the passion for accumulation as an end in itself. The capitalist is not a Mandevillean philosopher. He does not accumulate in order to consume or enjoy life. He accumulates to satisfy his craving for power. Like Luther's usurer (whom Marx quotes) the capitalist wants to be God: love of power is behind his desire to get rich.[53] This concept of capital was fully formed in the manuscripts of 1844, well before Marx applied himself to the study of political economy.

One is tempted to dismiss this conception as a figment of the author's imagination and many have yielded to this temptation. To preclude such inference, however, stand the hundreds of pages *documenting* the factual bases of the "blind, unbridled passion" and its effects on workers and capitalists alike. What happened is that these facts and reports fell on a revolutionary epistemology that turned everything it chose to touch into the opposite of what conventional modes of thought had judged it to be. The central theme of this epistemology—already stressed in the often vicious polemics of the earlier writings—is that social thought should deal with man, *live* man, not with the ego-spun image of man. Consequently, history and economics became areas of investigation of the activities of real men, while before they had been largely explorations in the power of the Cartesian ego to relate its own products to each other. This methodological viewpoint enabled Marx to discover that history is as much the behavior of humble men as of kings and diplomats and that horrors and inhumanity are to be found not only on the battlefield but in everyday life too. The fact that the philosophical vision of *Capital* was fully formed in 1844, just as the vision behind the *General Theory* was fully formed in 1919, suggests how great is the power of a philosophical outlook. It was this outlook that, brought to bear on familiar questions, yielded an unconventional analysis.

53. *Capital*, 1:491n.

Many orthodox economists, methodologically biased in favor of geometrizing, have emphasized the formal elements in Marx over the truly meaningful ones. To consider Marx' pseudosymbolism (which undeniably exists) as the essence of his economics is as gross an error as to consider his economics as if it were independent of his philosophy. His differs from the conventional economics in that with Marx symbols are not the masters of the subject matter but are subservient to it. And the subject matter is real man in real society. His so-called scientific terminology betrays its human roots: the term "surplus value" may be less connotative than alienation, but it is hardly neutral. It is not "time preference." "Organic composition of capital," by its biological simile, reminds one of capital's vampire-like tendency to feed on human blood. The firm, in hyper-classicism a fiction which the most clear-minded economists refuse to hypostatize, was for Marx a real organization. He speaks of the divorce between management and ownership, of the tendency of management to plunder stockholders, of their recklessness with the savings of others, of their sagacious financial malpractices, of the parasites management breeds, well before Veblen, Berle and Means, and the Temporary National Economic Committee looked into the abscesses of the modern corporation.[54]

M. M. Bober, the author of a book on Marxian economics, asserts that Marx detests explanations "by the intangible, the spiritual and the subjective."[55] If by subjective he means explanations in terms of individual psychology (the great man theory of history, for example), then Bober is right, for Marx dealt with classes and hence with sociological forces and movements. And if the spiritual and intangible are the idealistic, the purely mental, then the judgment is also true. But if spiritual and intangible factors are non-material but important ones (like, for instance, the esprit de corps of an army), then the statement is a gross misconception of the Marxian method. What is alienation if not a spiritual, intangible state of mind caused, it is true, by outside objective material conditions? What is the prime mover of capitalism if not greed, a non-rational, immaterial element, but a real one nonetheless? "Modern society, which, soon after its birth pulled Plutus by the hair of his head from the bowels of the earth, greets gold as its Holy Grail,

54. Marx' observations on the corporation are to be found especially in *Capital*, 3:386 ff., 436 ff.
55. *Karl Marx's Interpretation of History*, p. 398.

as the glittering incarnation of the very principle of its own life."[56] Marx' capitalism is little less than a system of passions comparable in intensity to those we find in young religious sects. Marx himself more than once found an elective affinity between capitalism and Calvinism, thus foreshadowing Max Weber's eminently "spiritual" analysis of the development of the former. And in his essay in 1843 "On the Jewish Question" he likewise points to a similar affinity between the *spirit* of Judaism and that of capitalism—thus anticipating Sombart's famous reply to Weber! Marx was too good a Hegelian to ignore the non-quantitative, the intangible, and the spiritual. In his emphasis on these elements he is in touch with the nineteenth-century revolt against mechanicism. The intangible is, to some extent, the chancy, the uncontrollable, the blind. Their importance in *Capital* is obvious in the working of capitalism itself. In order to gain an advantage over their competitors, entrepreneurs eagerly introduce new machines. This increases the organic composition of capital, but reduces profits and causes crises. Capitalistic innovations, the embodiment of blind passions, are blindly undertaken and lead ultimately to the negation of the present order. There is in Marx a lively awareness of the tragedy of the unrelated, unplanned, individual decision-making process. In innumerable social and political contexts we have recently come to recognize that reason and good will on the part of the few are of no avail. No matter how great the "social consciousness" of a few landlords in a city block, they can do little by themselves to stem the blight: if they try they usually go bankrupt. No matter how pacifistic the American (or Russian) government happens to be at a given time, it will be compelled to pursue the arms race if Russia (or America) continues hers. The cobweb theorem, which is an oddity, a footnote in orthodox economic analysis, is the essence of Marx' system. There is, however, a teleological optimistic note. Throughout man's tragedy, the "cunning of reason" is still at work: and it advances toward the ultimate freedom.

After listing Marx' and Engel's major economic works, Bober concludes that they are "flaming with descriptions on the cunning, treachery, cruelty and lasciviousness of the master classes, and of the pettiness, vacillations, shabbiness, hypocrisy and chicken-heartedness of the middle classes. Especially are these pages groaning or thundering with pained outcries over the lot of the laboring

56. *Capital*, 1:133.

poor, dehumanized, degraded, foul-mouthed, deprived of decent impulses, derelict, selling their wives and children into wage slavery, reduced to automatons, to fractions of human beings."[57] May one ask what cunning, treachery, pettiness, vacillations, dehumanization, etc., are if not spiritual and intangible elements that defy the Benthamite calculus? In Marx, "verbal flaming" and logical algebraic relations are two different styles to express the same historical phenomenon. They are consistent with each other. This is why there is not in Marx (as there is in classical economics) a distinction between positive and normative thought; between science and history, between static and dynamic analysis. There is no dualism in his economics for the simple reason that thought and matter had been reconciled in his epistemology. He avoided the extremes of both materialism and idealism by the assertion that matter and thought interact on each other and by the conviction that, as there had been a progress of freedom in the historical ascent of mankind, so this progress would continue and eventually ensue in communism. Thus, Marx needed no fictions to work out his history and his economics.

Just as no schism exists between history and economics, so within economics there is no schism between value theory and business cycle theory: the same concepts used in the former are the mainstay of the latter. Surplus value, or rather its absence after periods of capital accumulation, causes depressions. The treatment of monetary relations requires no different point of departure than value theory, for Marx deals with historical capitalism from the outset and has no need to dream up a kingdom of barter, Robinson Crusoes, Say's Law, diminishing marginal utility, or diminishing returns to land. These laws he recognized as the children of premises that remove capitalism from its historical setting and place it in the realm of the everlasting essences where all is stability.

Money is hardly a "veil" or even a "lubricant": it is the objectification of a passion, an infernal instrument of slavery of man to man and of man to himself. Indeed, it is little else than the theological *turpe lucrum* of the Catholic Fathers. Only under communism it will become a "veil," a mere *numeraire*, a unit of account. This last observation suggests a major difference between orthodox economics and Marx' vision. The former was compelled to see the kingdom of rationality in the present. Marx, too, envisaged a ra-

57. *Marx's Interpretation of History*, p. 94.

tionally organized world but saw it emerging in the future. The present was anarchic though, happily, it contained the seeds for its own abolition. The blindness and wastefulness of the capitalist modes of production are evident not only in his theory of cycles but even in his value theory. Under perfect market competition, the capitalist hires labor time and produces commodities, but only after the sale will he know whether he employed "socially necessary" labor. And it would be miraculous if he had, for the Marxian entrepreneur is not endowed with the Cartesian attribute of perfect foresight of his classical counterpart. The consumer is indeed "sovereign" (to the extent that he can be divorced from his also being a worker!) but his sovereignty, far from producing "optimum allocational efficiency," creates crises of overproduction and underproduction as a matter of course. In fact, what Marx is exposing is the inherent contradiction between the classical slogan "the consumer is king" and the axiom of Say's Law. They are antithetical since one acknowledges disruptive changes in tastes (kings, after all, are fickle!), while the other implies an ideal and perfect balance between production and demand. To Marx' mind there is no doubt whatever that "there is . . . no necessary, but only an *accidental* connection between the volume of society's demand for a certain article and the volume represented by the production of this article in the total production, or the quantity of social labor spent on this article." In modern jargon, his is an ex ante analysis. Neither does Marx forget that in addition to monetary (effective) demand there is actual social need and that, for the vast majority of the population, the former is only a fraction of the latter. He does not forget this because science and ethics are one in his system. Demand stems from the use value of commodities, their utility in sustaining life, but this notion of utility is vastly different from that of hyperclassical economics where it is only a formal concept, the one a child implicitly uses when asked why goods are bought: "Because they are useful." For Marx the freedom of the marketplace is philosophically an empty formalism and economically a blind, anarchic, and wasteful process. It creates crises, bankruptcies, monopolistic concentrations, and alienation. Given the nature of capitalistic accumulation and exploitation, "overproduction" is endemic and even sets the stage for an expansion of capitalism beyond its national boundaries—an insight which the theory of imperialism exploited. Just as there is no perfect allocational efficiency within a country, so there is no delicate "international division of labor" maximizing social utility among trading nations.

Not following the Cartesian method, he did not indulge in tautological derivations. On the contrary, he exposed them in others. While dealing with so-called crises of underconsumption (and as if referring to today's economic theory!) Marx observes: "It is sheer tautology to say that crises are caused by the scarcity of effective consumption, or of effective consumers."[58] Marx was an accomplished logician and was aware of the superficiality of making explicit what is already in the premises, in the axiom of supply and demand analysis. Marx avoids this fallacy by constantly relating his theories to the sociological, institutional, and historical characteristics of the system, characteristics which he does not take as "given." To assert that economic activity falls when ex ante savings exceed ex ante investment is the crudest of tautologies, once aggregate demand is defined as consisting of consumption and investment, and supply of consumption and savings. The mind that craves for true (as against merely formal) understanding is not content with such ad hoc, retrospective "explanations" which are, at bottom, only relations among definitions. Marx knew that economics can avoid being tautological only by bursting through its customary boundaries and rooting itself on social experience. Unlike conventional economists he made no distinction between data and variables of the system—a distinction that we saw born out of the dualism of Descartes. Nothing of importance (the structure of industry, the nature of the state, the arrangements of foreign trade, the legal relations of society, the techniques of production, the prevalent economic and social theory) is regarded as a datum. At the center of the Marxian system are historical men and classes. Related to them, with varying degrees of proximity, are the institutions, habits, organizations, modes of thought, theories that make these classes what they are and push them to change the class-relationship or to resist changes. From the point of view of historical change, everything human is a variable, though, of course, some variables are more important than others. This is why Marx' business cycle theories are not built around the impact of interest rate changes, as they are with classical economists. They are simply not important enough to thwart more powerful forces affecting capitalism.

58. *Capital*, 2:410.

(In time, conventional economics was to recognize the irrelevance of interest rate movements as causes of depressions.) The spiritual element of capitalism in its oppressive manifestations is what Marx dealt with. And true spiritual facts are notoriously difficult to portray by mathematical symbolism. Those who interpret Marx as if he were a naïve Benthamite (the essence of which is that the non-measurable is made measurable via fictions) find Marx full of contradictions. They do not recognize that most of these contradictions belong to the mathematical medium they use to interpret Marx.

Shortly after Marx' death, a number of thinkers stressed the value of intuition to burst through the barriers set by narrow logic to understand reality. In Bergson, as we shall see, intuition is nurtured by constant contact with life. Marx' journalistic work, his continuous interpretations of contemporary events, his work for the Socialist Internationale, his reading of factual economic reports, falling on his noteworthy classical learning and on his understanding of the Greek tragedies, Shakespeare, and Dante, sharpened his intuitive grasp of the workings of society. All this, and the fact that he exploited the Hegelian system thoroughly, enabled him to overcome the conventional gap between mind and matter, theory and practice, subject and object. The innumerable "contradictions" with which capitalism is riddled would not have been discovered by Marx had he adopted either a rationalistic or a strictly teleological, evolutionary viewpoint. Many of the contradictions to which he calls attention are history's "cunning" at work—the antithesis stemming from the apparent peacefulness of the status quo.

Yet it must be admitted that Marx did yield occasionally to the temptation of following the chimera of algebraic symbolism. Not only did he discover nothing by it, but his "law of the falling tendency of profit" has been rightly ridiculed as tautological ever since. The logic of algebra is Aristotle's, not Hegel's; it is eminently unsuited to deal with movement and "contradictions." Ultimately, however, the overt emphasis on political action and the clear didactic purpose of his work saved Marx from being just another classical economist. Marx' intellectual vision was a world without alienation, and this vision determined his analysis of the past and present: "As philosophy finds its material weapon in the proletariat, so the proletariat finds its intellectual weapon in philosophy. . . ." A few years later, he substituted "economics" in a broad sense for philosophy, but his economics retained a philosophical and didactic aura.

In stressing the didactic ethical nature of Marx' teachings, we appear to run counter to Marx' and Engel's many protestations of being "scientific," of dealing with the "laws" of motion of capitalism. These claims should be put in proper perspective. They represent a willful attempt to divorce their writings from an ethics (the Christian one) which, by its sycophancy and subservience to the material interests of the powerful, had betrayed its original calling of leading men toward true justice, charity, and love.

The ethical-religious element in Marxism is recognized by Toynbee in the quotation already given. Those who do not recognize this spirit find it easy to turn Marx into a set of rigid axioms, largely in contradiction with each other. Induction and observation go by the boards and deductive axiomatic reasoning takes their places. Freedom gives way to determinism and Marx' man becomes hardly distinguishable from the *homo economicus,* all bent to achieve the greatest satisfaction with the least possible outlay. Then Marxism becomes another intellectual straitjacket, a blind engine of manipulation, a vile jargon, and his system, a substitute for thinking.

Marx' theory threads a delicate balance between opposing viewpoints that have been debated since the beginning of philosophy. This being the case, it is not surprising that the controlling element in the interpretation of Marx is the reader of Marx, his outlook and philosophy.

In previous chapters we have noted that analogies are an expression of fictional thinking. Marx' writings are full of imagery. Does it follow that his thought is as fictional as that of conventional economics? Let us examine this question by considering one image noticed by many commentators: the Promethean myth. It appears for the first time at the beginning of Marx' doctoral dissertation on the materialism of Democritus and Epicurus when he quotes the answer of Aeschylus' Prometheus to Hermes: "Know well I would never be willing to exchange my misfortune for that bondage of yours. Far better do I deem it to be bound to this rock than to spend my life as Father Zeus' faithful messenger." In *Capital,* referring to the industrial army of unemployed, he says that they chain "the worker to capital even more effectually than Prometheus was fastened to the rock by the fetters forged by Hephaestus." Repeatedly the workers' conditions are referred to as "fetters" or "chains" and just as often they are enjoined to revolt for "they have nothing to lose but their fetters."

In harmony with the idea that capitalism is a step forward toward a rational social organization, Marx imputes to capitalism the power to have broken the "fetters" (or the "sentimental veil") surrounding relations in the Middle Ages: "for exploitation veiled by religious and political illusions, it has substituted naked, shameful, direct, brutal exploitation," he writes in the *Communist Manifesto*. Of his imaginative style Marx himself was aware when, having described factory conditions, he remarks: "Dante would have found the worst horrors of his Inferno surpassed in this manufacture."[59] We hold, however, that these and innumerable other examples of allegorical writings do not qualify as fictions. The fictions of conventional economics consist of this: something exists in a certain sphere of intellectual endeavor, e.g., the concept of force in mechanics. Economic theory appropriates it for its own use. Or else fictions are non-existent entities which happen to be serviceable as links in the chain of reasoning from axioms to conclusions. Marx' references to clearly fictive figures (mythological, literary, etc.) have the sole purpose of impressing *facts* on the reader's mind.[60] His references to well-known literary creations, rather, support what we have been at pains to illustrate: that Marx did not build a dead system but dealt with real existential men. Literature and even myths have exactly this advantage. They deal with the *particular*, the individual hero and the individual situation. They therefore avoid drowning moral issues in a morass of philosophical hairsplitting.[61]

We have recently discovered that imaginative literature is, after all, a vehicle superior to philosophy and to academic psychology in portraying and dealing with ethical problems. Nietzsche,

59. Dante is also quoted in *Capital*, 1:103 and in the prefaces of both *Capital* and of *A Contribution to the Critique of Political Economy*.

60. The innumerable examples of imagery in Marx have interested many scholars who have tried to apply the techniques and devices for the interpretation of dreams to an understanding of Marx' meaning. The results of such efforts are generally dream-like.

61. Recall Schopenhauer's observation: "University philosophy is, as a rule, mere juggling": *The World as Will and Idea*, 2:364. Schopenhauer was certainly referring to Hegelian hair-splitting. Marx was even more graphic with his well-known aphorism, "Philosophy stands in the same relation to the study of life as onanism to sexual love." Compare this with Arendt's characterization of Cartesian reasoning as "the playing of the mind with itself." See above, p. 21.

Camus, Kafka, Dostoevsky, Shakespeare, Goethe, and Ibsen are more effective interpreters of man's real ethical predicaments and problems than positivists, pragmatists, and assorted twentieth-century philosophical schools. It is no surprise, therefore, that Marx, whose works "drip ethics from head to toe," often used literary characters and imagery to convey his interpretation of facts.

11

Breaking the "Mind-Forg'd Manacles"

> *Cried Alyosha, "I think everyone should love life*
> *above everything in the world."*
> *"Love life more than the meaning of it?"*
> *"Certainly, love it, regardless of logic as you say,*
> *it must be regardless of logic, and it's only then*
> *one will understand the meaning of it."*
>
> *Dostoevsky*

T HE VAST majority of economic theory is based on the implicit identification of the laws of thinking with the ways of reality. This identification was the essence of naïve Cartesianism, while some Enlightened philosophers (especially Bentham and Kant) saw clearly that it was only a useful myth. What was a risqué view in the eighteenth century became almost conventional in the nineteenth. A new theory of knowledge emerged then, characterized by the conviction that truth, which Descartes found outside the stream of time (in geometry), could be discovered only *in* the stream of time and worldly experience. The very meaning of consciousness (ego) changed: from a process of drawing inferences from self-evident truths, it became awareness of the world and of oneself through involvement. William James' negative reply to the question "Does 'Consciousness' Exist?" merely gave the Cartesian ego its coup de grace.[1]

1. See below, pp. 221–22.

Nineteenth-century philosophy, by disowning the Cartesian viewpoint, shook the foundations of all disciplines that were based on its methodology. The latecomers among the social sciences easily adapted themselves to the new outlook. Even Spencer, the apostle of mechanicism in sociology, was in the end obliged to confess that life in its essence cannot be conceived in mechanistic terms. But those social sciences with deep epistemological roots in Cartesianism could not shake their methods too easily. Economics in particular continued along its pre-charted path. Its very method of analysis was exceptionally time-consuming: by mid-century, means had not yet perfected themselves although they held the promise of so doing. Accordingly, economics deviated more and more from the new intellectual outlook being forged by European and American philosophers. Just as once-bustling harbors, cities once thriving with commerce, and communities once envied for their wealth sink into poverty with the discovery of new trade routes, new technologies, new sources of supply, so intellectual systems may fall on "hard times" when new intellectual currents appear. A new approach to man and society, a "revolt against formalism," occurred in the second half of the nineteenth century. It affected philosophy and social thought, but it did not influence economic theorizing which continued to develop in a manner incongruous with the new way of conceiving reality. The Great Depression showed how unbridgeable a gulf had developed between the ways of economic theorizing and the new outlook. In America, Franklin Delano Roosevelt dealt with the crisis by surrounding himself with men whose modes of thought were inimical to those of conventional economics. And in England, Keynes started his long "struggle of escape from habitual modes of thought and expression."[2]

It may be useful to reiterate that in judging economics to have been unaffected by the new intellectual outlook,[3] we are passing judgment on neither the former nor the latter: we are merely recording a fact of intellectual history. We shall be brief in dealing with this major revolution of thought—even more radical than the overthrow of scholasticism by Cartesianism—for its main characteristic, the devaluation of reason, is commonplace. We undertake this summary, first, because even Schumpeter's magnum opus on the

2. *General Theory*, p. viii.
3. The science/art dichotomy, we pointed out, emerged partly in response to the new outlook.

history of economic analysis, despite its moderately catholic viewpoint, fails to call attention to the receding tides of rationalism; second, because we are convinced that this phenomenon eventually influenced J. M. Keynes who is responsible for temporarily moving economic theory away from the eye of the storm of axiomatic thinking and toward the confused periphery of experience; and, third, because the spirit of anti-Cartesianism is still with us. It has by now percolated down to the masses and is the source of some problems of interest to economists. For example, it is the source of that inability of college students to learn economic theory which was detected some years ago by the American Economic Association. Despite Keynes' work, today's economics is as rationalistic as ever, while the mood of students is romantic, emotional, activistic, and political. They prefer "involvement" to the detachment of theory and logic and acting to thinking. Their spirit and values being the exact opposite of those upheld by and embodied in economics as a reasoning process, it is no surprise that they cannot understand, let alone appreciate, economic theory.

Schopenhauer set the mood of the attack against reason by unerringly detecting its millennial source: "all philosophers before me . . . place the true being or the kernel of man in the *knowing* consciousness, and accordingly have conceived and explained the I [ego], or, in the case of many of them, its transcendental hypostasis called soul, as primary and essentially *knowing*, nay, *thinking*." But this is an "ancient and universal radical error," a "proton pseudos" (basic error), which must be set aside if thought is to make any true advances.[4] What two thousand years of philosophizing conceived as the essence of man—rationality—actually is "the mere surface of our minds, of which, as of the earth, we do not know the inside but only the crust."[5] Beneath consciousness, Schopenhauer holds, stronger and primary lies the will. *It* is the substance of man. The intellect does not rule our behavior. It is a "mere tool" of the will, a "parasite" of the rest of the organism, a "mere accident of being." It is not that reason leads the will, but that the will leads reason. The latter is "the strong blind man who carries on his

4. *The World as Will and Idea*, 2:409. Emphasis in the text.
5. Ibid., 2:328.

shoulders the lame man who can see." "The will alone is the thing in itself."[6]

By stressing the primacy of reason, philosophical and social thought has put the cart before the horse: Bentham's calculus does not determine action. To believe that knowledge really and fundamentally determines behavior is like believing that the lantern which a man carries by night is the *primum mobile* of his steps.[7] A fundamental error of causality has been committed which has vitiated our understanding of reality for centuries. For instance, it led the philosophers of the Enlightenment to view institutions as the embodiment of neat, rationalistic covenants, contracts, and reason. Schopenhauer sees them as ultimately stemming from nonrational motives.

Fully conscious of the blow that such a view deals to established ways of thinking, Schopenhauer searched far and wide for instances of the primacy of the will in the world of nature and in the world of man. His lengthy illustrations comprise a good part of *The World as Will and Idea,* to which we refer the interested reader. Suffice it to say that Schopenhauer's philosophical insights were later appropriated by empirical psychology. That this discipline never reached any firm conclusion pertaining to the innermost "springs of action" of man merely proves our point, that Benthamism is a fiction, and that "laws of behavior" exist only in the conceiving mind and break down when deduction (based on fictions) is abandoned and we let facts "speak for themselves."

One need not belabor how Schopenhauer's will is the negation of Descartes' ego. The French thinker, it will be recalled, regarded affections, emotions, passions as the arch-enemies of "clearness and distinctness" of ideas. To this normative standpoint, Schopenhauer opposes his own positivism. Passions and emotions do cloud reason (narrowly conceived) but they exist and their existence must be faced.

Unlikely as it may seem, some economists, a century after Schopenhauer, have incorporated into their writings, by sheer coincidence, his vision of the will as the motor of history. Not only is this true of the "Schumpeterian entrepreneur," but it is also true of Keynes' view of the nature of the decision to invest, a decision normally taken *despite* the better judgment of a rational weighing

6. Ibid., 2:411, 412, 421, 418.
7. Ibid., 2:440.

of pleasures and pains.[8] It is patent, however, that theoretical economics could not truly absorb these insights without destroying itself in the process. This is why Schumpeter's entrepreneur lives an uneasy life at the periphery of economics: in economic history and development economics. As for Keynes' observations, the post-Keynesian restoration made short shrift of them.

If Schopenhauer were an exception in nineteenth-century thought, he would not command our attention. But his attack on the identity of thinking and being was a common theme of most thinkers of the century. What sparked the attack was Hegel whom many philosophers, like Marx, regarded as the prototype of a mind gone berserk in the delusion that the Idea reflects reality. In re-volting against Hegel, some thinkers discovered his intellectual ancestor, Descartes, and found his Achilles' heel, too. (In so doing, incidentally, they support our interpretation that Hegelianism is a blown-up form of Cartesianism.[9])

Kierkegaard, for instance, levels the same weapons at both. He calls the identity of Hegel's dialectical thinking with the world "the one lunatic postulate" by which philosophy bankrupted itself. Hegel never proved that thought reflected reality: he assumed it, and this assumption Kierkegaard regards as a sham, a trick, which only enabled the German philosopher to say whatever he wanted, unchecked by reality without or moral law within. Just as his iden-tity of thinking and being is a trick, so the movement he claimed for his dialectic is specious. Where does the mediation of thesis and antithesis come from? "In logic, no movement *becomes*; logic and everything logical can merely *be*."[10] The world of logic is a dead world. Similarly specious, indeed tautological, is Descartes' *cogito ergo sum*, whose critique by the Danish philosopher deserves to be quoted at length: "The Cartesian *cogito ergo sum* has often been repeated. If the 'I' which is the subject of *cogito* means an indi-vidual human being, the proposition proves nothing: 'I am thinking, *ergo* I am; but if I *am* thinking what wonders that I *am:*' the asser-tion has already been made, and the first proposition says even more than the second. But if the 'I' in *cogito* is interpreted as mean-ing a particular existing human being, philosophy cries: 'How silly; here there is no question of yourself or myself but solely of the pure

8. See chap. 13.
9. See chap. 9.
10. Quoted by Hermann Diem, *Kierkegaard: An Introduction*, p. 75.

ego.' But this pure ego cannot very well have any other than a purely conceptual existence; what then does the *ergo* mean? There is no conclusion here, for the proposition is a tautology."[11] It is, of course, the second interpretation offered by Kierkegaard on which Descartes built his system: the "I" in *cogito* was to him the essence of a human being, a pure concept, I-as-thought. But to conclude from the existence of this thought-entity that thought thereby exists is clearly a tautology, "a play on words," as Kierkegaard wrote elsewhere.[12]

Neither Hegel nor Descartes can unify thinking and being because thinking via concepts and essences does not possess the categories of reality: it abstracts from reality. "The attempt to infer existence from thought is . . . a contradiction. For thought takes existence away from the real and thinks it by abrogating its actuality, by translating it into the sphere of the impossible."[13] Searching for economic laws by delving into one's own consciousness only succeeds in creating the impossible: a world of petty egoistic shopkeepers from whom all sorts of wondrous things (optima) derive.

Descartes' very premise of universal doubt, Kierkegaard notes, is an abstraction. In existence, in real life, "the presupposition of universal doubt . . . would require an entire human life; now [in Descartes and his followers] it is no sooner said than done."[14] This doubting is a fiction. Within a few pages, Descartes professes to doubt everything and then proceeds to reconstruct the universe! And by "letting itself go," the Hegelian mind also reconstructed the universe. No better proof of the fictiveness of both systems exists than this ability of theirs to start from diametrically opposed premises (universal doubt and total trust) and yet arrive at the same result!

It is a commonplace that Kierkegaard, like Nietzsche, rebelled against rational systems from love of the freedom of the individual.[15] In particular he saw man as led astray by a belief originating in the Renaissance and culminating in Hegel and the natural sciences —the belief that man possesses within himself (that is, in his

11. *Kierkegaard's Concluding Unscientific Postscript*, p. 281. We have interpreted Descartes' *Cogito* in the second sense suggested by Kierkegaard.
12. See above, chap. 2.
13. *Postscript*, p. 282.
14. Ibid.
15. See Cornelio Fabro, "Faith and Reason in Kierkegaard's Dialectic," in *A Kierkegaard Critique*, pp. 156–206.

reason) the source of all truth about God, nature, and man. This seemed to Kierkegaard the highest form of conceit: that man's range of knowledge and depth of understanding coincides with God's. Despite such madness (or perhaps because of it, for madness makes one blind), rationalistic thinking did not even scratch the surface of understanding. Existence transcends logic.[16] The whole world of "ideas-as-such," essences, and the like is a false world: "The *concept* existence is an ideality, and the difficulty is precisely whether existence [as a fact] is absorbed in the concept." Spinoza's motto, *essentia involvit existentiam,* only means that essence includes the *concept* existence, existence in ideality, but not in actuality. Spinoza's motto, too, then, is tautological.[17] Facts in their existential (real) setting should be the raw material of thought. Any system makes us forget what it means to be a human being, says Kierkegaard in tones reminiscent of Marx. "Not human beings in general, but what it means for you and me and him, each for himself to be human beings."[18]

The contemplation of existence under the guidance of the ego leads, *eo ipso,* to isolation, Kierkegaard remarks,[19] and we know how true this is in regard to economics. Both the actors of economic theory (consumers, businessmen) and its creators (the economists themselves) were deeply isolated beings. The latter, of course, were isolated from their fellow men because of the unpopular and often abhorrent policy suggestions the theory compelled them to make.

If existence cannot be understood by pure thought, action and that awareness that comes from self-reflection give the possibility of attaining, if not ultimate, at least immanent, useful truths. This emphasis on action over detached thinking is a common theme of the anti-rationalistic tide. Marx, although he managed to build a self-contained sociological system, made action the test of truth, as also do the pragmatists. Kierkegaard also calls attention to a tragic conflict to which the habit of following the guidance of logic rather than of *Existenz* leads and of which classical economists in particular have been the victims. Reason cannot help creating ideals and ideals then demand to be implemented. But matter and existence set barriers to the actualization of the ideal, and a clash ensues.

16. *Søren Kierkegaard's Journals and Papers,* p. 1054.
17. Ibid., p. 1057. Emphasis in the text.
18. Quoted by Löwith, *From Hegel to Nietzsche: The Revolution in Nineteenth-Century Thought,* p. 319.
19. *Journals and Papers,* p. 1034.

An expression of this clash is the economist's wish (still existing today in certain quarters) to impose a competitive economy, or free trade, or a cut in money wages on an existential real setting characterized by monopoly, powerful lobbies, commercial and political jealousies, and powerful unions. Paradoxically, Marx, since he was not as idealistic and narrowly logical as his classical predecessors, avoided this clash: he calls for revolutionary implementation of "scientific" socialism, that is, of a social order that is practically already here. As for Keynes, his prescriptions are avowedly *sub specie temporis*; he specifically repudiated logical modes of thought that, proceeding *sub specie aeternitatis*, could only lead to catastrophe.

Possessing a deeply ethical nature, Kierkegaard, who attacked established religion as hypocritical, hit on the peculiarity of his times and of ours: "In times like these [he observed] everything is politics," hence ethics, but people do not know it. He detected the "sickness unto death" of the Europe of his days to be the "debasement of man" as an individual, due to both the socialist and the liberal outlook. By addressing themselves to mere institutional and parliamentary changes (leaving the whole sphere of the spirit and a morality untouched) these creeds only tend toward a "leveling" of the individual. In economic theory this denigration of man was brought about unintentionally by the inner dynamics of ideal thought and by the "kingdom of laws" which any science sets up to push its thought forward.

Nothing better summarizes Kierkegaard's belief than the quotation chosen as the epigraph of this book. It suggests that life cannot be thoroughly understood by logic and by adhering to a balance between pleasure and pain. Existential truth, unlike logical truth, is practical, unfinished, and essentially paradoxical. It is practical because it deals with the ethical order, with the actions of individual men in a given environment. It is unfinished because it is not a body of essences frozen and true forever, but a relation between a changing individual and changing circumstances. Finally, it is paradoxical, for the less profoundly we think the more likely we are to approximate the truth.[20] Profound thought is actually superficial thought since it tends to stress the trivial and ignore the truly important. Economics' ultimate truths are possible only when everything of importance (the structure of industry, the organization of

20. *Postscript*, Book 2, chap. 2.

production, tastes and habits, the goals of the state, etc.) is regarded as a datum and is hence unchanging (or is somebody else's business to explain).

Nietzsche, to whom we now turn, also found truth "in that which is embodied here-and-now."[21] To Nietzsche, ultimate knowledge is unnatural. It leads to blindness to the obvious, a fact of which, Nietzsche observes, Greek sages were aware and illustrated by the myth of Oedipus.[22] Like Kierkegaard and James, Nietzsche holds truth to be a process which is never final: not a process of "discovering" the truth but a process of "conferring" truth on something. He calls for a reorientation of researchers' interests, away from ultimates and toward "the little things": food, climate, recreation, the casuistry of self-seeking. They are "incomparably more important than everything that has been regarded as important up to now."[23] The trouble is that these "little things" are not amenable to rationalistic understanding.

Nietzsche's break with the tradition of the ego is as complete as Schopenhauer's and Kierkegaard's: "The only rationality known to us is the tiny bit that belongs to man" where, in any case, it is only a fraction of his being.[24] The error of philosophy (and economics, we may add) has been to take this little bit of reason and to stir it into everything. Descartes' *cogito ergo sum*, he notes, should actually read *cogito, ergo cogitationes sunt,* for his famous proof is the most banal of tautologies.[25] Having shorn reality of all its distinctive characteristics, it was easy for the ego to create those "mirages . . . which with all the deceptive force of magic provide the solution to every riddle." How much should a government tax? Marginal social benefits and alternative costs give the answer. How does one promote "development" in poor countries? By "little pushes" (or "big pushes"—there seems to be disagreement). What is the optimum population of Bengal? We don't really know, but we know the *principles* determining the optimum population of *a* country.

21. Karl Jaspers, *Nietzsche: An Introduction to the Understanding of His Philosophical Activity,* p. 199. Nietzsche's reaction against rationalism is brought out also by Walter Kaufmann, *Nietzsche,* chap. 2.

22. Jaspers, p. 233, quoting Nietzsche. Oedipus, the most intelligent of men (he solved the riddle) was blind to the obvious and ended by committing parricide and incest.

23. Ibid., pp. 187, 199–200.

24. Ibid., p. 213, quoting Nietzsche.

25. *The Will to Power,* No. 484.

"Rationality at all costs" is the motto of the man of science. But, as Kierkegaard has noted, rationality and the scientific spirit run counter to certain strong cravings of man. The true man of science must efface his personality and deal wholly with the object of analysis. More often than not, this object, being drained of all ethical significance, is also trivial, and therefore may hardly appear worthy of absorbing one's life. Thus the scientist eventually turns into a social philosopher. Examples of this leap abound in economics. The classic one is provided by Pareto, who, in many letters to his friend the economist Maffeo Pantaleoni, refers to sociology as offering "greater satisfactions" than economics.[26] The reader who is familiar with current economic writings and interests will provide other examples of the same *ennui* sooner or later gripping the theorist and turning him into a social philosopher.

All logical thinking—Nietzsche remarks—owes its existence to the "condition that alone makes thought possible, viz., that something remain *identical* with itself. Only things that remain the same (e.g., identical substances and static entities) have true being for thought." The laws of identity and self-contradiction all stem from a philosophic ego that regards itself as self-identical and unchanging because it, too, is an abstraction. The ego is "not contrived to understand becoming; it strives to demonstrate the cold inflexibility of everything,"[27] thus disqualifying itself from dealing with the real which is "incapable of being expressed in formulae." In a manner reminiscent of Kant, Nietzsche found value in this error. By becoming a condition of life and by facilitating action, superficial and even erroneous thinking vindicates its right to exist.

Since Bergson's criticism of mechanistic thinking and of the concept of time in science has so pervaded our review of economic theory, a lengthy discussion of his ideas would be repetitious. Suffice it to say that in Bergson's view neither mechanistic nor teleological (Darwinian or "stage" theories) modes of thought come to grips with life. Bergson is thus led to glorify the power of what he calls "intuition." As to what intuition is, Bergson is rather vague. He cannot help being so, for a rationalistic analysis of intuition is a contradiction, as are "decision theories under uncertainty" (a contemporary booming area of economics). Intuition is a higher

26. N. Bobbio, "Vilfredo Pareto's Sociology in His Letters to Maffeo Pantaleoni."
27. Jaspers, *Nietzsche*, pp. 211–12, quoting Nietzsche.

form of instinct: it is "instinct that has become disinterested, self-conscious, capable of reflecting upon its object and enlarging it indefinitely."[28] Rationalism cannot conceive of the unexpected, but intuition "naturally" courts it. It is neither mechanistic nor naïvely teleological[29] exactly because it is awed by the newness of living forms. Intuition is not the foe of intellect. It transcends it, taking over from intellect's failures. At the very least, intuition amounts to a "vague feeling" that mechanistic and finalistic modes of thought fail to understand life. By building on this realization we may hope for real progress in social thought. The precondition for understanding life is to make Hamlet's admonition to Horatio one's own: "There are more things in heaven and earth, Horatio, / Than are dreamt of in your philosophy."

According to Bergson, intuition has hitherto been cultivated by the saint, the artist, and the mystic. They "stand at junctions of openness and freshness. Necessity, obligation, and formalism close minds and close society. Genius and vision open new roads and new perspectives."[30] In economics we have experienced the truth of Bergson's ideas in the Great Depression (a failure not of reality but of economic knowledge that for a century had contributed in "closing minds and societies") and in Keynes who, abundantly endowed with intuition, temporarily opened "new roads and new perspectives."

The revolt against conventional modes of thought was not limited to continental Europe. In time, America, too, made its contribution, especially through the pragmatic outlook. By comparison with continental philosophy, pragmatism has a certain aura of Bostonian urbanity which, however, does not altogether hide its fundamental happy-go-lucky anarchistic character, as William James says.[31] Schopenhauer, Nietzsche, Kierkegaard, and Bergson repeatedly asserted that scholarly activity is none too rational, displaying the same mixture of passion, fantasy, and bias that one finds in everyday life. James, too, gives what he regards as a historical, factual, and dynamic account of how truths actually originate. To the static, ego-centered epistemology of conventional philosophy he opposes

28. *Creative Evolution*, p. 194.
29. See Bergson's reference to Huxley, chap. 6 above.
30. From Irwin Edman's foreword to *Creative Evolution*, pp. xiv–xv.
31. *Pragmatism: A New Name for Some Old Ways of Thinking*, p. 259.

his realistic, "paleontological," evolutionary one. What is conventional philosophy's definition of truth? James asserts that philosophers have defined truth to consist of "those judgments which we find ourselves under obligation to make by a kind of imperative duty," or of "that system of propositions which have an unconditional claim to be recognized as valid." These classical definitions (which the reader will recognize to be identical to those of the deepest economic methodologists) James regards as question-begging, for nobody defines precisely what is meant by "duty" and by "claim" (pp. 227–28).

In accordance with these definitions, rationalistic epistemology regarded truth (and reality) as a "petrified sphynx" whose veil men progressively lift. This view of truth, James says, echoing Bergson, might well describe the way "prehistoric geniuses" made up explanations, but it is not a historically accurate view of how men like Galileo, Dalton, and Faraday attained truths. For what they did was to create "things" utterly invisible and impalpable, indeed, non-existent: atoms, electrons, and magnetic fields (p. 185). When thought reached this crucial stage, realism died. A new age opened to the intellect, what we would call the age of fictions, of constructs to be interpreted on an "as if" basis, which, in time, will be superseded by other "as if" systems. Following distinguished philosophers of science (especially Mach, Ostwald, and Duhem), James calls a hypothesis but a "way of thinking." The term " 'energy' does not even pretend to stand for anything 'objective' ": it is "*as if* reality were made of ether, atoms or electrons, but we mustn't think so literally" (p. 216; emphasis in text). The only reality is the phenomenon itself in its chaotic flux, heat, and other sensations it produces. All the rest, and especially the highest creations of the mind, the full-blown theories, are mere standpoints (pp. 190–91).

The process of attaining truth as conceived by conventional philosophy is naïve. The true is not what is felt to be clearly and distinctly such by "inner necessity"; it is only "the expedient in the way of our thinking, just as 'the right' is only the expedient in our way of behaving" (p. 222). It has always been so, and it is time we acknowledge it. Survival seems to be the test of ideas: as long as they live, they are true; when we reject them, they become false. What is true of the law is also true of theories: so long as a pronouncement by court or legislature is not challenged it is true. Like bank notes, truths, if they are not refused, pass (p. 207).

The shaky foundations of theories explain why they are so easily challenged. When challenged, the minds of men become a battlefield. A new truth has to appear consistent with all other beliefs we have. It must carve its place, so to speak, in men's hierarchy of other beliefs causing only a minimum of rearrangement of old and useful truths. If the new truth is important, it will take time before it will attain its place in the universe of other beliefs, and in the process other knowledge, too, is modified. Knowledge grows "in spots" for we let the new "spread as little as possible: we keep unaltered as much of the old knowledge, as many of our old prejudices and beliefs, as we can. We patch and tinker more than we renew. The novelty soaks in; it stains the ancient mass; but it is also tinged by what absorbs it. . . . It happens relatively seldom that the new fact is added raw. More usually it is embedded cooked, as one might say, or stewed down in the sauce of the old" (pp. 168–69). Basically, new truths arise in the same way as new legislation: through a process of "wheeling and dealing" and compromise. New theories plus old truths combine and naturally modify each other, just like Keynes' theory plus the old hyperclassical viewpoint gave us the "neo-classical synthesis." This process may be none too reasonable, but this is how things go. Perhaps this is why illogical constructs (of the type we have pointed out in relation to economic thought) arise.

The thinker, who was supposed to keep himself and his feelings in the background (in reality he was all-powerful, given that all theories stem from the ego unchecked by reality or self-knowledge), acquires his rightful place in the subject-object equation of the pragmatists. For the phenomenal world at best provides us with only a few basic facts of experience. Only man's imagination organizes them in a theory, system, or model. Just as the same constellation appears as a "dipper" to some, as a "bear" to others, and as "Charles' Wain" to others yet, so any sensations can be organized in different ways, yielding widely different conclusions and prescriptions.

With pragmatism, the Western intellect took another step forward in the unmasking of fictions. The "coincidence of thought with the object" was viewed by pragmatists as epistemological make-believe; and Descartes' consciousness, the ego, William James flatly calls "the name of a non-entity."[32] In denying the existence of con-

---

32. "Does 'Consciousness' Exist?" (1904), reprinted in *Essays in Radical Empiricism: A Pluralistic Universe*, p. 2.

sciousness, James makes clear that he is not attacking thought as a function or process but solely the hypostatized (idealized) Cartesian view of this process.

We saw that Descartes (and, a fortiori, his followers) ignored the actual process of thought-formation, inventing, instead, an all-rational ego as the creator of theories. This ego, this consciousness, is to James a "fictitious" entity,[33] and, like Kierkegaard, Nietzsche, and others, he imputes all the perverse philosophizing of the previous centuries to this original invention and concomitant neglect of the real process of the formation of ideas. "There is . . . no aboriginal stuff or quality of being,"[34] that is, there is no ego endowed with geometrical properties and, likewise, there is no geometry-laden matter.

Despite all this, the pragmatist attack on rationalism seems rather bland and flat when compared with that of European thinkers. Its greatest interest for us rests on its having arisen in total ignorance of the work of continental philosophers (it was rather influenced by the direction physical science was taking), sufficient proof that the times were ripe for a revolt against formalism, just as they had been ripe for a revolt against scholastic realism two and a half centuries before.

Marx suggested that harmonious social development consists of the "superstructure" of morality, jurisprudence, political philosophy, economics—in one word, of ideas, faithfully reflecting the changing "substratum" of economic relations and production modes. Something of the same nature must occur within the narrower field of the "superstructure" itself: conflicting methodologies in sociopolitical thought cannot be tolerated for long. The ways in which sociology, philosophy, economics, and politics look at the world have to move in step. A situation in which sociology is empirical, psychology is intuitive, economics is formalistic, and history is ethical is a "house divided within itself" and cannot endure long. But the increasing narrowness of scope and interests of each discipline makes it possible for deviations from the common path to continue for a fairly long period, which will be characterized by discordant voices and the cacophony of methodological battles. Neither will these disputes achieve compromises or generate greater understanding.

33. Ibid.
34. Ibid., p. 5. The sentence quoted also contains the following footnote: "similarly, there is no 'activity of consciousness' as such."

They rather tend to take the form of the conversation between the bird and the duck in Prokofiev's *Peter and the Wolf*.[35] Ultimately, however, one methodology will prevail, and any discipline that absolutely persists in working and reworking its old categories, unaware or uncaring of the revolution of thought that is going on around it, will be looked upon as an intellectual fossil. Its practitioners will find themselves increasingly isolated prophets of "thoughts out of season," incongruous representatives of a stream of thought that was. And although this isolation has its appealing loftiness, it also has its dangers.

The nineteenth century is a watershed in the intellectual history of the West comparable in importance to the century of Descartes. It destroyed what the latter had enthroned, namely, the belief that reason rules life. While the categories of the Enlightenment were eternal and independent of time and space, those of what we may loosely call existentialism and pragmatism were merely relative and historical. Accordingly, the nineteenth century broke the "mind-forg'd manacles" symbolized by mechanistic thinking and in the process discovered a new freedom: freedom from the fetters of its own past perspectives.

The attack on consciousness often became an attack on its own creatures. Pareto, for instance, wrote that democracy is a sham, a rationalization of primitive instincts. Behind all changing ideologies are always the elites of which the masses are hapless victims. History is the succession of one elite after another, climbing on the backs of gullible people. Together with Sorel, Sombart, D'Annunzio, and a score of other thinkers, Pareto was regarded by those who indulge in analogical parallels between the Idea and reality (really a form of Hegelianism) as the intellectual ancestor of fascism. It is interesting that of the twin fictions of the Enlightenment—popular sovereignty and consumer sovereignty—the former gave way while the latter is still well entrenched, at least in economic theory. The reason for this is that political philosophy never developed that rigid formalistic methodology that instead sprang up around the idea of consumer sovereignty. A tight medium of discourse precludes

35. Circling a pond, the bird asked the duck: "What kind of bird are you who can't fly?" Replied the duck, "What kind of bird are you who can't swim?" Most of the debate between mathematical and non-mathematical economists has exactly this character.

that flexibility of thought that is necessary for thought to overthrow its own creations. This is why the attack on mechanicism was initiated by the loosest of all disciplines, philosophy, and succeeded in affecting the methodologically weakest forms of study, history, sociology, and psychology.

It is, of course, beyond the scope of this study and, in any case, unnecessary, to trace the devaluation of narrow logic in the whole range of Western intellectual life. It is preferable to sketch it in a few intellectuals, who are representatives of a mighty group that shaped the climate of opinion of the past century. For the connection between the few thinkers with whom we concern ourselves and the larger area of Western intellect, we may trust Kaufmann, who points out that Nietzsche's thought is linked with that of Jaspers, Heidegger, Sartre, H. Hartmen, Max Scheler, Spengler, Freud, Adler, Thomas Mann, Herman Hesse, Stefan George, Rilke, Shaw, Gide, and Malraux.[36] Since each of these thinkers is clearly linked to others—e.g., Spengler to J. Burkhardt, N. Danilevsky, A. Toynbee, P. Sorokin, etc.; Shaw to Ibsen; Gide to Dostoevsky, Kafka, Camus—it is evident that what is generally regarded as most advanced in Western literature and in social and philosophical thought is captured by the small sample of thinkers with whom we dealt in this chapter.

The scholarly works of Oswald Spengler are a good instance of the new philosophical outlook influencing history. The method of the "systematic," cause-and-effect historian is criticized. Rationalism is of no avail in understanding events. "The more men tried to think, the more they forgot that in this domain [historiography] they *ought not* to think." In forcing the rigid scheme of a spatial and anti-temporal relation of cause and effect upon something alive, Spengler said, they "disfigured the visible face of becoming with the construction lines of a physical nature-picture."[37] Analogical thinking led historians astray. And again, "becoming has no number. We can count, measure, dissect only the lifeless and so much of the living as can be dissociated from livingness. Pure becoming, pure life, is in this sense incapable of being bounded. It lies beyond the domain of cause and effect, law and measure. . . . Every event is unique and incapable of being repeated. It carries the hallmark

36. Walter Kaufmann, *Existentialism from Dostoevsky to Sartre*, introduction.
37. *The Decline of the West*, 1:151–52.

of Direction ('Time'), of irreversibility."[38] The cause and effect approach does not understand events because not cause but "Destiny" operates in history and destiny does not work with blind mechanical (Cartesian) or teleological (Hegelian) logic. Destiny is a word whose content one "feels." It is essentially "mystery" and it discloses itself only to an "intuitive" mental immersion in the age under study. It is "sensed," not dissected by systematic logic. Only a few thinkers are given this intuitive power.[39]

Quite clearly, this methodology betrays affinity with Bergson's theory of truth, and it led Spengler to reconstruct imaginatively what he calls the "genius of cultures," not so much by a recital of battles and diplomatic treaties but by imitating the form of expression of art. This need not detain us, but we may call attention to an interesting conflict between the body of Spengler's work and the charts which he appended to the end of volume one of his study. The text itself derives its power by the very vagueness of the parallelisms between cultures; that is, the parallelisms are suggestive because they are loose. The author's intuition is supplemented by the reader's. But in the charts he portrays chronologically definite parallel stages in the development (political, spiritual, and artistic) of the four cultures he examines. The analogies necessarily become rigid; they appear forced and occasionally absurd, much like assigning a date to the inception of the Industrial Revolution. The reason for this conflict is clear: the mere method of tabular presentation "kills" that imaginative intuition that pervades the body of Spengler's work. The medium is inadequate to reflect the product of his imagination, just as mathematical models falsify *The General Theory*. There simply are certain things in life that numeration cannot grasp. One of them is the "destiny" that pervades history and another is the uncertainty and ignorance of the future that pervade economic life.

The consequences of the new outlook in America are well brought out by Morton White's *Social Thought in America*, a book which deals with the theories of O. W. Holmes, T. Veblen, J. Dewey, C. A. Beard, and J. H. Robinson. All of them were exponents of a "revolt against formalism" (the subtitle of White's book) in historiography, in legal writing, in philosophy, and in economics. Holmes attacked the belief that the actual, historical de-

38. Ibid., 1:95.
39. Ibid., introduction, pp. 36–41.

velopment of the law was a logical process that could be explained by logic. "The life of the law has not been logic": "The felt necessities of the time, the prevalent moral and political theories, intuition of public policy, avowed or unconscious, even the prejudices which judges share with their fellow men, have a good deal more to do than the syllogism in determining the rules by which men should be governed."[40] Thus the idealistic view of the progress of the legal wisdom died.

Dewey's attitude is sufficiently summarized by his criticism of conventional logic as the *"fons et origo malorum* in philosophy." Logical derivations of the type post-Cartesian thinkers indulged in while writing history were attacked by J. H. Robinson and C. A. Beard. As for Veblen, he objected that economics had reached merely a taxonomic stage and that its categories had to be filled with historical and "anthropological" facts. Mill, in a quotation given before,[41] speaks of "wealth" as anything that is the object of economic activity. Veblen wants economics to question itself. What *specific* items qualify as the highest expression of wealth at a given time in a given country? *How* has society come to "choose" them? What *means* are used to attain such items? What *classes* thrive on their provision? What *habits* and *institutions* arise around them? And, finally, what does the true analysis that can answer these questions suggest about the future evolution of society?[42] He called for an evolutionary economics, one, that is, which enveloped facts in a "theory of process, of unfolding sequence."

All the themes of continental and American philosophy can be found in these writers. In them we find a criticism of reasoning from axioms via syllogistic inferences and an emphasis on historical and cultural factors as explanatory engines, a distrust of setting artificial barriers to thought by reasoning in a vacuum about a "natural man," an "economic man," a "political man," etc. They all believed that the whole of man was involved in any given activity. They viewed themselves as scientists who, however, rejected the traditional standpoint of scientists: detachment from the object of study. Their reflections convinced them that men were not rational but somehow they tended to neglect this aspect of experience when

40. Holmes, *The Common Law,* p. 1, as quoted by White, *Social Thought in America: The Revolt against Formalism,* p. 16.

41. See above, chap. 4.

42. Veblen gave his answers to these questions in *The Theory of the Leisure Class.*

they set forth plans for a more rational and benign organization of society. Perhaps because of this self-contradiction, history has not been kind to them: with all their realistic, scientific, and historical outlooks, they apparently failed to foresee either the Great Depression (Veblen is the exception) or World War II. These facts and the atomic bomb seem to have cast a pall on their belief—perhaps the remnant of Enlightened optimism—that science and reason can solve social ills.

12

Keynes I

Oh, life is terrible. We do not rule it. It rules us.
Oscar Wilde

I N A suggestive essay on the Jews in modern Europe, Veblen notes
that Jews have contributed an unusually large number of social
thinkers, philosophers, and reformers.[1] In these areas, Jews are to
be found "particularly among the vanguard, the pioneers, the uneasy guild of pathfinders and iconoclasts." Why has this been the
case? Because, says Veblen, the Jew's traditional education, centering on Talmudic studies,[2] inculcates values and an outlook that are
diametrically opposed to those that he will eventually find in the
gentile world by which he is surrounded. The scheme of conventions into which the Jew is born and reared begins to totter as soon
as he becomes aware that what he has been brought up to believe
and what happens around him in the gentile world clash with each
other. The intellectually gifted Jew's "psychological equipoise" is
disturbed and he himself may become a disturber of the intellectual
peace, but only at the cost of becoming "an intellectual wayfaring
man, a wanderer in the intellectual No Man's land, seeking another

1. "The Intellectual Pre-eminence of Jews in Modern Europe."
2. Those who have no experience with Talmudic scholarship may obtain
a glimpse of its rigor in a modern novel, *The Chosen* by Chaim Potok (New
York, 1967).

228

place to rest farther along the road, somewhere over the horizon,"
rejected by both gentile and Jewish societies.

More than just a clash of values is involved. There is, above
all, the clash of metaphysics. The Jew's modes of thought, according to Veblen, stress the imponderable, the miraculous, the spiritual;
the Gentile's, the mechanical and scientific. Under these two outlooks, events are amenable to opposite interpretations, thus creating
a skeptical personality, in fact, a renegade Jew, who rejects the fictions of both Hebraic and gentile thought. On the ashes of the discarded fictions, he creates his own original and realistic system and
world view.

The originality of John Maynard Keynes probably springs from
the same psychological roots. His formal education at home, at
Eton, and at Cambridge was the parallel of the Jew's Talmudic
scholarship in rigor and conventionality. The Great War and the
British economic catastrophes of the 1920s and 1930s progressively
put him at odds with the mechanistic ways of thinking of society
in general and of his economic colleagues in particular. But we
cannot strain the parallel too much: Keynes was no Spinoza, Marx,
or Freud. To him, friendships meant too much to enable him to
become an "intellectual wayfarer." And he always had a keen appreciation of the practical. After the publication of *The Economic
Consequences of the Peace*, the ostracism of the "establishment"
awakened him to the dangers of too much originality. He decided,
very pragmatically, that intellectual independence comes only with
financial independence, and he proceeded to accumulate a fortune
through securities and exchange speculation.[3] Simultaneously, he
made himself independent of the whims of publishers by acquiring
a periodical, *The New Statesman*. The flood of articles that came
from his pen probably detracted from the depth to which Keynes'
thought was capable of arriving. It is a measure of his greatness
and, at the same time, of the shallowness of conventional economics,
that despite these not wholly propitious circumstances he still managed to affect the course of a discipline that was crying to sever
itself from the intellectual chains of the past.

Worshipping him as a great social thinker, however, will not
do. His broader philosophical statements have a half-baked quality.
A good example is his closing paragraph of *The General Theory*,

3. R. F. Harrod, *The Life of John Maynard Keynes*, p. 297.

where he reasserts the primacy and power of ideas to move history.[4] Some of his other concerns, e.g., eugenics, reflect a kind of unthinking faddism.

The intellectual climate surrounding young Keynes' education has been sketched by his biographer, Roy F. Harrod, who brings out the main characteristic of this environment: its relative isolation—shattered in 1914—from the currents of thought of Continental Europe. After Locke, British intellectuals thought they were following the empirical method. No Hegel arose and consequently no antidote to Hegel was needed. British social conditions in the nineteenth century also did much to generate a feeling of self-satisfaction and complacency with the arrangement of society. For success was the outward hallmark of Great Britain: she believed herself to be the arbiter of Europe's destiny, indeed, of world affairs. Internally, after the Chartist movement, social strife never seriously threatened her institutions. Under these conditions social criticism was naturally skin-deep, being concerned with such comparative trivia as the role of women in society, the narrowness of Victorian morality, or the morality of keeping one's university chair after having lost belief in God.[5]

An idea of the environment and values in which Keynes was reared may be gained by considering the letter Professor Foxwell wrote to Dr. John Neville Keynes, Maynard's father, dissuading him from leaving Cambridge for Oxford:[6]

> Pray don't go. It is much better that a study should be concentrated in a particular place. There arise many of the same advantages as in the localisation of an industry. Your departure would leave a nasty ragged wound in our Moral Sciences Organisation.
>
> What is the use of being a settled family man if you are to drift from your moorings in this fashion? Think of the effect your move may have on your son. He may grow up flippantly epigrammatical and end by becoming the proprietor of a Gutter Gazette, or the hero of a popular party; instead of emulat-

4. The closing paragraph of Whitehead's *Science in the Modern World* expresses the same conviction. Whitehead was one of Keynes' teachers.

5. Henry Sidgwick resigned his Fellowship at Trinity "on grounds of religious doubt" (Harrod, *Keynes*, p. 2).

6. Quoted ibid., p. 9.

ing his father's noble example, becoming an accurate, clear-headed Cambridge man, spending a life in the valuable and unpretentious service of his kind, dying beloved of his friends, venerated by the wise and unknown to the masses, as true merit and worth mostly are.

In this age of dizzying mobility among university teachers, Foxwell's letter may seem to have been written in jest. It is not so. Foxwell simply expressed the deep conviction that nothing is as disruptive of our "intellectual equipoise" as the coming into contact with new ideas, values, presuppositions, and viewpoints, even when they emanate from a university a few miles away, one hardly noted for iconoclasm. But things and events do lose that inner connection that only the customs and traditions and outlook of a closely knit group give them. Substantially, this was also Veblen's view, with the difference that Jewish certainties had a more determined foe than Oxford could possibly prove to be for Neville's son. And for Veblen, this clash causes greatness (though not happiness) at least as often as it causes "flippancy."

John N. Keynes stayed in Cambridge. He is the author of two scholarly works that also throw light on the qualities of Maynard's intellectual environment. His *Formal Logic* is a "notable work: thorough, lucid, and authoritative. . . . It is an exposition of the system of deductive logic of which Aristotle was the inventor and which for some twenty-two centuries has constituted the main part of what teachers and scholars have understood by logic."[7] Working in such a well-plowed field, Neville Keynes had not much opportunity to contribute original ideas. His is a work of systematization, not advance. It not only ignored the antirationalistic tide sweeping Europe, but it appeared on the eve of a revolution in logic that turned its back on Aristotle, that is, mathematical logic.

Neville Keynes' other work is also a definitive statement; like the *Logic*, it came at the twilight of an era. *The Scope and Method of Political Economy* displays the same thoroughness, erudition, ability to render balanced judgments characteristic of a work that deals with issues that have been debated for decades and which have left everybody intellectually exhausted. History is full of unexpected turns: John Neville, being in the classical tradition, held dear the dichotomy between positive and normative, real and mone-

7. Ibid., pp. 6–7.

tary economics. His son destroyed both. John Maynard came to maturity while historical undercurrents of no mean import were undermining the preconditions of British stability, political and intellectual. For a while, these undercurrents were interpreted as strength. Imperialism, for instance, brought about an "alliance between mob and capital" (as Hannah Arendt puts it) which diverted social discontent and gave a new lease on life to outworn social arrangements. The "moral currency" of the nation (in Hobson's words) might well have been "debased" by the explanations of this phenomenon current in British society (white man's burden, spreading civilization and religion among ignorant natives, etc.). But this was exactly its advantage: so long as hypocrisy is catholic, it, too, becomes a cohesive element of society. Meanwhile, those whose education made them fit to serve one's country were asked early to think deeply about lofty issues. Young Keynes at Eton (age 16) was asked to write an essay on the "Responsibilities of Empire."[8] *Noblesse oblige.*

The world war brought to an end this era of genteel balance and self-conscious possession of the truth, and Keynes was one of the first to recognize the passing of an epoch. To him the war was not only a historical event, but a deeply personal one: many of his friends had debated whether to serve their country or to assert their classical humanistic values and claim pacifist convictions. Some of them died in battle. Keynes became the head of a treasury department where he kept a close eye on movements of gold and foreign exchange. To see such holdings dwindle to nothing so that the whole flow of imported foodstuffs and strategic goods was more than once on the verge of being halted must have given him the first realization of the ephemeral nature of human arrangements and institutions. After the 1918 armistice, the Prime Minister took him along to Paris as official representative of the treasury, as financial advisor in the peace negotiations, and as a member of the Supreme Economic Council of Allied Powers.

In Paris, Keynes suffered as he probably never did before or after. Despite his high-sounding titles, he held a purely advisory role, a civil service position. Real power reverted to the politicians and what they did with their power was what Keynes learned in Paris. A fundamentally pragmatic animal, only interested in his own survival, the politician is the inevitable foe of those principles that

8. Ibid., p. 21.

found intellectual expression in Enlightened social thought and in the humanistic tradition: the principles of justice, order, and reason. These same principles did underpin Wilson's Fourteen Points but in Paris they were betrayed. When this happened, the values under which Keynes had been brought up also collapsed. The philosophy of G. E. Moore, the "preconditions of Harvey Road,"[9] the belief in the power of reason, the idea of a providential order of things all fell *as explanatory principles of reality*.[10] Yet proximity to the politician does not have a totally negative effect. His very actions deny that determinism on which most Enlightened social thought was based. Being himself not the slave of any principle, the politician reasserts the un-Cartesian notion that man is free.

Thus it was that Paris taught Keynes two related lessons: that naïve rationalism was powerless to explain political reality, and that man is the maker of his destiny. The personal experience of Paris, in other words, did for Keynes what many years of study of the Hegelian system and observation of political events did for Marx. And this is why the mature thought of both social theorists is remarkably alike in its movement away from rationalistic habits of mind, in its rejection of natural law fictions and in its stress on real man, his needs and psychology.

Like Marx, Keynes starts with a re-interpretation of the past. While his classical predecessors had found the economic organization of nineteenth-century capitalism to be natural, reasonable, eternal, and simplicity itself (it was so portrayed by general equilibrium theory), Keynes writes in *The Economic Consequences of the Peace* that, on the contrary, it was "unusual, unstable, complicated, unreliable, temporary." The "appearance" of stability was purely due to man's ability to become "habituated to his surroundings" (p. 3). What Keynes brings to an understanding of reality is a "historical sense" and, in addition, a feeling for the spiritual. For, he adds, whatever stability the system had was largely due to psychological, not material or economic, reasons. Neither efficiency[11]

9. Harrod uses this phrase very often to signify the pre–1914 "stable values of the civilization in which Keynes was bred" (ibid., p. 1). Harvey Road in Cambridge is Keynes' birthplace.

10. Not, however, as goals to aim for. Like Marx, Keynes had a dim view of current society, but never gave up striving for its betterment, and for the emergence of a reasonable, just world.

11. Indeed, the war proved that "we did not exploit to the utmost the possibilities of economic life" since production increased greatly in war time with fewer resources! (*Economic Consequences*, p. 4.) A more determined blow

nor justice held the system together but rather "a double bluff or deception": those who produced most of the national output were given the *hope* of personal betterment, while those who appropriated most of it were supposed not to enjoy it too conspicuously. "And so the cake increased; but to what end was not clearly contemplated."[12]

This view of the capitalist process is certainly not Walrasian. Neither the mechanistic nor the teleological (Smithian) overtones of classical economics are present. Rather, the economic system is shown to be the ephemeral product of chance, of explosive forces temporarily held at bay, a synthesis between two antitheses. The war and the Paris aftermath laid bare the "sandy foundations" of this order. Keynes realized sooner than most other thinkers that the past could not be recaptured. In 1919 an age was over, although neither England nor America was especially aware of this. Both were guilty of the ultimate pride: the belief that they stood outside of Europe, that Europe's "times of trouble" were not theirs.

Our brief review of philosophical modes of thought in the nineteenth century has touched on this relative isolationism of Anglo-Saxon thought. The pragmatist attack on logic and formalism came many decades after the Continental reaction to Cartesian reason, and by comparison with it seems rather anemic. Whatever delusion Keynes might have had that reality is ruled by the Idea and by Ideals was dashed in Paris. A better scenario could hardly have been conceived by anybody wishing to test the power of natural laws, reason, and covenants in the affairs of men. For the Big Three arrived in Paris with a "ready made compact" (Keynes' words) full-blown from the head of Wilson. The Fourteen Points were the extension of the principles of the American Declaration of Independence and of the Rights of Man from the realm of national to that of international relations. They were reason incarnate. They had been proclaimed from a somewhat detached White House as the condition to lay down their arms. The conference was called merely to implement the Idea.

Alas, in Paris, passions thwarted reason. Probably never has the annihilation of reason by passion been better described by any historian than it is in the pages of *The Economic Consequences.*

---

at the heart of economic theory (which "proves" the existence of maximum efficiency) can hardly be conceived.

12. *Ibid.*, p. 20.

And this is so exactly because Keynes' descriptive "tools" are the categories of modern psychology and *realpolitik*. Wilson turned out to have "no plan, no scheme, no constructive ideas whatever for clothing with the flesh of life the commandments which he had thundered from the White House" (p. 43). Moreover, his temperament was essentially "theological" in its righteousness. His attitude toward his colleagues soon became "I can do nothing that is not just and right, and you must first of all show me that what you want does really fall within the words of the pronouncements which are binding on me" (p. 51). Thus began the weaving of "that net of sophistry and Jesuitical exegesis" that eventually became the Paris Treaty, as Clemenceau and Lloyd George joined hands to show Wilson that "fair is foul, and foul is fair" (p. 51). Wilson might still have rescued something of his original covenant if he had not been so inept in the agilities of the Council Chambers. But, like all believers in the power of reason, he probably loathed the political process and thus became its victim, "a perfect and predestined victim to the finished accomplishments of the Prime Minister" (p. 41).

Many readers of Keynes' rendition of Wilson's character and nemesis have concluded that the economist did not do him justice. And it is undeniable that the President emerges as something of a fool. But if our interpretation is even close to being correct, the reason for Keynes' dislike (which bordered on hatred) becomes clear. At Paris, we said, it was not only the Fourteen Points that proved to be a fraud but *all of Keynes' explanatory classical baggage*, too. In describing Wilson's agonies, Keynes is describing his own. He, too, arrived at Paris with high hopes for mankind and mankind let him down. Never in his book does Keynes describe his role at the conference, but the letters Harrod collected in his biography enable us to surmise that what happened to Keynes is, in a rough sort of way, what happened to Wilson. Starting from high ideals, he contributed more and more to negating them by accepting "necessary" compromises. While Wilson never understood what he was instrumental in bringing about (i.e., a prostitution of the Fourteen Points by the higher exigencies of expediency), Keynes did and rather quickly.[13] But he kept silent. Then he re-

13. In a letter to his mother (14 May 1919) John Maynard Keynes acknowledged, "I suppose I have been an accomplice in all this wickedness and folly" (Harrod, *Keynes,* p. 249).

proached himself, felt wretched for working toward perpetuating injustice and insanity in the name of justice and wisdom and accommodation, and felt wretched for feeling wretched. Throughout he hoped against hope. At length, a few weeks before the conference finished its work, he slipped away from that "scene of nightmare" and in two months of frenetic writing gave vent to his accumulated frustrations. Wilson, whose pre-Paris wisdom he admired (he refers to the Fourteen Points as "a wise and magnanimous program for the world") is only Keynes' alter ego, the embodiment of his own shattered ideals. How else can one explain the intimate psychological details of the character of Wilson and of his nemesis if not by saying that Keynes recognized his own tragedy in Wilson's? It is not given to man to enter into somebody else's soul and depict its tragedy and travails. Much easier is it to describe one's own psychological states, and impute them to another.

Our purpose is not to criticize *The Economic Consequences* and least of all to criticize Keynes. We are examining his early book in an effort to find a clue to certain fundamental modes of thought that can possibly assist us in understanding his great economic work, just as Smith's *Theory of Moral Sentiments* and Marx' early *Philosophic and Economic Manuscripts* gave us clues to the nature of their economic thinking.

We believe we have found this clue in Keynes' realization that the realm of reality is not the realm of reason. The former is the domain of dark and mysterious forces. Contradictions are the rule in life. The proceedings of Paris "had this air of extraordinary importance and unimportance at the same time."[14] These forces, their confused power and hold on men, can be conveyed not in rationalistic language but in that of modern psychology and fictive literature.

Clemenceau's character, too, is described in the language of psychology (men of past standards might even say in the language of a gutter gazette). Clemenceau suffered from delusions of grandeur. Keynes wrote, "He felt about France what Pericles felt of Athens—unique value in her, nothing else mattering . . . he had one illusion—France; and one disillusion—mankind, including Frenchmen and his colleagues not least" (p. 32).

As for Lloyd George, his character and role in the conference

---

14. Keynes, *The Economic Consequences,* p. 6.

were more complex. Keynes' interpretation discredits not only the Prime Minister but, it seems, the idealistic notion of democracy as well. The end of hostilities spelled the end of the Prime Minister's leadership by causing a break-up in the old political blocks upon which his power was based. England's financial difficulties, the inevitable legacy of the war, furnished his opponents with powerful munitions. The people's natural desire for a change would have done the rest. But the Prime Minister was an ambitious man and exceedingly clever. He soon realized that his chances of survival rested on a continuation of the state of war. In an act of "political immorality" he called for a general election when there was no public interest that necessitated it. The Prime Minister wanted a personal "mandate." As history had it, however, the ensuing electoral campaign betrayed his weakness and brought to the surface the most ignominious traits of the masses. The opposition's accusation that the Prime Minister was for "letting the Hun off" touched a responsive chord in the electorate, as also did cries of "hanging the Kaiser" and demands that Germany be made to pay for the "whole cost" of the war. George understood which way the wind was blowing and decided to parry these attacks by himself adopting the hard line of his opponents. Thus the election became another historical and personal tragedy. It "affords a sad, dramatic history of the essential weakness of one who draws his chief inspiration not from his own true impulses, but from the grosser effluxions of the atmosphere which momentarily surrounds him. The Prime Minister's natural instincts, as they often are, were right and reasonable. He himself did not believe in hanging the Kaiser or in the wisdom or the possibility of a great indemnity." But as the election campaign progressed, he began "warming to his work" and finally a few days before the election issued a six-point program calling for, among other things, a trial of the Kaiser and for England's right to demand an indemnity covering the whole cost of the war.

Lloyd George's political instincts were sound: he was returned to office and carried with him "a lot of hard-faced men . . . who look as if they had done very well out of the war" as one of Keynes' "conservative friends" put it (pp. 136–45). Can any description of the world of reality be conceived in terms more diametrically opposed to Cartesian modes of thought? Both Wilson's and Lloyd George's original ideas were in the tradition of the ego: they were "reasonable." Originally, both of them probably viewed the Great War as an unnecessary and temporary aberration of the ideals of reason, justice, self-determination, and individual freedom. And they combated this aberration by reiterating the traditional ideals. But when well-meaning abstractions came into contact with facts (national jealousies, revenchist feelings, and other "obscure and confused ideas"), when "the people" (as an abstraction) became the British electorate and the opposition party, the abstractions proved unable to give birth to a reasonable and just settlement. The pleasure/pain calculus broke down and the peace, from a rationalistic point of view, turned out to be "war by different means."

The tragedy was not only a historical one but a personal one: The Prime Minister suffered in the realization that he was an instrument of unreason, while Wilson lived in a "fool's paradise."

Men like Wilson, George, and Clemenceau have always existed; the unique thing is that a man brought up as a classical economist recognized them and wrote about them. This feat, to repeat, was accomplished by overthrowing familiar modes of thought and adopting those of psychology and power politics.

The peculiar advantage of these modes is their ability to remain at a superficial level. They succeed in describing the real exactly because they are superficial, shunning ultimate questions. Thus, in a sense, Keynes approached the problem of understanding the events of Paris in the spirit called for by Kierkegaard, Bergson, and Nietzsche. Where Keynes stumbles is when he tries to attain "deeper understanding," that is, understanding of the "historical forces" behind personalities. Indeed, some of his utterances are then naïve. He is, for instance, indignant at the establishment of a Reparation Committee with, in his view, "dictatorial powers over all German property"; at the taking away of her merchant marine, of her coal fields, of her colonies in China, Siam, etc.; of interferences with her tariff policies and taxation prerogatives. These arrangements constitute an "unprecedented interference with a country's domestic arrangements" (p. 107).

Actually, when Keynes was a young student writing essays on the responsibility of Empire, such "interferences" were rather common. After the Manchu dynasty was toppled in China in 1911, a loan was made to the Chinese Republican government under a four-power consortium. The terms of the loan can be inferred by the objections of the "Presbyterean" (as Keynes calls Wilson in *The Consequences*) in the White House. The President wrote that the conditions of the loan "seem to us to touch very nearly the administrative independence of China itself; and this administration does not feel that it ought, even by implication, to be a party to those conditions. The responsibility on its part that would be implied in requesting the [American] bankers to undertake the loan might conceivably go the length in some unhappy contingence of forcible interference in the financial, and even the political affairs of that great Oriental State. . . . The conditions include not only the pledging of particular taxes, some of them antiquated and burdensome, but also the administration of these taxes by foreign agents."[15] The "forcible interference" at which Wilson hints occurred innumerable times in the relations between Western countries and their colonial victims. One of Keynes' friends, Leonard Woolf, at the same time that Keynes was writing *The Consequences*, was documenting British "interference" in the affairs of African countries.[16]

R. H. Tawney, referring to the situation in China in the 1920s and 1930s, recognized that "over one-quarter of China's railway mileage, over three-quarters of her iron-ore, mines producing more than half her output of coal, more than half the capital invested in cotton mills, and a smaller but not negligible proportion of that invested in oil mills, flour mills, tobacco factories, motor factories and banks are in the hands of foreigners. Dr. Sun Yat Sen's description of China as an economic colony is, from an economic point of view, not inappropriate."[17] If China could be so described, by what terms could the relation between Western powers and their colonies be characterized? Many of them hardly existed as independent entities in Keynes' own days. But he apparently had no inkling of this. Indeed, in an article in 1909 he criticized "current opinion in India, when a considerable part of the educated classes seems to desire with patriotic fervor the industrialization of their country." Keynes scolds them for not knowing the basic principles of economics which for well over a century have taught that the true road to prosperity was through international specialization and trade.[18] In time he became wiser.

15. Quoted by Frederic Clairmonte, *Economic Liberalism and Underdevelopment: Studies in the Disintegration of an Idea*, p. 172.

16. Leonard Sidney Woolf, *Empire and Commerce in Africa: A Study in Economic Imperialism*.

17. R. H. Tawney, *Land and Labour in China*, p. 129.

18. John Maynard Keynes, "Recent Economic Events in India."

In marked contrast to his explanation of politics, Keynes' early ideas of foreign economic relations were wholly unhistorical, in the tradition of Ricardo's law of comparative advantage. It is because he was under the influence of the myth of classical trade doctrine —which, needless to say, idealizes the reality of national relations— that Keynes was shocked at the "interferences" of the victorious allies with German sovereignty. A more historical outlook should have told him that the techniques employed in Paris by France and England toward Germany were the same ones refined by white nations in their economic relations with non-white countries too large or too civilized to be taken by outright force.

The outlook, categories, and principles of classical economics are also responsible for the knightly role in which Keynes casts Germany vis-à-vis her Eastern neighbors. With the usual keenness that characterizes his criticism of political means, he notes that the Western powers' policy toward Bolshevism is hopelessly contradictory. Though fearing it, they really promote its ascendancy in Germany by exacting large reparations that will cause the breakdown of society in that country. The alternative, aiding in the rebuilding of Germany under the leadership of the most determined anti-Communist class (the Junkers), was also rejected at Paris, for this class stands for militarism. The way out brewed by the "calculations of diplomacy" consisted of creating an independent Poland as a buffer between Russia and Germany and promoting Poland's alliance with France. But, Keynes points out, the vision of an independent Poland, "prosperous and magnificent between the ashes of Russia and the ruin of Germany," is "cheap melodrama." Poland is an impossibility without prosperous neighbors: it has "no industry but Jew baiting"![19] So far so good, but then Keynes proposes his own way out of the impasse and lands in "cheap melodrama" himself. We should help in the rebirth of Germany, he wrote, by encouraging its middle class which is equally opposed to militarism and Bolshevism. A democratic Germany will eventually bring Russia back to the fold of Western civilization. For Germany "has the experience, the incentive, and to a large extent the materials for furnishing the Russian peasant with the goods of which he has been starved for the past five years, for reorganizing the business of transport and collection, and so for bringing into the

19. Keynes, *The Economic Consequences,* p. 291.

world's pool, for the common advantage, the supplies from which
we are now so disastrously cut off" by the blockade.[20]

The lost sheep of Western civilization must be brought back
into the fold and the middle class (it did not behave too honorably
during the British general election) and Adam Smith are cast in
the role of the good shepherds. "It is in our interest to hasten the
day when German agents and organizers will be in a position to
set in train in every Russian village the impulses of ordinary economic motive." Therefore, "let us encourage and assist Germany to
take again her place in Europe as a creator and organizer of wealth
for her Eastern and Southern neighbors." Rhetoric is a dangerous
tool. It often bamboozles the reader, but it can also do the same to
the author. Germany's middle classes a few years later (after the
treaty was revised) were given adequate chance to play these noble
roles. History records their deeds.

Keynes is at his best when he tracks down the practical implications of the economic consequences of the peace. He handles the
Cartesian fictions like a consummate master, showing their hopeless
contradictions. If coal is taken away from Germany, her industries
will collapse and she will be unable to raise the foreign exchange
demanded by the victors. Neutral countries like Switzerland whose
economies rely heavily on imports of coal from Germany will likewise be adversely affected. The disruption of her transport system,
following the turning over of her rolling stock to the Allies, can
only accentuate this dislocation. If she is prevented from imposing
import duties on allied goods, her foreign exchange will be wasted
on buying silks and champagne (amidst so much poverty?) and the
reparation bill will not be met. The grossest dilemma of all is this:
if by a policy of Spartan deprivation and high taxes, Germany
should succeed in raising the large indemnity demanded of her, at
the end of a generation she would have the Allies in her power.
For she would have taken all their markets away, their populations
would be reduced to the supine state of Boeotian pigs, with low
taxes, dying industries, and declining efficiency. Success might then
turn into a nightmare for the victors.[21]

Eventually the Paris Peace *was* revised in favor of greater leniency. As Harrod says, "In the final upshot, [Germany] obtained
relief beyond the wildest dreams of Keynes, for, on her external

20. Ibid., pp. 293–94.
21. Ibid., pp. 93 ff.

account, loans from America *exceeded* her disbursements in reparations, so that she was a *net receiver* of money until the period of
world slump, when her obligations were suspended." And what,
Harrod asks, was the result? "Hitler."[22] Unfortunately for social
thought, no single event or individual—certainly not Keynes or the
leniency of the Cowles Commission—had much to do with the rise
of Nazism. As Keynes remarked in one of his most mystical moments, events have at the same time an air of importance and unimportance. Each of them, in retrospect, may be interpreted
rationalistically and dialectically as a step toward the final outcome. Yet it is unthinkable that the final outcome would have been
averted but for it. It is this intuitive feeling for the unexpected that
Keynes lacked in 1919. He is generally believed to have had
wizard powers to foresee events. *The Economic Consequences
of the Peace* does not bear this out, for the economic sections of
the book betray the most orthodox, mechanistic mentality. He
was a modern thinker when dealing with what we may call the
first echelon of reality, e.g., man and his motives. The more
he moved away from psychological analysis, the more obvious becomes his dependence on obsolete modes of thought. His practical
proposal as to how much Germany was able to pay is an exercise
in bookkeeping, the most simple-minded tool of mechanicism.

Thus *The Economic Consequences* betrays the two sides of
Keynes' personality, two sides which will never be fully reconciled:
that of the detached scholar casting flashes of light on the past and
present because he implicitly assumes men to be free even of laws,
and that of the mechanistic, classical thinker. In his major work,
The General Theory, both these personality traits are present in
their pure form, but there is more of the former and less of the
latter than in his earlier book. The key to understanding *The General Theory* is the realization that it is not "an engine of blind
manipulation" (which is what mathematical models are) but, quite
simply, a book which does what the whole tradition of Cartesian
thought claimed it was doing but never did: explain reality. As the
latter is free from subservience to ultimate principles, axioms, and
mechanistic causes and effects, so is Keynes' mature economic work.
The long analyses of expectations, the un-Benthamite psychologizing, the stress on the confused relationships which "may" prevail
in the real world, the weaving of the theoretical structure with the

22. Harrod, *Keynes*, p. 269. Emphasis added.

"facts of political life" are all expressions of this old desire clothed in novel forms of analysis.

But Keynes also needed to be systematic and coherent. And he addressed readers whose modes of thought were systematic, rigorous, and formalistic in the utmost. So he made concessions to tradition. Then, realizing that he had gone too far in this direction, he reverted to his chance-ruled outlook. The result is that *The General Theory* is a difficult and badly organized book because it does not follow a fixed methodology. Indeed, from a methodological point of view, it is a muddle. Intuition, practical details of commercial life, history, induction, modern psychologizing, hunches, popular philosophy and philosophy of history, polemical *ad hominem*, mathematical scholarship and attacks on mathematical economics, reality and fictions are all rolled together. The following interpretation of *The General Theory* is avowedly one-sided. It stresses only the neglected spirit and outlook of Keynes' work, which is, however, its soul.

13
Keynes II

*Here the ways of men part: if you wish to strive
for peace of soul and pleasure, then believe; if
you wish to be a devotee of truth, then inquire.*

Nietzsche

THE OUTWARD expression of the Cartesian ego in pre-Keynesian economics was Bentham's pleasure/pain calculus on which all the "real" relations of theory were based. The "Keynesian revolution" consisted of overthrowing this balancing mechanism by an appeal to what Keynes repeatedly called the "facts of observation." His attack on Benthamism was an attack on the century-old tradition of inventing axioms and making logical derivations from them. And it brought economics methodologically within twentieth-century modes of thought. Keynes himself felt an intellectual kinship with those thinkers who relied on "intuition" and "preferred to see the truth obscurely and imperfectly rather than to maintain error, reached indeed with clearness and consistency and by easy logic but on hypotheses inappropriate to the facts."[1]

1. Keynes, *The General Theory of Employment, Interest and Money*, p. 371. Keynes, therefore, does not agree with Friedman's method of inventing hypotheses. (Page references in the text of this chapter are to *The General Theory*.)

Immediately in chapter 2 of *The General Theory* we have an example of Keynes' new methodological outlook. The second classical postulate he rejected was one of the best products of the ego-centered hyperclassical method, which, in its drive to go back to fundamental causes, got tangled up in paradoxes. The postulate asserted that men offer their services to employers up to the point where an extra unit of real wage just balanced off the "irksomeness" of an extra unit of work. As in all other cases with which the marginalist calculus dealt, the world was divided into two "forces" pulling in the opposite directions and equilibrating at one point. On the one hand, there was the satisfaction of earning a greater real income by working more (a satisfaction that, by the axiom of diminishing marginal utility, decreased). On the other hand, there was the increasing pain associated with working longer hours. Thus, the employee's calculus was fundamentally that of judging whether an extra pence was worth an extra backache. It follows also that an infinitesimally smaller increase in pay per unit of time would have induced the worker to extend his offer of labor time an infinitesimally small amount till the intensity of the new stronger marginal backache again balanced off the infinitesimally small extra pay. Not that this effect was certain, for, as Robbins discovered in his search for generality, the worker's rationality might well dictate a non-pecuniary response, inducing him to prefer "leisure" over greater real income. But the natural desire to be able to give practical advice forced this discovery out of classical macroeconomics and confined it to the more speculative branches of the discipline.

Both demand and supply of labor were related to real wages. This was the necessary consequence of the metaphysics of reason: labor, the creature of the omniscient Cartesian, was himself omniscient and thus capable of piercing "the veil of money" and of fathoming the true essence of economic reality. This ultrarationalistic standpoint led to the usual paradoxes. One was that every minute price change would cause chaos in the labor market by causing a change in the supply of effort. A slight price increase, for instance, by lessening real wages would reduce the incentive to work and hence decrease the available labor force. Keynes objected to all this by appealing to the facts of "ordinary experience"—that experience Cartesian philosophical speculation had found deceitful. Ordinary experience "tells us, beyond doubt, that a situation where labour stipulates (within limits) for a money-wage rather than a

real wage, so far from being a mere possibility, is the normal case."
Workers hardly leave the labor force whenever there is an increase
in prices. Their reactions may be illogical, but "whether logical
or illogical, experience shows that this is how labour in fact behaves" (p. 9). Reality, neglected by the Cartesian sway, is granted
a new dignity in the Keynesian order of things.

That Keynes' "labour" is a realistic concept, different from the
eternal, abstract one of classical economics, is also obvious from
his observation that labor does not exist separately from an individual or group of individuals all trying to defend and improve
their *relative* income position. These considerations of emulation
and intergroup reactions were clearly alien to classical economists:[2]
their analyses, characterized by the absence of the time concept,
really assumed simultaneous actions and reactions, thus clearly
obviating the necessity of splitting a concept (labor) into sub-
groups. On the contrary, we saw that it encouraged collapsing
together heterogeneous classes like labor and capital, treating them,
for certain theoretical problems, as if they were the same. It is impossible to exaggerate the importance of Keynes' rejection of the
"homogeneity postulate." As we shall see at the end of this chapter,
Keynes was aware that in overthrowing it, he was rejecting the
method of classical thought—the method that demanded clearness
and distinctness of *ideas* at the cost of common observation of *facts*.

Another brainchild of Cartesian reason was the money market
mechanism which provided superficial backing to Say's Law. In
speculating that this law was based on a "false analogy" with a
non-exchange Robinson Crusoe–type economy, Keynes showed that
he was aware of economics' roots in natural law fictions (p. 20). He
attacks the unrealism of this delicate balancing mechanism by introducing the time concept once again into the picture and thus causing delayed reactions. In the classical view of things, a shift in the
savings function was no cause for a shift in the investment function
since no income change was allowed to occur. For all the alleged
changes to which the verbal medium of analysis referred actually
took place simultaneously, since, as we saw, logic and mathematics
compress the past, present, and future into the instant "now." Thus,
given, for example, an autonomous increase in savings, three things

2. For simplicity of expression we will henceforth use the term classical
economics to cover what *Keynes* meant by it. It is synonymous with what we
called classical and hyperclassical economics.

occurred simultaneously: a fall in the interest rate, a decrease in the volume of savings due to the movement along the new function, and an increase in the volume of investment caused by the fall in interest. All of this occurred "in the blink of the eye" and the total change in investment was just enough to compensate for the total change in savings (autonomous plus induced). Since the former change must occur simultaneously with the latter, no change in income and hence in the marginal efficiency of investment took place, and Say's Law was upheld.

Keynes discredited this mechanism by implicitly breaking the process at a chosen point, that is, by introducing again the time element. His is a "stop-watch" analysis: his "time" concept is not the continuous absorption of the present by the past with which we are familiar in life. It is nevertheless an infinitely closer approximation to reality than the non-entity of classical thought. Viewing the process sequentially as links on a chain, Keynes can stop to observe the effect of the shift in savings on income and *then* on investment, an effect which the "timeless" analysis of classical thought precluded. By adopting this method Keynes is justified in concluding that a change in savings by affecting consumption must influence the marginal efficiency of investment and hence output. Methodologically, Keynes' criticism is a criticism of the ceteris paribus assumption which, as in the case of Marshall's demand curve, produces self-contradictions.

It is, however, the treatment of expectations that renders the mechanistic fabric of classical theory beyond repair, and which best reveals the intellectual kinship of Keynes with the anti-rationalistic tide of the nineteenth centry. Emphatically, Keynes stresses the "outstanding fact" of economic life: that uncertainty which surrounds every business decision. Reflecting such fact, all the functions of his economics rest on a state of ignorance and are therefore vulnerable to the slightest sociopolitical wind. The precariousness of human arrangements of which Keynes had become aware at Paris pervades his mature economic writings. Methodologically, this stress on ignorance is a great innovation, the by-product of the shift of viewpoint from the ideal to the real. Where reason and perfect foresight prevailed, now there are the "dark forces of ignorance." Just as in philosophy Descartes' Ego and Hegel's Absolute gave way to Schopenhauer's Will, so in economics the all-rational, calculating animal of classical economics gave way to one which is prey to psychic states, feelings, and opinions, often of a delusory nature. Keynes well understands the reason for the failure of his predecessors to analyze carefully what he calls the "state of confidence" of the business community. The a priori method cannot deal with it: "there is . . . not much to be said about the state of confidence *a priori*" (p. 149). Yet the failure of this method should not be allowed to become a failure of scholarship, and least of all should reality be scolded for not fitting our a priori preconceptions. It should instead challenge the intellect to finally come to grips with reality by abandoning deductive reasoning. What method Keynes substitutes for it is obvious from his own treatment. It is basically the method of imaginative induction and observation and personal experience. What deprives this methodology of its inherently iconoclastic tendencies (that is, of the tendency to deny the "kingdom of laws") is a superb handling of the literary medium and a liberal sprinkling of psychological "propensities." These "propensities," more than anything else, have hitherto beclouded an understanding of Keynes' work. Post-Keynesian economists, by stressing them, have mistaken the form for the substance. In Keynes, these propensities are rhetorical benchmarks, succinct summarizations of "facts of observation" aimed at assisting the understanding of his work. They may be compared to those brief statements on the margin of the pages of old-fashioned and weighty books: they are there to help the reader. They are to *The General Theory* what an index is to a book. Post-Keynesian economists read this index, built a theory on its basis, and called it Keynesian theory.

Keynes' starting point is the realization that businessmen's (and our own) knowledge of the future "amounts to little and sometimes to nothing" (pp. 149–50). That he erected a consistent system without losing sight of this premise is a tribute to the depth and clearness of his intellect. Where others, for good reasons, displayed a "remarkable lack of any clear account of the matter," Keynes proposed to make clear what is unclear but important. Chapter 12 especially is a literary tour de force: he must be intelligible while dealing with behavior that does not lend itself to rationalistic descriptions. Ignorance, deceitfulness, and a profit motive turned antisocial are the materials with which he erects his structure. Realizing that it is in danger of crashing down, he shores it up with the help of "more stable" long-term expectations, "conventions" of business life, "laws of human nature," and the like. Fearing that this may be interpreted as a reversion to well-trodden paths of thought, he falls back again on the obscure but powerful cravings, fears, and self-delusions of men. What Keynes dreads most is that the probabilistic calculus will swallow up and recast his insights. This is why he is at pains to stress (as he also was in his 1937 article) the difference between what can rightfully be subjected to the conventions of statistics (e.g., the game of roulette) and the *inherently unknowable*, like the yield of a transatlantic liner or the likelihood of obsolescence of a piece of equipment within ten years. A by-product of this fear is the warning that we should not assume that in an atmosphere of ignorance errors tend to offset each other: "the assumption of arithmetically equal probabilities based on a state of ignorance leads to absurdities" (p. 152). In fighting the fiction of certainty and the misapplications of probability theory, Keynes was fighting nearly two centuries of evolution of economic thought. The remarkable thing is not that his work was distorted, but that it survived at all.

There are very good reasons why businessmen are in the dark in estimating the prospective yield of an undertaking whose fruits are to be reaped in the future. The whole universe, social and physical, affects the future profitability of an investment. To quantify and give relative weight to these elements in the double-entry bookkeeping of pleasure and pain is sheer fantasy. Keynes detected the logical fiction whereby uncertainty was circumvented by the classical school. In describing the marginal efficiency of capital (the outward expression of the calculus of whether to invest or not) classicists considered only the first member of the series of a stream of returns, Q_1. This is legitimate, Keynes notes, only in a static theory, where all the Qs are constant and identical, but it is incorrect in a theory of employment rooted on existential time (pp. 138–39). We know that the reason why all the Qs collapsed into one was that time as such was ignored in classical analysis. If there is no time, there is no uncertainty. There are no clocks in heaven because God sees past, present, and future simultaneously. Once the decision to invest was taken, the new stock of capital that thus came into existence paradoxically immediately died (in the mind of the economist), for no revision of expectations is possible or necessary in a timeless world. Certain fictions of life, however, allow businessmen to carry on their activities even in the face of ignorance, and Keynes analyzes these fictions. For one thing, they fall back on certain "conventions," the most important of which is the tendency to assume that the present state of confidence, whatever it is, will continue unless there is strong reason to believe that it will not.

Realizing that this consideration threatens to reinstate through the back door what was previously thrown out—stability and the kingdom of reason—Keynes hastens to add that businessmen's confidence in this fiction is so weak as to be destroyed by the slightest turn of events. In the stock market, for instance, behavior based on convention simply *intensifies* the tidal movement from a bullish to a bearish outlook and vice versa. For probably the first time in economic theory attention was paid to this peculiar institution of capitalism, the stock exchange, hardly the altar of reason. Keynes' treatment would have pleased Veblen, for Keynes portrays financiers as "sagatious saboteurs." Instead of being engaged in evaluating the long-term prospects of an investment as objectively as possible, speculators, investors, and financial intermediaries are interested only in forecasting changes in the conventional basis of valuation a short time ahead of the masses. "They are concerned not with what an investment is really worth to a man who buys it 'for keeps,' but with what the market will value it at, under the influence of mass psychology, three months or a year hence" (pp. 154–55). Financiers act under the spur of the profit motive but their activities do not lead to, but rather threaten, the general welfare. Mass psychology, which first compelled a conventional (i.e., unanimous) evaluation of the securities, now causes a uniform reaction of the general public to even the most trivial event. This is why the market is subject to "waves of optimistic and pessimistic sentiment, which are unreasoning and yet in a sense legitimate when no solid basis exists for a reasonable calculation" (p. 154). The conventional and psychological reactions of the public owe their existence exactly to lack of knowledge.

Just as Keynes well understands why classical economists fell into the error of considering the annual flow of capital returns as constant, so he appreciates the behavior of speculators: their actions are unreasoning since they are not based on firm knowledge. Yet they are reasonable since they are to be expected in an environment of nearly total ignorance! There is a Hegelian hint here that what appears as irrationality is actually reasonable, when the peculiarities of man's real environment are taken into account. This is why

Keynes avoids making those accusations of irrationality that mark classical works. What professional investors try to foresee are exactly these waves of mass "thoughtless" revaluations of securities. Instead of trying to defeat the forces of ignorance, they attempt to capitalize on them. With grim humor, Keynes compares the behavior of bankers, brokers, and professional investors with that of competitors for certain magazine prizes in which the contestant is asked to choose the six prettiest faces from a hundred photographs, the prize being awarded to the person whose choice comes closest to that of the mass of competitors. Obviously each participant will choose not on the basis of his own esthetic standards but on the basis of what he regards the esthetic standards of the majority to be. Mutatis mutandis, this is true of the clever investor, with the difference that the esthetic standards of men are much more uniform than the forecasting of countless chancy events and unintelligible moods. And there are some, Keynes adds, who devote their intelligence to anticipating what average opinion expects the average opinion to be, while others practice the fourth, fifth, and higher degrees (p. 156)!

This maelstrom of cunning on a foundation of ignorance destroys everything in its wake. The rational investor whose decisions are based on a thorough study of the probabilities of the long-term success of an enterprise is likely to meet with disastrous setbacks, especially since it takes more intelligence to assess rationally the probability of gain of a venture than to try to "beat the gun." Truly professional behavior, being in the minority, is also labeled eccentric, unconventional, and rash. Far from intelligence leading ignorance, ignorance forces intelligence underground. And Keynes wryly notes that "worldly wisdom teaches that it is better for reputation to fail conventionally than to succeed unconventionally" (p. 158). The bad fairies, he noted elsewhere, are so much more powerful than the good ones, and, he could now add, their standards prevail in the world.

Now, if this speculative game were divorced from the rest of the economy, limiting itself to a "battle of wits" among investors, no damage would result. But Keynes sees its pernicious effects spreading throughout the economic body and infecting it. In particular, enterprise, the task of producing goods and services, is disrupted by the valuations and revaluations that the stock market produces. Enterprise becomes the "bubble on a whirlpool of specu-

lation," and the promotion of the development of the country, the
by-product of the activities of a gambling casino (p. 159). We have
here nothing less than Veblen's distinction between industry and
finance and the clear suggestion that the latter, centering on the
exchange, is a hindrance to the former.

It is a measure of what we may call the "hyperclassical restoration" that economists' interest in the stock market has not been
whetted by Keynes' long essay on speculation. Indeed, this most
important section of *The General Theory* has been methodically
ignored. The *L-M* curve resembles Keynes' treatment of the financial aspects of capitalism as Apollo resembles a satyr. For the *L-M*
curve re-enthrones, as geometry always must, naïve calculation and
stability where neither exists. Stock market studies are still not considered to fall within the province of economic theory, though
Keynes was of contrary opinion: "These considerations should not
lie beyond the purview of the economist" (p. 158).

We have noted above that Keynes regards speculative activity
as all-pervasive in its effects because of the impact it has on enterprise and capital formation. But there is another fundamental "propensity," the propensity to consume, that is similarly affected.
Keynes himself gives contradictory accounts of his consumption
function manifesting the antithetical desires to portray life (which
ill fits mechanistic molds) while still being coherent and rational.
His heart, we may say, was with life and reality, but expediency
and "worldly wisdom" dictated lip service to stability, certainty, and
Benthamite calculations. Thus, at times he writes that consumption
is based on relatively stable psychological characteristics, while
often he relates consumption to "windfall changes in capital values,"
thus linking it to the vagaries of the stock market. Windfall effects
"should be classified amongst the *major* factors capable of causing
short-period changes in the propensity to consume" (p. 93; emphasis
added). Recalling the chaos that grips capital valuations, the conclusion is inescapable that consumption itself is drawn into this
"whirlpool" and is as unstable as speculative moods themselves.
Keynes returns to this theme again and again. Perhaps the most
important influence on the readiness to spend out of a given income
is the paper appreciation or depreciation of securities and other
financial assets. If a man is enjoying a windfall increment in the
value of his capital, he is prone to spend more liberally, while if he
is suffering a paper loss he will be more careful with his spending

(p. 94). Later he notices that people who indulge in stock market investment—and Keynes clearly does not think that they are an innocuous minority—"are perhaps even more influenced in their readiness to spend by rises and falls in the value of their investments than by the state of their income" (p. 319), a statement that relegates even current income as an influence on consumption to a secondary plane, at least in the short run.[3] Just as the influence of the rate of interest on investment is secondary by comparison with the innumerable subjective factors summarized under the *rubrica* of marginal efficiency of capital, so the influence of current income on current consumption is often swamped by windfall effects operating through changes in the paper value of securities.

A strange metamorphosis has fallen on the Keynesian theory of consumption. The windfall effect was first "objectified" by linking it to interest rate changes. This assumes that the relation between stock prices and interest rates is clear and definite while empirical evidence suggests the contrary.[4] Then the interest rate was turned into a variable affecting consumption on the same footing as income. That is, consumption was made a function of both income and the rate of interest. Finally, this interest rate was judged to affect consumption both directly and inversely, each force offsetting the other! These metamorphoses stemmed from the "healing-the-wounds syndrome" that produced the whole neoclassical synthesis. We dislike schisms. As soon as a radical theory arises, a process noticed by William James starts: the intellect goes to work to show that the new is "only a special case" of the old. The post-Keynesian dependence of consumption on the rate of interest is solely a throwback to classical modes of thought. In the process the windfall effect disappeared from the literature.

How do we reconcile the windfall effect with Keynes' "logical theory of the multiplier, which holds good continuously, without time lag, at all moments of time" (p. 122)? Here Keynes seems to adhere to as strict a mechanistic view as can be found in any classical writer. We believe, however, that Keynes' words have been misunderstood. What Keynes says is simple: the *logical* theory of

3. We may note that, by everyone's admission, Keynes' theory is fit to explain only *short-run* changes in national income.

4. See Frederick R. Macaulay, *Some Theoretical Problems Suggested by the Movements of Interest Rates, Bond Yields, and Stock Prices in the United States since 1856:* "There is no real similarity between the long-term trends of the two series," bond yields and stock prices (p. 156).

the multiplier is a perfect tautology—a useless "fifth wheel" (as someone later discovered). *Within the domain of pure logic*, where time is neglected, it holds good continuously. Within the realm of reality, the reaction of income to change in demand must be discovered empirically.

A brief consideration of the investment function will confirm our thesis that deductive logic took a back seat in Keynes' system of thought. That investment is a highly unstable element of aggregate demand was generally conceded, at least in business cycle studies. But Keynes found investment to be more than simply unstable. He deemed it the result of irrational forces which are, at bottom, *unintelligible*. "Most, probably, of our decisions to do something positive, the full consequences of which will be drawn out over many days to come, can only be taken as a result of animal spirits—of a spontaneous urge to action rather than inaction, and not as the outcome of a weighted average of quantitative benefits multiplied by quantitative probabilities" (p. 161). The "urge to action," the "animal spirits," the "nerves, hysterias and even the digestions and reactions to the weather" of businessmen are the Keynesian equivalent of Schopenhauer's Will or Bergson's élan, all concepts notoriously unwilling to be caught in the pincers of the Benthamite pleasure-pain calculus. Indeed, the tables are turned against rationality: if the animal spirits are dimmed and the spontaneous optimism falters so that business depends on nothing but a "mathematical expectation," enterprise will fade and die (p. 162). Keynes would agree with the philosopher who said that man is a species of monkey who, suffering from megalomania, acts despite his better judgment.

Keynes' theory of interest also makes a clean break with classical theory. Dealing with essences, the classicists addressed themselves to the question of the ultimate nature of interest, to its raison d'être. Keynes is not so profound. He took interest, the phenomenon, as a deep-rooted *fact* of social and economic life and was interested in explaining its movements, not its nature. Post-Keynesian economics, looking at *The General Theory* from the standpoint of the ideal, did not know what to make of his theory in which the current interest rate is determined by people's opinion of what the "normal" rate is. Obviously this conception leaves interest hanging by its bootstraps (as Robertson pointed out), a criticism which implicitly assumes that Keynes' purpose was to explain the ultimate

nature of the phenomenon of interest. But Keynes is not a rationalist. To his practical bent the fact that interest has existed for so
many centuries is sufficient justification for its existence. He was
concerned with explaining movements in the rate of interest, movements that he finds caused by the usual elements of uncertainty,
expectations, conventions, mass psychology that underlie his other
functions. This is why he calls the interest rate "a highly psychological phenomenon" (p. 202), and later, a "highly conventional"
one—conventional because it is based so thoroughly on customary
ways of looking at the future.

Quite clearly, the interjection of uncertainty, existential time, ignorance, and antisocial intelligence (on the part of financial opera-
tors) makes a mockery of the kingpin of economic analysis. Equilibrium in Keynes is an emperor without clothes. One need only
recall Keynes' description of the "several slips between the cup and
the lip" by which he shows the uncertainty pervading traditional
monetary policy. The conventional view was simplicity itself. Should
unemployment develop (how?), an increase in the money supply
would lower interest rates and stimulate investment, discourage
savings, and encourage consumption, thus restoring full employment
equilibrium. But in the Keynesian framework, things are not ruled
by such unilinear logic. An increase in the stock of money will not
reduce interest rates if the liquidity preference of the public increases more rapidly than the quantity of money. Even if a decrease
in the rate of interest does occur, it will have no influence whatever
on investment if the marginal efficiency of capital falls more rapidly
than the interest rate. Even if investment is stimulated, employment
may not be favorably affected if the propensity to consume is falling.
Finally, even if all these obstacles are overcome and employment
does rise, upward pressures on prices and wages will absorb some
of the increase in the quantity of money with no favorable effect
on investment and consumption.

What can be learned from this gloomy exercise? Simply this:
that to Keynes shifts in the functions were more important than
movements along the old functions: ceteris paribus does not apply
to the world of men. To assume reactions to be predetermined is
tantamount to falling back on the Benthamite calculus as underpinning the economic world. There is no concept of equilibrium in
Keynes because his framework of analysis rests on facts, and on

the fact par excellence: the ignorance that pervades decision-making. If the very actors of economic life are ignorant, it ill befits the students of this aspect of life to be dogmatic.

Just as monetary policy is discredited, so is classical trust in a cut in money wages as a means to restore full employment. Keynes had already outlined the unreality and contradictions of this suggestion in his attack on the first classical postulate. And he devotes the whole of chapter 19 to exposing the superficial mechanicism embodied in the classical medicine. There is, he asserts, no detailed account in classical works of the effect of a wage cut. After reviewing the probable reasoning behind the prescription, he notes: "if this is the groundwork of the argument (and if it is not, I do not know what the groundwork is) surely it is fallacious" (p. 259). The "groundwork" seems to have consisted of a superficial reasoning by analogy from the firm to the industry and from the latter to the economy.

Keynes stresses that the bargaining process takes place on an industry-wide basis. And he also points out that there is no demand schedule for labor, but only "demand schedules for particular industries [which] can only be constructed on some fixed assumption as to the nature of the demand and supply schedules of other industries and as to the amount of aggregated demand" (p. 259). The ceteris paribus once again misled the classicists. A cut in wages was not expected to change demand, but only costs and profits. Demand, to the classical economist, was as much an idealized category as consumption is today: they have existence independently of wages and money supply, respectively, since they are part of real, not monetary, economics. Keynes himself did not know what to make of the classical false analogy between the firm and the economy. It must be the basis of classical reasoning—he asserts— for if it is not, then classical thought has "no method of analysis wherewith to tackle the problem" of national income level (p. 260). Our whole survey of the development of classical theory confirms that, in fact, classical thought not only had no such method of analysis but was simply not interested in explaining business fluctuations, but only the higher logic of economic life. Keynes' awareness of the deceptiveness of the ceteris paribus assumption is illustrated by his remarks prefacing consideration of the effect of a cut in money wages within the framework of his own theory. With the punctilio of one who has learned that in debating with scholars nothing can be taken for granted, he defines what ceteris paribus means: that the three fundamental functions of his theory are stable. Even in the context of this conscious fiction, he finds a wage cut to open up such a Pandora's box of uncertain and unpredictable reactions that his suggestion to leave wages alone is eminently reasonable. Expectational effects can be favorable or adverse: "we can only guess" what they will be. Where the classical methodology left no room for uncertainty, Keynes' emphasis on the "facts of experience" lead him naturally to an agnostic position. By comparison with the classicists' unwitting radicalism, his thought can be truly labeled conservative. As noted repeatedly, this outlook stemmed from his realization of how thin the crust of civilization and human knowledge is.

Ironically, Keynes finds that the way a wage cut operates is identical to the way an increase in the money supply is supposed to work, so that now the various "slips between the cup and the lip" that he noted before can be unleashed again. Given this substantial identity between the effects of wage cuts and monetary policy, Keynes argues that only "a foolish person," or an "unjust person," or an "inexperienced person" would prefer the former to the latter (pp. 268–69)! By splitting the classical generalized demand and supply for labor into their basic industry components, Keynes once again abandons the path of aggregative thinking. Disaggregation is the hallmark of most of his analysis, despite the misleading adjective "general" on the title page. Logically, Keynes appears to agree with Nietzsche's opinion that concepts overlook what is individual and real.[5] Marx, too, often abandoned his two-class framework whenever he needed greater realism.

It is in the theory of prices that Keynes plays havoc with the generalized ideal reasoning of classical thought. In the most puerile rendition of The General Theory, it is asserted that an increase in demand is felt first on output, then, after full employment has been reached, on prices. Such a turn of events *is* portrayed in The General Theory but it is predicated on a number of simplifying assumptions that Keynes actually *ridiculed*. Their retention in post-Keynesian macroeconomics leads to a kind of modified quantity theory of money which still retains its basic Cartesian characteristic, i.e., certainty of results because tautological. And, from the

5. Karl Jaspers, *Nietzsche: An Introduction to the Understanding of His Philosophical Activity*, p. 319.

standpoint of reality, it leads to frustration since the whole post-war experience in America has shown price stability and full employment to be not easily attainable simultaneously.

Whatever advances have been made in solving the conflict between full employment and price stability have occurred because of changes in the subject, not the object; that is, economists have succeeded in changing their *outlook* via a number of self-deceiving beliefs. One such belief is the defining of full employment as that rate of unemployment that is considered normal for the sake of price stability! So that, if prices begin to rise at an "unacceptable rate" while unemployment is, say 4 per cent, then 4 per cent unemployment becomes 0 per cent (for policy's sake). Another trick to conjure the problem away consists of exploiting thoroughly the classical concept of "frictional unemployment," which broadly defined may well include nine-tenths of the unemployed in 1933.[6] Finally, the conflict between full employment and inflation, far from being interpreted for what it is—a serious shortcoming of scientific knowledge—is enshrined in the folklore of the discipline and it is given a name: it is a trade-off, almost a law of nature.[7]

The make-believe nature of these exercises has made it inevitable for the most untheoretical of all animals, the politician, to deal with the problem in his own pragmatic, unprincipled, short-sighted way. During the Kennedy-Johnson administrations, a battery of ad hoc price control techniques were devised, from wage-price guidelines to the unleashing of the antitrust division of the Justice Department on recalcitrant corporations. And President Nixon has been pushed willy-nilly in the same direction.

Had Keynes' analysis of price movements been given more than perfunctory consideration, postwar economic events would have caused neither surprise nor frustration. For Keynes, in what we take to be a mocking remark, "having . . . satisfied tradition by introducing a sufficient number of simplifying assumptions to enable [him] to enunciate a quantity theory of money" (p. 296), quickly proceeds to the more relevant task of considering the actual factors which, in fact, influence events and prices. Cognizant of the natural tendency of the mind to concoct fictions that have no bearing on

6. Roger C. Van Tassel, *Economic Essentials: A Core Approach,* pp. 146–47, does exactly that.

7. There is another trick but this is very old. It is to hail inflation as causing growth.

reality, he makes some interesting methodological remarks. He notes, for instance, that the object of his analysis is not to create a machine or "method of blind manipulation, which will furnish an infallible answer" but rather to provide "an organized and orderly method of thinking out particular problems." Even the technique of isolating the "complicating factors one by one" is suspect, for at a higher stage of analysis the probable interactions of the factors among themselves must be taken into account. A well-known blast against the "symbolic pseudo-mathematical methods of formalizing a system of economic analysis" follows. This technique leads to a loss of the "complexities and interdependencies of the real world in a maze of pretentious and unhelpful symbols."

A volley of shots seriously maiming the quantity theory of money comes from an attentive reading of this section of *The General Theory*. "Bottlenecks," time as a concept of experience, the "psychology of the workers and the policies of labour unions," lack of proportionality between the rise in the quantity of money and the rise in effective demand, lack of homogeneity of resources, expectations of future changes, "discontinuities," abrupt changes in the income velocity of money (which in itself is "merely a name which explains nothing") are some of the concepts unleashed by Keynes which not only destroy the innocence and freshness of the quantity theory of money but also suggest that *The General Theory* itself is not a ready-made, handy tool of forecasting. Of this Keynes was aware: "These factors [he notes wryly] do not lend themselves to theoretical generalizations" (p. 302) just as the factors summarized as "state of confidence" do not. But such is life.

In restating and briefly summarizing *The General Theory* (chapter 18, sec. 2) Keynes, after listing the basic relationships of his model, remarks: "there is not one of the above factors which is not likely to change without much warning, and sometimes substantially" (p. 249). His "psychological functions" are "fundamental" in the sense of being non-economic in nature. But they do not have the essential characteristic of all that is fundamental in idealistic philosophy, namely, stability.

Our study, thus, leads us to this conclusion: the essence of *The General Theory* is not the discovery of the liquidity preference, of the consumption function, of the inelasticity of investment, etc., but the *repudiation of the traditional methodology of economic theory, the method of the ego which had prevailed since Adam*

Smith. Only those who interpret Keynes' work through the neo-classical income-expenditure model will be surprised by this conclusion. Yet it is clear that Keynes' stress on "experience," the "facts of life," the "world we live in" compelled him to consider many factors that are all important to an understanding of the economy but that "do not lend themselves too well to theoretical generalizations." With Keynes the economic mind reasserted the primacy of substance over form. And if the price to pay for attaining the truth is the abandonment of that "peace of soul and pleasure" that rationalism gives, Keynes leaves no doubts as to his preference. For the mechanicism of his predecessors he substitutes an economics more consonant to that "instability due to the characteristics of human nature" (p. 161), which the first third of this century had made clear and which philosophers had discovered a century before.

Occasionally, Keynes uses the word equilibrium in a rather original sense. In connection with his theory of interest he notes that "for every rate of interest there is a level of employment for which the rate is the 'natural' rate, in the sense that the system will be in equilibrium with that rate of interest and that level of employment" (p. 242). Robbins tried to eliminate the normative element of equilibrium by rhetoric ("equilibrium is just equilibrium"). Keynes did so more effectively by creating an inflation of equilibria.

It is generally stressed that Keynes was a good classical economist and it must be admitted that here and there are echoes of classical fictions. He believed in the falling rate of profit (as did Marx) and he used the law of diminishing returns whenever convenient. The concept of "an hour's employment of ordinary labour" is a heuristic fiction (like Smith's unit of toil and trouble), but an innocuous one of which he makes no practical use. That it is fictional in nature is indicated by the paradoxes to which it leads if reality adhered to this concept. For instance, it would follow that governmental attempts to "upgrade" labor through education, etc., only result in an expansion of the labor supply, thus making the very attainment of full employment more, not less, difficult! Keynes' occasional methodological confusion is perhaps best illustrated by his own parable of the two queens which seems to suggest that his own analysis is based on quantitative concepts. We saw repeatedly that he instead attacked the mock precision of hyperclassical pleasure-pain calculations and relied heavily for his own construct on qualitative, ephemeral, psychologically unstable elements.

J. S. Schumpeter was in error when he called Keynes' fundamental concepts dei ex machina. Viewing *The General Theory* from the classical end of the binoculars, he naturally found its method perverse and illogical. For Schumpeter as for classical thought, psychology is an excuse to introduce stability in life; for Keynes, psychology is a license to undermine classical constructs.

Keynes recognized that in an existential context "anything can happen." But despite this awareness he almost always held a tight grip on his subject matter. In 1919 he employed psychological insights into the nature of statesmen to discredit their work. In 1936 he used the same engine of expression to discredit the work of his classical predecessors. Not that he analyzed the psychological roots of economic thought (although there are a number of psychological insights on this matter in *The General Theory* and in other works of his), but he examined the psychology of the actors of economic life: businessmen, consumers, workers, and financiers. The stress on the paradoxical confused nature of life is evident in *The Economic Consequences*: in *The General Theory* the contradictoriness of economic life is elevated to a methodological principle.

Throughout his life, Keynes simply reveled in paradoxes: one has the clear impression that he agreed with Kierkegaard's admonition on how to attain true understanding: examine what the conventional beliefs are and assume truth to be the exact opposite. Given the nature of what he was criticizing, this spirit served him well. One further example of Keynes' unorthodoxy will suffice. Cutting through a century of learned discussions on the usefulness of foreign loans to the recipient country, he asserted that they will always be desirable for the recipient country, for when the burden of repayment will become too heavy, an economic or political crisis will occur and the indebtedness will be canceled![8] Evidently, the mature Keynes realized that the 1930s had shown the hollowness and futility of his 1919 exercises in the German "burden."

A 1937 article by Keynes in the *Quarterly Journal of Economics* answers the criticism of four economists by reiterating the main areas of difference between his own theory and the classicists. These areas are two: the abandonment of general, all-comprehensive principles and axioms when dealing with the behavior of different groups, e.g., consumers, entrepreneurs, and speculators, and the

8. Harrod, *The Life of John Maynard Keynes*, p. 566.

abandonment of the classical fiction of certainty and its substitution by the facts of life, above all, by the uncertainty and ignorance that pervade our knowledge of the future and by the "conventions" (practical fictions) developed in business life to function effectively in the face of lack of knowledge. Addressing himself to Leontief's criticism, Keynes acknowledged that he rejected the classical homogeneity postulate but added that he "thought" experience contradicted it. "In any case, it is for those who make a highly special assumption to justify it, rather than for one who dispenses with it, to prove a general negative."[9] Keynes' characterization of the homogeneity postulate as a highly special assumption is significant: for it is such only from the standpoint of reality. From the standpoint of the ideal, the postulate is not special and narrow but general and fundamental. Nothing better reflects Keynes' existential viewpoint than his denigration of this product of rationalism as a special and narrow and false assumption. It is geometrical thinking and the postulate of reason that he so describes. Alternatively, one may say that the difference implied by Keynes is this: that the classicists were convinced they understood "human nature" while he, Keynes, was not so sure.[10] Not Keynes but the classicists were dogmatic. A familiarity with life makes one aware of its contradictory and multifarious manifestations and generates intellectual tolerance. While logic is a system of *must*'s, Keynes' is a system of *may*'s. Equilibrium may be at full employment, but it need not be so. A wage cut may help but there is no reason why it must. Money supply expansion may generate an increase in demand, but not necessarily. Keynes knew that an outlook on life cannot be taught to others and therefore resorted to the language of the courtroom. It is the burden of those who make special and exceptional assumptions to prove them. The classical defenders did not take up this challenge, for to prove the classical economic axioms is out of the question. On the other hand, those who came to call themselves Keynesians converted his "may's" into "must's" by re-introducing those special assumptions that Keynes felt were the burden of economists to prove factually. That literally dozens of mechanistic models have been inspired by the "Keynesian revolution" is an expression of this metamorphosis of Keynes' standpoint.

9. Keynes, "The General Theory of Employment."
10. This split, of course, parallels the one between Benthamism and modern psychology. Only the former is dogmatic.

It is a gross misunderstanding of the nature of both classical and Keynesian economics to assert that "in sinking its foundation deeper in the world of experience than does the Keynesian analysis, the traditional theory is able to use a smaller number of separate assumptions and thus to achieve a more integrated system of conclusions."[11] Classical economics did achieve the goal attributed to it by Leontief, not because it was grounded on the facts of experience, but rather because it avoided them. The whole corpus of classical thought is held together by the classicist's ego, not by facts. It and the logic of intellectual mechanistic thought created an integrated, if unreal, system of relations.

In his 1937 article Keynes does not answer the criticism of details set forth by the four economists in the *Quarterly Journal.* He rather uses his space to emphasize matters of methodological approach.[12] Thus he proves that our interpretation is the correct one: to wit, that *he* considered the originality of his work was in the method, in the world view implicit in *The General Theory* and not in any particular "tools" he forged. He himself describes this world view: "We have, as a rule, only the vaguest idea of any but the most direct consequences of our acts."[13] A dispassionate analysis of the past reveals that the objective world holds no promise of certainty. The unique assumption of classical economics, he goes on to say, is that "at any given time facts and expectations were assumed to be given in a definite and calculable form; and risks, of which, though admitted, not much notice was taken, were supposed to be capable of an exact actuarial computation. The calculus of probabilities, though mention of it was kept in the background, was supposed to be capable of reducing uncertainty to the same calculable status as that of certainty itself; just as in the Benthamite calculus of pains and pleasures or of advantage and disadvantage, by which the Benthamite philosophy assumed men to be influenced in their general ethical behaviour."[14] Such a well-ordered, clock-like universe is not within man's reach—for which we must be grateful.

Keynes, for whom "the study of the history of opinion [was] a

11. Vassily Leontief, "Postulates: Keynes' General Theory and the Classicists," in *The New Economics: Keynes' Influence on Theory and Public Policy,* ed. S. E. Harris, p. 234.
12. "The General Theory of Employment," pp. 211–12.
13. Ibid., p. 213.
14. Ibid., pp. 212–13.

necessary preliminary to the emancipation of the mind,"[15] knew that man behaves the way he does not because he has god-like knowledge but because he must. A vast part of his decisions as an economic agent or a social being is taken in an environment of uncertainty. And, as if to avoid misunderstanding, Keynes repeats that by " 'certain knowledge' . . . I do not mean merely to distinguish what is known for certain from what is only probable. The game of roulette is not subject, in this sense, to uncertainty; nor is the prospect of a Victory bond being drawn. Or, again, the expectation of life is only slightly uncertain. Even the weather is only moderately uncertain. The sense in which I use the term is that in which the prospect of a European war is uncertain [in 1937!], or the price of copper and the rate of interest twenty years hence, or the obsolescence of a new invention, or the position of private wealthowners in the social system of 1970. About these matters there is no scientific basis on which to form any capable probability whatever. We simply do not know."[16]

One can hardly ask for greater clarity. While the prospect of a man of a certain age dying within a certain number of years is calculable, the possibility of a revolution occurring is not amenable to scientific analysis. Maybe Bergson's intuition would help. But certainly not the Benthamite calculus. Keynes' original work on probability under the guidance of Russell and Whitehead bore fruits and affected his economic thinking. But above all, we think, Keynes was so often wrong in his economic and political forecasts that he had learned to be humble vis-à-vis reality. He knew, as peasants whose livelihood is in the grip of the vagaries of the weather know, that "man proposes and God disposes."

However, this perennial state of ignorance in which economic man lives does not paralyze him, Keynes continues. The necessity for action and for decision (the "animal drives") compel him as a practical being to act overlooking the "awful fact" of ignorance, and to behave as if he had gone through a sound Benthamite weighing of advantages and disadvantages.[17] If this were all, then classical economics would accurately portray economic life. Its own "as if" would coincide with the "as if" of life, of economic men's behavior. But Keynes' observations go further. Practical men, in their drive to

15. Keynes, *The End of Laissez Faire,* p. 16.
16. "The General Theory of Employment," pp. 213–14.
17. Ibid., p. 214.

act in the face of uncertainty, create, and adhere to, certain fictions which, though usually helpful in good times, often break down and accentuate crises. What fictions do businessmen rely on? First, there is the fiction that the present is a more reliable guide to the future than a candid examination of the past would suggest. Memories are short. Second, there is the fiction that the existing "state of opinion" correctly takes into account future changes (just as the current yield takes current opinion as to future risk into account). Third, there is the fiction that "others" are better informed than we, as individuals, are, so that we endeavor to follow their judgments and to behave "conventionally."[18]

Action and decisions based on such flimsy foundations are bound to be unstable in the extreme. The least social and political tremor leads to a "revision" of expectations by all parties. A distrust of the very fictions that supported action sets in. In time, a new "conventional" way of viewing the future sets in only to be destroyed by the next revision, and so on. It is the task of correct thinking to analyze both the fictions of men and their breakdowns, and this analyzing must be done continuously for the experience of the past is never exactly repeated. We see now the tremendous burden Keynes places on the true intellectual. He asks that he be historian, sociologist, psychologist, statistician, philosopher, and economic theorist all at the same time; to be an academician and a man of action; to read scholarly treatises and newspaper reports; above all, to have a world view and to be cognizant of the world views of bankers and of the general public for *they* make history. *Systematic* knowledge would hardly be possible if every thinker followed Keynes' prescriptions. That is why practical knowledge relies on genius *and* on the army of his followers who systematize his thoughts, "trading off" some of his commitment to the truth for some of *their* commitment to precision, symmetry, beauty, and manipulative ability.

Keynes calls the fictions upon which economic behavior is based "pretty, polite techniques made for a well-panelled Board Room and a nicely regulated market." They work when the social order moves with clock-like precision, that is when we do not need them! Scholars interested in understanding reality and possessed with a "candid knowledge of the past" should not be the slaves of

18. Ibid., p. 215.

fictions as practical men are.[19] For a century, however, classical economic theory has itself been "one of those pretty, polite techniques which tries to deal with the present by abstracting from the fact that we know very little about the future." Keynes seems to agree with Marx that the orthodox economist is a victim of "false consciousness." What is more, he agrees with the socialist philosopher that the source of this perverse thinking lies in their neglecting a "candid" examination of the past.

19. In defense of economists (and without laying claim to a wide knowledge of the literature of the other social sciences), we may add that we doubt very much that sociology and psychology have shown much interest in exploring the fictions supporting business life, or, for that matter, any other aspect of life.

Keynesian Economics

The same effort by which ideas are connected with ideas, causes the intuition which the ideas were storing up to vanish.

Bergson

W E SHOWED that Keynes regarded the originality of his work as the granting of a legitimate place within economic analysis to those elements of life which had previously been ignored because they eluded rationalistic modes of thought. In so doing, Keynes had to deny economics its century-old pride: clearness and certainty of conclusions. He effected within economics a major revolution paralleling the denigration of logical reasoning by nineteenth-century philosophers.

Keynes' metaphysics of chance, as we may call it, was inimical to everything economics had stood for since Ricardo: monism, clearness, beauty, symmetry, and certainty. And, in concentrating so single-mindedly on *understanding* economic life, Keynes' economics was not a tool fit to guide political action. The stress on the precariousness of expectations, on shifty psychological states, on the ease with which conventional views break down, warns the would-be manipulator of socioeconomic reality that the results of his actions might be catastrophic through the impact on business psychology, liquidity preferences, the stock market, and the marginal efficiency of capital. A world war, the social and economic upheavals of the 1920s and 1930s, the rise of communist and fascist governments in many European countries, and, not least, his personal involvement in the world of finance (where, at least once, he came close to bankruptcy) made Keynes skeptical of the customary ways of looking at reality. The experience of the 1930s cut the precarious thread that in 1919 still linked Keynes to his classical predecessors. It is generally recognized that Keynes denied that the economy has the capacity to "naturally" produce full employment and social optima.

In this respect his outlook is not different from Marx'. Where the two thinkers part company is in their approach to what "should" be done. Marx' thought was still tinged by at least one Enlightenment characteristic: he believed in the perfectibility of man. In some respects he was the precursor of many later intellectuals who trusted in the power of education to solve social ills. Given appropriate guidance and teaching, must not the working class understand what is wrong with society and act to redress these wrongs? Keynes was too fiercely independent a thinker to lean, psychologically, on any creed founded by others. And it must be acknowledged that the first third of the twentieth century is more notable for having destroyed old idols than for having created new ones. Neither the individual, nor the state, nor the masses came out of those decades very honorably. The open-minded observer could not possibly trust innate a priori goodness.

Thus, the same quality that allowed Keynes to look at reality with such keenness (i.e., his *un*philosophical bent) now stood in the way of his building a model or iron-clad system of relations. He had no philosophico-social a priori. He knew that the nineteenth century was right in criticizing systems as superficial since all systems are rooted on presuppositions that are not questioned. The system-builder refuses to think beyond a certain point, as Walter Kaufmann put it in his rendition of Nietzsche's critique of conventional philosophy.[1] Keynes went beyond the traditional starting points of orthodox economics. He rejected the homogeneity postulate, questioned deductive modes of thought and mathematical models, had little use for the law of diminishing returns, exposed the implicit fictions of stability, perfect knowledge, etc., on which classical theory had been erected. He did all this *without* settling

1. See above, chap. 8.

down to one methodological standpoint: he emphasized the value of observation *and* of deduction, he used the principles of homogeneity *and* of diversification, he exposed false analogies *and* himself relied on analogical thinking. He looked "now out of this window, now out of that" and refused to adhere consistently to one methodology. He thus cut himself off from the very possibility of presenting a new model or system. His critical outlook prevented him from starting from a set of unquestioned assumptions. *His tone is not axiomatic but dialectical, like Socrates'.* He did not create an engine of analysis that would give a blind answer to every question but tried to inculcate into the economist a *habit of mind*: the habit of questioning that which is universally accepted.

These same reasons that made Keynes fail as a model-builder also stood in the way of his giving policy suggestions. An accurate and unbiased reading of *The General Theory* reveals this work to contain no radical proposals, no panaceas. Where the classicists called for the breaking up of large corporations to enforce a competitive market, Keynes limits himself to suggesting that interest rates be kept at a low level, something he rightly viewed as the continuation of what had been occurring for a long time. Whenever Keynes refers to deficit spending, he scorns it as "wasteful";[2] pyramid and cathedral building, digging holes in the ground in search of gold, producing to destroy as in wartime are the examples he gives. Why did an obviously humane person like Keynes shy away from making policy recommendations? The answer is implicit in our assessment of the spirit animating Keynes. We asserted that Keynes viewed his theory as approximating reality with its complications, paradoxes, unexpected turns, complex economic and social interrelations, only the surface of which the human intellect can scratch. It follows that vis-à-vis reality Keynes must have felt like an intelligent psychiatrist dealing with a psychopath: he knows that there is no way of being certain how the patient will react to his ministrations and is therefore happy enough to leave him alone, trying to eliminate only the most obvious sources of annoyance (in an economic context, the actions of statesmen brought up on the principles of classical economics).[3] But there is another reason for

2. The quotation marks are Keynes'. Was he thinking, perhaps, that some of these "wasteful" expenditures (the Pharaohs', popes', and Medicis' grandeur) produced something of which men can be more proud than of all the economic writings from Smith onward?

3. *The General Theory*, p. 129.

Keynes' shyness. He knew that occupying men "by building them houses to live in"[4] is preferable to keeping them busy goose-stepping or hurling grenades at each other. But he also knew that economics by itself can do little to implement such rational ideas. Isn't it unrealistic and conceited to expect economic theory to succeed where Christianity and natural law philosophers have failed?

We have repeatedly asserted that ideas are navigational charts assisting man's voyage. We do not demand that they reflect accurately the configuration of the whole region. We only want to see clearly and unequivocally outlined routes. Keynes gave mankind a rather confused map: paths crisscross in labyrinthine fashion. The very boundary between terra firma and quicksands is not clearly marked. To change the metaphor, Keynes' book can be compared to those early charts of the interior of Africa adorned with the warning "*Hic sunt leones.*" It does not help anybody but the man who is committed to truth at all costs and who is not afraid to face it to know that economic and social life is full of pitfalls and "slips between the cup and the lip." Neither is it encouraging to be told that economic theory as such can do little to restore sanity to the world. More positive creeds are necessary to support life, and especially politics, the essence of which is action.

The deep-rooted esthetic and political cravings of economics would have sufficed to convert Keynes' thought into a model helping statecraft. The soil on which *The General Theory* fell accelerated this process of "rationalization." For by the middle of the century American pragmatism had ceased to be an academic philosophy, and, duly simplified, acquired the status of an unofficial state philosophy. Presently, popular pragmatism breathed its activistic spirit on Keynes' economics quickly transforming it into Keynesian economics. About the pragmatic outlook, one may say what Keynes said of Ricardian economics: it conquered America as completely as the Holy Inquisition conquered Spain. Lloyd Morris thus describes the pervasiveness of pragmatism: "By the midnineteen forties, pragmatism had touched the lives of two generations of Americans. Perhaps never before had a philosophy been applied so hopefully, over so wide an area, to shape the minds of youth to the uses of a greater freedom. If social power and insight

4. Ibid., p. 131.

were developed in the young, must not society eventually be perfected? Whether or not they knew it, most Americans born in the twentieth century played some part in this experiment. For it had taken place in the most universal of their institutions. In less than fifty years, pragmatism had transformed the American school."[5]

We now understand the reason for a certain occurrence to which many Keynesians have called attention, the fact that *The General Theory*, although it caught everyone by surprise, soon came to be accepted by the relatively young economists while those beyond the age of fifty rejected it.[6] The common interpretation is gerontological: it suggests that one cannot learn past the age of thirty-five. The true reason is that the young economists had gone through the "pragmatic experiment" in the schools and had imbibed its activistic philosophy, while the older ones (many, perhaps most, the product of European schooling) had been brought up under the now antiquated spirit derided as "ivory tower" intellectualism— the spirit admirably expressed by Professor Foxwell's letter to John Neville Keynes. But before the "young" could embrace Keynes, his mature world view had to be rejuvenated. In particular, *he had to be shown to have a model that could be used for purposes of social and economic reconstruction.* The process of "rationalizing" Keynes began. In describing this process, we will be dealing with well-known aspects of contemporary economic thought. We shall, therefore, be very brief.

1. To Keynes, investment was the *causa causans* of economic change. He never tired of stressing the utter fickleness of the bases on which decisions to invest are taken. Movements along the investment line shrink into insignificance in the face of sudden and unexpected shifts. A functional relation based on the ceteris paribus assumption is absurd. Instinctively, the economic mind passed to the counterattack and carried the day by divorcing investment decisions from their flimsy psychological underpinning and by rooting them again on physical concepts amenable to being expressed in Benthamite, calculable form. Ignorance, blind faith, hope, and a touch of megalomania were replaced by income (or sales) as the main element determining investment. The accelerator—as this principle came to be called—is one of the most stringent mecha-

5. *Postscript to Yesterday,* pp. 368–69.
6. Paul A. Samuelson, "The General Theory," in *The New Economics: Keynes' Influence on Theory and Public Policy,* ed. S. E. Harris, p. 146.

nistic relations ever to enter macroeconomics. The marginal capital/ output ratio is a fiction in the best hyperclassical tradition. It goes a long way toward clamping on the mind those manacles that Keynes had broken.

2. Appropriate surgery, as indicated in the preceding chapter, divorced consumption from the stock market, its windfall effects, and its "whirlpool of expectations." Consumption was turned into a pillar of stability, hailed as the "heart of the Keynesian system," and, aptly enough, compared to Marshall's demand. Following its own momentum, however, the rationalistic mind ended by destroying all appearance of stability by its discovery of so many variables theoretically affecting consumption that one must conclude that there is no such thing as *a* consumption function. There are merely fictive hypotheses all fighting against one another in the market-place of scholarship. *Practical* economic suggestions, of course, do find their way through the scholarly maze by returning to the simple-minded, sophomoric conception of $C = f(Y)$. Top-heavy with variables, the academic consumption function is useless; too mechanical, the practical one is useless. Throughout the 1960s consumption has behaved erratically, thus foiling the calculations of government economists. Keynes took into account the unpredictable element in the relation of consumption to disposable income when he warned that for short-period income changes, the impact falls on savings.[7] And his frequent qualifications (e.g., "if there is no change in the propensity to consume"[8]) suggest that he was skeptical about the elsewhere trumpeted "fundamental law of human nature." Unconsciously referring to their own recasting of Keynes' economics and somewhat disappointed by events, the Keynesians often lament that "Keynes' relationships are less constant than he cared to admit." The only cure for such interpretations is a rereading of *The General Theory*.

3. A large portion of post-Keynesian literature addresses itself to the question of whether Keynes "proved" the possibility of under-employment equilibrium in a system of price-wage flexibility. We know this to be beside the point, for Keynes limited himself to proving the inherent *instability* of the system. Equilibrium he viewed as a fiction. But the historic standpoint of the ideal could not do without this will-o'-the-wisp. Having deprived Keynes' work

7. *The General Theory*, p. 97.
8. Ibid., p. 30.

of its life, it reduced it to a mere skeleton and rediscovered in its middle a throbbing heart: the equilibrium concept. Once Keynes' thought was uprooted from its natural humus of existence, it was easy to reread classical theory into it. The many loose ends that in *The General Theory* simply reflect the doubts of an honest and imaginative scholar groping through life were neatly sewn together. Relations were frozen in a graph and the hypothetical method ("let us assume . . .") could start again on new raw material. Existential time and stop-watch time disappeared altogether. Naturally, it is generally held that Keynes did not prove the possibility of under-employment equilibrium persisting forever (whatever that may mean). Apparently, however, most economists, motivated by prag-matic considerations, eventually came to regard this issue as a "purely scholastic" one which should not be allowed to influence policy recommendations. Thus the old dichotomy between the theoretical and the practical reappeared.

4. While some economists were thus busy re-interpreting Keynes' comments in the light of classical method, others were bent on showing that the classicists, too, possessed the very notions that Keynes had alleged to have discovered. Keynes' true discovery— the weakness of the rationalistic calculus—having gone unobserved, this exercise consisted of a comparison of Keynesian and classical "tools" of analysis. Viner found a liquidity preference in the classical treatment of the velocity of circulation of money,[9] although this opinion is contradicted by others who assert that in classical thought "hoards" were considered to be unresponsive to the rate of interest. D. G. Chapernowne "reconciled" Keynes' and the classical theory of wages,[10] while others emphasized that nobody "really" believed in Say's Law (which, from the point of view of *practice*, is true enough).

5. The addition of real wealth to Keynes' savings also became a useful device to restore full employment equilibrium. That it is a fiction is betrayed by the fact that the conception of savings on which Pigou relied to uphold equilibrium (savings as a "desire for possessions as such, conformity to tradition or custom and so on"[11]) is thoroughly unclassical: an *unthinking* "desire for possession as

9. "Mr. Keynes on the Causes of Unemployment," p. 152.

10. "Unemployment, Basic and Monetary: The Classical Analysis and the Keynesian."

11. "The Classical Stationary State," p. 346.

such" is the negation of rational conduct. It more accurately reflects the way Marx' capitalist behaves.

6. The re-emergence of equilibrium in macroeconomics has been accompanied by the usual split between real and monetary economics, the former neatly portrayed by the *I-S* relationship, the latter by the *L-M* curve. Just as it was once customary to deal first with the theory of value and then superimpose on it a money economy that conformed to the methodology and discoveries of real economics, so now money relations are eventually added to the real demand/supply aggregates, their effects and influences being rigidly circumscribed by the equilibrium conclusions of the real variables.

Having eliminated ignorance, expectation, considerations of social psychology, etc., and having re-enthroned Bentham, aggregate demand became a relatively stable function. A definite marginal propensity to consume follows automatically and yields a definite multiplier. That this mechanical multiplier is fictional is suggested by the paradoxical conclusions to which it leads. For instance, in its balanced-budget version, it suggests that an increase in taxes and government spending by equal amounts will lead to an increase in national product by that amount. If reality behaved in this fashion, treasury heads would lose their jobs and all economic problems would fade away. For out of the now higher national income, taxes and government spending could again increase, causing incomes to increase, and so on forever. Somewhere Kierkegaard remarks that a sense of humor and a dose of ataraxia are necessary to any scholar approaching Hegel. The same quality is of great help to an individual approaching many economic theorems.

Since savings is generally portrayed as related to both income and rate of interest, formal elegance suggests that investment be so related also. The accelerator hypothesis rides on this analogical attraction. But here mathematics plays one of its usual tricks: stable equilibrium demands that the savings function be more responsive than the investment function to income changes. Now, this mathematical condition seems to contradict the usual assertion that dS/dY has a low statistical value, while responsiveness of investment to income (the marginal K/O ratio) is normally given as high.

7. That interest is due to a desire for liquidity emanating from men's realization of how precarious their expectations are was found to be too radical a break from classical rationalism. Post-Keynesian economics re-introduced the "real" traditional factors of

productivity and thrift. As Modigliani pointed out, both real and monetary factors determine the level of interest.[12] The old dichotomy of "real" and monetary economics again reappeared. In interest rate theory, other attempts at "reconciliation" have been tried: they created the incredible complexities of the loanable fund theories, largely due to ignoring time because it cannot too well be squeezed into a Cartesian graph. Neither has the econometric approach been more promising. In one such study, Bronfenbrenner and Mayer confessed that they knew not whether they were measuring the demand or the supply of money or a "hybrid monstrosity."[13] Some textbook writers are not so guarded: they plot historical liquid holdings against the rate of interest only, thus reading into reality the ceteris paribus assumption of their minds.[14]

8. Emphasis on the "real" factors of aggregate supply and demand justifies Friedman's characterization of the Keynesian system as one in which "money does not count." But those who recall Keynes' emphasis on money as the asset that "lulls" that disquietude about the future that is the fundamental fact of life will regard Friedman's assertion as absurd. And yet once disquietude, fears, ignorance, doubts, etc., are emasculated from *The General Theory*, it is not false to assert that money is an irrelevant appendage, insofar as the "model" is concerned. On the contrary such a conclusion is the necessary consequence of the reading of "real" economics into *The General Theory*.

Keynes' own treatment of financial assets is itself an oversimplification. Money competes with a wide range of ever changing financial and tangible assets to "lull" our disquietude. The way to come closer to the truth is certainly not by emphasizing a stable velocity of circulation of money—as in the modern quantity theory. This theory has recently gained more acceptance not because of any positive merits of its own, but because the stability of the multiplier has proven to be a delusion. The mechanistic multiplier was buffeted by reality. Reason abandoned it and returned to another mechanistic principle—the one proposed by Locke and Hume.

9. The idealistic habit of classifying interrelated things in neat, mutually exclusive categories led to a clear-cut split between aggregate demand and aggregate supply, the former the active, the latter

12. "Liquidity Preference and the Theory of Interest and Money."
13. "Liquidity Functions in the American Economy."
14. Joseph P. McKenna, *Aggregate Economic Analysis*, p. 168, fig. 10:4.

the passive element in the equation.[15] This concept is responsible for a large portion of the inept policies being pursued in times of inflation. These policies are based on the delusion that they affect demand *only* and thus bring about a reduction in prices. If the aggregate demand/aggregate supply relation were understood for what it is (a subjective mode of ordering reality but in no way portraying it), it would be clear that anti-inflationary policies affect negatively both the demand *and* the supply of goods, with the result that the price level need not fall at all (although production, and hence employment, *must* fall). Why should the price of houses fall if anti-inflation policies cut their supply? And why should the price of industrial goods be reduced if capacity creation (the precondition for an output increase) is discouraged? In part 1 of orthodox textbooks (microeconomics) we teach that when both demand and supply fall the price outcome is indeterminate. In part 2, under the spur of the need for action, we forget these well-known lessons. Once again we live on two sides of the moon, as Keynes noted.

It may well be that the conventional anti-inflationary policies, *thought* to affect demand, actually accomplish whatever they accomplish by lessening the pressure of labor costs on profits and by teaching the workers the "discipline of unemployment." If this is so, we must conclude that, from a political and social point of view, Keynesian economics has added nothing to what was practiced a century ago.

10. Paralleling the translation of Keynes' thought into more familiar language and ways of thinking, there has occurred a denigration of the man's intellectual powers. Paul Samuelson remarked that "until the appearance of the mathematical models of Meade, Lange, Hicks, and Harrod, there is reason to believe that Keynes himself did not truly understand his own analysis"![16] He finds Keynes guilty of the theorist's ultimate sin: Keynes was "fuzzy on one important analytical matter through all his days: the relationship between 'identity' and functional (or equilibrium-schedule) equality; between 'virtual' and observable movements; between causality and concomitance; between tautology and hypothesis."[17] It seems

15. The passivity of supply clashes with the elsewhere much trumpeted "technology" (which in itself is but an empty word).

16. Samuelson, in *The New Economics*, p. 146.

17. Ibid., p. 156.

unlikely that Keynes would have received a doctorate under the direction of Russell and Whitehead with a study on probability characterized by such "fuzziness." Russell, incidentally, seems to disagree with Samuelson's opinion of Keynes. He judged Keynes' intellect to have been "the sharpest and clearest" that he ever came into contact with in his long life. "When I argued with him I felt that I took my life in my hands, and I seldom emerged without feeling something like a fool."[18]

And yet, *from the standpoint of economic classicism,* Samuelson's criticism is not wholly unjustified. Keynes *is* haphazard on these mathematical points in *The General Theory.* The reason is that, like his mentors Russell and Whitehead, he felt mathematics to be logical relations about nothing. Those who assume that mathematics correctly portrays social facts Keynes compared to Euclidean geometers in a non-Euclidean world, forever doomed to rebuke parallel lines for not keeping equidistant to each other.

It happened to Keynes what happened to Marx—what nearly always happens to genius. Marx' philosophy of history is an analysis of the *reciprocal* relation of material factors and of man's thoughts. The exigencies of political propaganda and agitation and the intellectual caliber of many of Marx' admirers have converted his theory into a grotesque, mechanistic cause-and-effect relation between the desire for wealth and everything that occurs in history. Many "Marxist" arguments are no better than the statement that the tradition of Halloween stems from a vast conspiracy of candy-makers. Gone from Marxism is its empiricism and its ethics.

The same transformation has fallen on Keynes' economics. His inductive and imaginative method was frozen into dogmatic, a priori "propensities," the new intellectual Pillars of Hercules beyond which the mind does not inquire. And just as "Marxism" has become a tool in the service of amoral and immoral causes, so Keynesian economics is indiscriminately placed in the service of the Great Society and in that of realpolitik. Keynes was an imaginative artist. Keynesian economics is a more or less involved tautology. In its simplest presentation, the statement $Y = C + I + G$ (on the basis of which policy decisions are taken) is no better than Hume's direct and proportionate relation between money stocks and prices.

Keynesian economics has, on the surface, been rendered more powerful by its conquest of governmental statistics bureaus. For

18. *The Autobiography of Bertrand Russell,* 1:97.

the first time in the history of economics, the practical (statistical) categories through which we claim to understand the economic world have been framed in accordance with the underlying (macro-) economic theory. But just as the first part of the twentieth century (or whatever portion of it was not dominated by a war) refused to be straitjacketed by the classical world view, so our own decade refuses to be straitjacketed by either Keynesian theory or by the (statistical) social accounts. That these accounts are actually anti-social in their capacity to hide the truth and to encourage thought-less policies (e.g., growth at all costs) has recently been recognized. Less understood is the fact that macroeconomic theory (the alleged underpinning of the accounts) has actually contributed nothing to the attainment of even the traditional economic goals. *Indeed, recent economic policies are not supported by any analytical backbone—they do not draw their sustenance and justification from economic theory: on the contrary, they spell the death of economic theory.*

Let us review the traditional economic problems as detected by economists and politicians during the past decade. First, there has been the unemployment problem. It has been tackled by using certain corporations as the government's proxy-employers. The state manufactures money which it then distributes to select corporations. The latter, to supply the government with goods nobody else can, or wants to, buy, will employ people. In Elizabethan times things were more direct and thus more intelligible. Then the government simply put the unemployed to work in its own workhouses. After the phase of liberalism, the workhouses have naturally fallen into private hands.[19]

Second, there has been the problem of inflation. The traditional way to cope with this problem (a way that does rest on economic theory, albeit of a very old ancestry), that is, through monetary manipulations, has fallen into disrepute. Not even the Governor of the Federal Reserve System believes in it any longer. Since his appointment in 1970, Arthur Burns has been one of the most ardent advocates of wage-price controls. The experience of the past decade shows that traditional monetary policy (and hence theory) takes back seat to the setting up of wage-price guidelines and/or controls;

19. There *are* differences between Lockheed and a workhouse. But they are sociological, psychological, and technological in nature. They perform the same economic function and are backed by the same economic theory.

to the unleashing of the Anti-Trust Division of the Department of Justice on large corporations guilty of prices increases; to the selling of government stocks to force a price "rollback"; to more or less overt executive pressures on unions and corporations. The most important of these tools—wage-price controls—existed in Elizabethan times. None of the others rest on a foundation of economic theory. Indeed Keynesian theory ignores the link between wages and prices!

Third, there has been the balance of payments deficit. It has been attacked by a motley of ad hoc devices such as making it more difficult for financial corporations to exercise their rights to invest in foreign countries; raising tariffs and setting import quotas; legislative concoctions that artificially "equalize" American and foreign interest rates; applying political pressures on a country to induce it to hold on to its dollar stock indefinitely; forcing the recipients of United States loans, assistance programs, etc., to buy American products; by stopping convertibility of dollars into gold, first in regard to dollar stocks held by private institutions (which, ipso facto, are labeled "speculators"), and then in regard to dollars held by foreign governments.

Economic historians teach that most of these policy tools were common in prescientific (Mercantilist) days. From time to time they have been pursued by countries where the Smith-Keynes tradition never took hold, for instance, by fascist countries.

The common characteristic of the above policies is that they work by *legal* (realistic political analysts might even say, illegal[20]) fiat. They do not rest on any economic analysis whatever. They do not exploit "laws of behavior." No intellectual effort is necessary to come up with these devices. Certainly the efforts of geniuses like Smith, J. S. Mill, Marshall, and Keynes have nothing to do with them. These devices act *directly* on the presumed problem by cajoling or intimidating the "wrongdoer." They represent the destruction of that kingdom of "forces" that, throughout its long history, economics has so laboriously built up. They rest on a "kingdom of personalities" (just as Mercantilist policies did) and on a basis of political power.

---

20. The suspension of convertibility, for instance, is a breach of promise. It ultimately rests on political sovereignty and military might. It can be compared to the repudiation of public indebtedness. Not the least victim of "modern economics" is that sanctity of contracts that the *philosophes* had discovered.

And yet the conclusion that Keynesian economic theory has little to do with guiding practical policies will not come as a surprise to our reader. We have documented how economic thinking fell under the sway of an epistemology that scorned empiricism, observation, and facts. The umbilical cord which connected the original economic investigations to the world of practice was later cut. Certainly by Walras' time nothing was left of Adam Smith's tenuous empiricism. By Robbins' time a concern with social ends disappeared. Keynes was unable to reverse the tide. On the contrary, with Friedman, the inherent right of each economist to draw from his consciousness whatever "hypotheses" he wishes was reaffirmed.

"Tragedy," Herbert Spencer noted, "is a deduction killed by a fact." The unexpected fact of the Great Depression buried the beautiful deductive scheme of classical economics. Today's many economic problems are making the *IS-LM* deductive symmetry more and more obsolete. One can only hope that facts will be kinder to us than they were to our fathers in the 1930s.

15

The Logic of Cartesianism

*We can prove geometry because we make it; to
prove the physical we would have to make it.*

Vico

THREE TYPES of economic theory have been the subject of this
essay: those of the "orthodox" school,[1] of Marx, and of Keynes. The
style and substance of each theory was found to be influenced by
the view it had of the relation between thinking and being. If
Ricardo conquered England as thoroughly as the Holy Inquisition
conquered Spain (as Keynes says), it is because Ricardo's method
of analysis was the expression of, and harmonized well with, the
intellectual "climate of opinion" formed by Cartesianism. If Marx
succeeded in acknowledging the power both of ideas and of the
material environment as factors shaping history, it is because he
was influenced by Hegel's epistemological reconciliation of subject
and object. And if Keynes reacted against the "easy logic" of his
classical predecessors ("founded on assumptions inappropriate to
the facts"), it is because he carried out in economics the "revolt
against formalism" of the late nineteenth and early twentieth centuries. Although Keynes, unlike Marx, never contributed anything
to epistemology, he had an epistemology just as surely as the

1. In the "orthodox" school we are including what we called classical,
hyperclassical, and Keynesian (but not Keynes') theory.

Bourgeois Gentilhomme has a prose. His is the epistemology of the hurried businessman who never loses himself in the man-made logical conundrum of appearance and reality because he is too much a part of the world.

The economic thinking of orthodox economists, of Marx, and of Keynes represents the epistemological descent of the ego from stillness and peace to the confusion and complexity of the world of reality. What was gained in this descent is a superior understanding of the world. What was lost is the feeling of certainty that prevails in the realm of logical concepts and their derivations. Classical economic thought derived from classical philosophy (in its Cartesian tradition) a static concept of being and, accordingly, viewed reality as unchanging. Although cut off from the richness and ever changing nature of human experience, classical theory was able to "keep itself going" for two centuries because of the resourcefulness of the mind. Cartesianism, perhaps despite its original intentions, came to equate intelligence with ingenuity. It contrived purely abstract and even paradoxical problems whose solutions, while demanding much ingenuity, also created more problems which, in turn, provided further "food for thought." While all the time claiming to explore the ingenuity of economic life and of economic arrangements, classical thought explored instead the ingenuity of the mind. Von Mises, Robbins, Machlup, Friedman, and a few other classical writers came close to recognizing the psychic nature of economic theory but, lacking an appreciation of the historico-philosophic seventeenth-century background and of the "technology of the mind," fell short of detecting the origins and dynamics of economic theory. Both shortcomings of economic theorists were themselves by-products of the Cartesian outlook, which does not inculcate a "historical sense" and stresses the "logic" of thinking, ignoring what may be called its "pathology." Thanks to the work of philosophers like those surveyed in chapters 3 and 11, we now know that thought often advances *despite* logical rules rather than because of them. This is natural since logic is largely negativistic: it sets up warning signs along the reasoning path for which ingenuity has little use. Ingenuity "makes all the haste it can," as Locke said and as Kant and Bentham also recognized. The same mind that sets up rules then disposes of them if they prove to be stumbling blocks to further intellectual adventures. Fictions are the main tool of the ego to break the narrow confines of logic. They may be of an analogical, heuristic, ethical, poetic, practical, rhetorical, schematic, or mathematical nature. All of them are subjective, owing their existence to the ego rather than to objective reality.

Fictions may perhaps be compared to money. Both fictions and money evolve from simplicity toward greater and greater complexity. At an advanced stage, both are imaginary, representing nothing but themselves (modern money is a mere accounting entry). Modern money liberates great economic forces. Fictions liberate thought from the dictatorship of the given. But, just as our sophisticated money makes possible specious transactions ("financial swindles") sometimes leading to economic collapse, so do fictions often create mere intellectual make-believe, occasionally causing much hardship.

Paralleling the descent of the ego from the "logical" and eternal world of Ricardo to the historical and immanent worlds of Marx and Keynes is a movement away from intellectual ingenuity toward keenness of observation. Classical writings gave us the "autobiography of the mind." Marx and Keynes came close to giving us a biography of social life. As is customary with thinkers who find themselves in opposition to the intellectual status quo, both Marx and Keynes explore the workings of the mind itself—a subject which the ego, despite its constant use of the word "introspection," regarded "off limits." Marx' concept of "false consciousness" is in the critical tradition of Kant, Bentham, and Nietzsche, as also are the innumerable Keynesian criticisms of classical thinking. Marx' and Keynes' forays into the mechanics of thinking have been mistaken for "rudeness" (explainable in the socialist leader but unpardonable in a "Cambridge man"). They are, instead, the beginnings of an analysis of the dynamics of thought which is itself an important but neglected aspect of *life*. Both writers had no doubt that rationalism is irrational: its playthings are unreal. They regarded it their task to examine the extralogical faculties of the mind. Because of their critical standpoint, they effected in economics a reversal familiar to students of philosophy: the reversal from an idealistic to a broadly materialistic and empirical standpoint. Methodologically, Keynes lies *to the left of Marx*; witness the fact that the socialist thinker makes use of at least one fiction (an ethical one of great value in motivating action), viz., the fiction of communism, which Marx carefully placed in an abstract future. Also, Marx' theory is broadly evolutionary. Sufficiently emasculated, Marx' ideas stress laws which, once discovered, are as eternal as the

laws of classical thought. Keynes' reality instead is chaotic. The
Keynesian viewpoint would force every generation to refashion new
categories more in harmony with the facts. This is the inevitable
result of bridging the gap between appearance and reality. When
reality is made up of *intellectual* categories, these categories are
beyond history and hence may be serviceable for a long time. But
when reality is made up of actual human relations and arrangements, then the investigator must create new modes of thought to
"keep up" with the blossoming of historical facts. The Keynesian
standpoint takes the fun out of thinking. It is no wonder that post-
Keynesian economics found a way out of the painful prospect of
forever chasing an elusive reality. It did so by translating Keynes'
work into familiar symbols of mechanistic and mathematical relations on whose bases it then founded a "school of *thought*."

Actually, this transformation is not wholly caused by a desire
to escape from this Sisyphean task. Neither does the tendency of
means to overtake ends tell the whole story. The fact is that, at
bottom, the transformation of Keynes' economics into Keynesian
economics is caused by *the very logic of Cartesianism*. Since this
transformation is of some importance for the future of economics
and, possibly, for that of man himself, we should re-consider it.

As we saw, the prime mover of Cartesianism was doubt and a skeptical attitude toward observation as a means to discover truth.
Locke, Hume, and Adam Smith carried this skepticism into economics and Ricardo securely established a priori reasoning. With
this step, theorizing was anchored to the nature of the rationalistic
thought process rather than to the flux of an evolving society. The
severing of the link between matter and mind was, paradoxically,
accompanied by a reversal of the medieval hierarchy that placed
contemplative life (thinking) above active life. That is, thinking
became the ancilla of doing (acting, fabricating), even as philosophy had been the ancilla of theology in the previous age.
"*Reckoning with consequences*" (Hobbes) was the goal of the
philosophes, a goal most obvious in their political writings.

The activistic Cartesian man slumbered in classical economics
which, after all, had a negative, "let things alone" political philosophy. It lurks, however, behind the hypostatizing of concepts. This
logical error shows that, although the link between reality and
thought was cut, that between thought and reality was never ab-

jured. Theory always desired to rejoin the world of actuality, a fact most obvious in welfare theory. No matter how unempirical the process of theory-*building*, no matter how infinitesimally small the role attributed to facts in *framing* a theory, thought always hoped for coincidence of its mental constructs with reality. Here a problem appears, for if theory proceeds in willful ignorance of facts, it is unlikely that a meaningful test will reveal much coincidence of ideas with reality. But modern social thought in general and economic thought in particular seem to have recently found a way out of the problem *by exploiting to the fullest the implications of the very epistemology that leads to the construction of an unreal world in the first place.*

It will be recalled that Descartes saw more or less clearly that certainty can be obtained only when we deal with that which man himself has made.[2] Man made mathematics, so mathematical theorems are knowable and certain. But this initial insight leads to another: if man can make society, then society, too, becomes intelligible. We understand that which we make and especially that which we make by applying mathematical formulae. If we could only refashion the world along mathematical lines, we would understand it too. This is the driving spirit behind the *reductio scientiae ad mathematicam. The logic of Cartesianism drives all thought* (and not simply physical thought) *toward fabricating a world in accordance with its own mathematical ideas of it.* This desire was obvious from the very beginning of Enlightened thought. This is why Enlightened philosophers constructed a mathematical ethics and attempted a mathematical science of politics. Marx, too, saw clearly that "men make their own history" but, being a good Hegelian, was wise enough to add that they do not make it fully in accordance with their own aspirations. In our own days the possibility of making society in accordance with our own ideas is much greater. In economics, this aspiration is the ultimate reason why a work of scholarship which makes no claim of manipulating society (*The General Theory*) was recast into a mechanistic, rigid model capable of directing society toward certain ends and therefore *capable of proving the truth-content of the model itself.*

Obviously, by themselves, the ideas of popular Keynesianism could not bring about this design. By coincidence, however, there

2. See chap. 2.

is a power which is interested in order and predictable "laws of behavior" just as much as the economist is. This power is the state. If men and classes behave predictably, the state can attain its goals (whatever they may be) far more easily. Thus the marriage between economic ideas and political power was consummated with the founding of the Council of Economic Advisers. No conspiracy, it must be emphasized, brought the state and the New Economics together. Rather the marriage was based on a natural "elective affinity" for both parties share a common love for order and predictable reactions. To the practical man, order means ease in attaining his goals. To the theorist, order means automatic confirmation of his theories. And confirmation, let us stress, is the final and only test of truth demanded by current economic methodology. Having started by experimenting with the mind, economic theory is now in the process of experimenting with society. The step is a natural one.

The handicaps under which the social scientist labors have frequently been noted. He has no laboratory; he himself is the subject of the investigation and may become the victim of his biases; his measuring tools are very rough or nonexistent. But the peculiar advantage of the social scientist is less often noted. *He can make his theories come true.* If the planet strays from the course charted by man, the astronomer cannot rebuke it and push it back into orbit. The only thing to do is to come up with new formulae that take into account the planet's behavior. But men are more pliable than planets, exactly because they are influenced by the social "laws" of the scientist and, above all, by the policies derived from these laws. Did William James not say that we make theories come true?

In recent years there has also been a rapprochement between economic theory and the corporation as more and more theorists work as consultants. Much of this work consists of inventing intellectual devices which the client finds useful in better controlling its environment. Again, the economic mind has recognized in the corporation a kindred spirit. It, too, is interested in predictable and quantifiable reactions of the groups facing it: competitors, consumers, labor, and public authority.[3] It is no accident that the

3. A history of business could be written from the standpoint of corporate desire for order. The rise of monopolies would thus be viewed as an attempt to eliminate unpredictable price responses of competitors; advertising as

classical premise of selfishness (profit motivation) has lately lost many adherents to the new-fangled view that growth is more important than money-making.[4]

The Cartesian standpoint, despite its stress on thinking, has actually displaced homo sapiens and elevated homo faber, man as a maker. Even man's conception of God changed after Descartes. From a benign, wise father, He became, in the similes of the age, a watch*maker*. Paralleling the emphasis on doing is the abandonment of the old questions "why" and the emergence of the new questions "how." How things work holds no mystery if we make them ourselves. In this making, machines are of great assistance. In fact, when intelligence is identified with "reckoning with consequences," modern computers have obvious advantages. They can answer the question "how" better than man can, although they know nothing about "why." Hence the pre-eminence of "research" aided by computers.

Lately, however, the hope to direct society with the help of the New Economics has received some setbacks. In the realm of practical policy, the income-expenditure model has had a rather ephemeral life, having been supplanted by the motley crowd of ad hoc policies surveyed in chapter 14. Homo faber, we may say, has thrown away his mask. He has prevailed so thoroughly over homo sapiens that he now feels he needs no blueprint, no model, no *thinking* to act.

There is irony in this shift of economic theory from thinking as such to thinking as an appendage of doing (post-Keynes macrotheory) and, recently, to doing without much theoretical thinking. For, as long as economic theory contained the germ of an ideal (the ideal of justice, in hyperclassical thought), economics kept itself aloof from the world of men. Now that this ideal has been pushed into the background by half a century of "positivism" and has not been replaced by any other, economics strives to remake society.

---

an attempt to eliminate the fickleness of consumer choice; coffee breaks and music-while-you-work as attempts to render labor more docile. The means whereby the corporation tries to thwart the regulations of public authority are too numerous to be outlined here.

4. This new hypothesis was first advanced by William Baumol, *Business Behavior, Value and Growth*. It is not clear why growth and profit-making are antithetical.

The preceding observations, dealing as they do with contemporary intellectual history, are tentative. They merely bring out the *logic* of Cartesianism and are supported by necessarily spotty evidence. In practice, the logic of the ego may be thwarted by many other trends in social thought and in material history. For instance, the intellectual, antiformalistic trend associated with European philosophical thought of the late nineteenth century is still operating in our time, and is apparently enjoying something of a revival in America; witness the interest not only in Marx but also in the Nietzsche-Sartre tradition. Witness also a heightened social awareness in the universality of fictions.[5]

The new "mood" of the times may well lead to a reconstruction of economics. This reconstruction might even come not by destroying but by *exploiting* the possibilities latent in its Cartesian antecedents. The stress on introspection, for instance, is valuable, provided that it leads to a return to Socrates' "Know thyself." The adoption of this standpoint can only lead to detecting fictions, thus placing them in the service of man. Existential introspection should also overthrow the Cartesian opposition of thought (all reason) and reality (mostly passion), for thought might eventually come to see itself as not so thoroughly "rational." This, of course, should bridge the Cartesian bifurcation of mind and matter, leading to a better understanding of the latter. Meaningful introspection should also cause an examination of the realities of the environment within which thinking takes place. It is a remarkable fact that we have many descriptions of the "idea of a university" but we know practically nothing of its reality and of its possible effects on thought itself.[6]

Just as a moderate shift in the standpoint of Cartesianism can contribute something toward this reconstruction of economics, so can a re-reading of Keynes and Marx. Keynes' commitment to un-

5. To be sure, it is largely practical fictions that are being recognized and exposed. That democracy entails *popular* will is shown daily to be an ideal rather than the reality it purports to be. That public officials are enlightened, that the judicial process brings about justice, that hard work leads, if not to wealth, at least to well-being, are all recognized as myths. Indeed, it may dismay the intelligent reader to be told that our age is one of transition and thus comparable to Descartes' age (every age has been called transitional and every age has been compared to some other age!).

6. The motto "publish or perish," for instance, may well put a premium on the fabrication of fictions. It certainly leads to that proliferation of models that Hahn, Leontief, and others decry (see chap. 1).

derstanding material, historical forces is in the best tradition of the intellect. The richness of his discoveries is the result of a more sympathetic view toward reality and its problems, which become the problems of the investigator who regards himself part of society. In addition, Keynes suggests that thought is most prolific of insights when it lives *at the periphery of many* disciplines rather than at the center of one: history (contemporary and past), statistics, sociology, psychology, politics, philosophy, as well as economics all contribute to alerting the mind to the multifarious manifestations of life. So, also, do the history of ideas and the daily newspaper. This eclecticism, although unfamiliar to the present organization of graduate studies, exists, after all, among the supposed objects of economic investigations: businessmen, consumers, public bodies are hardly mathematical geniuses. They take very few things as "given." A healthy skepticism for settled opinion is another legacy of Keynes, as also is a certain humbleness vis-à-vis reality.[7]

An understanding of Karl Marx cannot but strengthen this Keynesian legacy and add others just as valuable. First, an abiding commitment not only to the "pursuit of happiness" but to its actualization; second, a sense of continuity of past, present, and future.

A synthesis of the three types of economic thought reviewed here should loosen the grip of formalism and restore a balance between means and ends, the subject and the object, theory and history, knowledge and manipulation, the "how" and the "why," science and ethics. Nor is it unrealistic to expect such a synthesis, for it is a commonplace worth repeating that nothing is more likely to happen than that which is not expected.

7. A common theme of the late-nineteenth-century continental philosophers (especially of Bergson) is that the intellect should adopt an attitude of *humility* (not of dogmatism) vis-à-vis the ever changing forms of reality. We are gratified to see the emergence of this attitude in no less a scholar than Walter Heller, once an enthusiastic spokesman and propagandizer for the New Economics. In his opening remarks at the Allied Social Science Association meeting in New York City in December 1973, he said, "The energy crisis caught us with our parameters down. The food crisis caught us too. This was a year of infamy in inflation forecasting. *There are many things we really just don't know"* (emphasis added).

References

Philosophical Aspects of Social and Scientific Ideas

Arendt, Hannah. *The Human Condition.* Chicago, 1958.

Bacon, Sir Francis. *New Organon.* Edited by Joseph Dewey. New York, 1902.

———. *Of the Advancement of Learning.* Edited by Joseph Dewey. New York, 1902.

Balz, Albert George Adam. *Descartes and the Modern Mind.* New Haven, 1952.

Barker, Sir Ernest. *Social Contracts: Essays by Locke, Hume and Rousseau.* London, 1947.

Bergson, Henri. *Creative Evolution.* Translated by Arthur Mitchell. New York: Modern Library Edition, 1944.

———. *Time and Free Will. An Essay on the Immediate Data of Consciousness.* Translated by F. L. Pogson. London, 1959.

Berkeley, George. *A Treatise Concerning the Principles of Human Knowledge.* In *The Works of George Berkeley.* Oxford, 1873.

Boas, George. *The Inquiring Mind.* LaSalle, Ill., 1959.

Brinton, Crane. *Nietzsche.* Cambridge, Mass., 1941.

Burtt, Edwin Arthur. *The Metaphysical Foundations of Modern Physical Science.* London, 1932.

Butterfield, Herbert. *The Origins of Modern Science: 1300–1800.* London, 1950.

Cassirer, Ernst. *An Essay on Man: An Introduction to a Philosophy of Human Culture.* New Haven, 1944.

———. *The Philosophy of the Enlightenment.* Translated by Fritz C. A. Koellin and James P. Pettegrove. Princeton, 1951.

———. *The Problem of Knowledge: Philosophy, Science and History since Hegel.* Translated by William H. Woglom and Charles W. Hendel. New Haven, 1960.

Cohen, Morris R., and Nagel, Ernest. *An Introduction to Logic and Scientific Method.* New York, 1934.

Descartes, René. *The Philosophical Works of Descartes.* Translated by E. S. Haldane and G. R. T. Ross. Cambridge, Eng., 1911. (The major works included in this volume are *The Rules, The Discourse on Method, The Meditations,* part of *The Principles of Philosophy,* and *The Search after Truth.*)

Dewey, John. *Logic.* New York, 1938.

——. *The Quest for Certainty: A Study of the Relation of Knowledge and Action.* New York, 1929.

Diem, Hermann. *Kierkegaard: An Introduction.* Richmond, Va., 1966.

Eddington, Sir Arthur. *The Nature of the Physical World.* New York, 1928.

Frank, Philipp. *Einstein: His Life and Times.* New York, 1947.

——. *Modern Science and Its Philosophy.* Cambridge, Mass., 1949.

Hartland, E. Sidney. *Primitive Laws.* London, 1924.

Hegel, G. W. F. *The Logic of Hegel.* Translated by William Wallace. Oxford, 1892.

——. *The Phenomenology of Mind.* Translated by J. G. Baillie. London, 1931.

Hobbes, Thomas. *Concerning Body.* In *The Metaphysical System of Hobbes.* Chicago, 1948.

Hume, David. *An Abstract of a Treatise of Human Nature.* Cambridge, England, 1938.

——. *Philosophical Works.* Oxford, 1874–75. (Among other works, these volumes contain *A Treatise of Human Nature, An Inquiry Concerning Human Understanding,* and the *Essays: Literary, Moral and Political.*)

James, William. *Essays in Radical Empiricism: A Pluralistic Universe.* Gloucester, Mass., 1967.

——. *Pragmatism: A New Name for Some Old Ways of Thinking.* New York, 1908.

Jaspers, Karl. *Nietzsche: An Introduction to the Understanding of His Philosophical Activity.* Translated by Charles F. Wallraff and Frederick J. Schmitz. Tucson, Ariz., 1965.

——. *Three Essays: Leonardo, Descartes, Max Weber.* Translated by Ralph Mannheim. New York, 1964.

Jeans, Sir James. *The Mysterious Universe.* New York, 1931.

Joad, C. E. M. *Philosophical Aspects of Modern Science.* New York, 1932.

Kant, Immanuel. *Prolegomena to Any Future Metaphysics.* Edited into English by Paul Carns. Chicago, 1902.

Kant's Critical Philosophy for English Readers. Translated by John P. Mahaffy and John H. Bernard. London, 1889.

Kaufmann, Walter. *Existentialism from Dostoevsky to Sartre.* New York, 1956.

——. *Hegel: Reinterpretation, Texts and Commentary.* New York, 1965.

——. *Nietzsche: Philosopher, Psychologist, Antichrist.* Princeton, 1950.

Kierkegaard, Søren. *Kierkegaard's Concluding Unscientific Postscript.* Translated by David F. Swenson. Princeton, 1944.

——. *Søren Kierkegaard's Journals and Papers.* Vol. 1. Edited and translated by Howard V. and Edna H. Long. Bloomington, Ind., 1967.

A Kierkegaard Critique. Edited by Howard A. Johnson and Niels Thulstrup. New York, 1962.

Klemke, Elmer D. *The Epistemology of G. E. Moore.* Evanston, Ill., 1969.

Knight, Isabel F. *The Geometric Spirit: The Abbé de Condillac and the French Enlightenment.* New Haven, 1969.

Koyré, Alexandre. *From the Closed World to the Infinite Universe*. Baltimore, 1957.

Lange, Frederick Albert. *The History of Materialism*. New York, 1925.

Lenin, Vladimir Ilyich Ulyanov. *Materialism and Empirocriticism: Critical Observations on a Reactionary Philosophy*. New York, 1927.

Locke, John. *An Essay Concerning Human Understanding*. In *The Works of John Locke*. London, 1824.

Locke and Berkeley. A Collection of Critical Essays. Edited by C. B. Martin and D. M. Armstrong. Garden City, N.Y., 1968.

Lovejoy, Arthur O. *The Revolt Against Dualism: An Inquiry Concerning the Existence of Ideas*. LaSalle, Ill., 1955.

Löwith, Karl. *From Hegel to Nietzsche: The Revolution in Nineteenth-Century Thought*. Translated by David E. Green. New York, 1964.

Mill, John Stuart. *A System of Logic, Ratiocinative and Inductive*. New York, 1872.

Montesquieu. *The Spirit of Laws*. Translated by T. Nugent. New York, 1900.

Nagel, Ernest. *The Structure of Science: Problems in the Logic of Scientific Explanation*. New York, 1961.

Nietzsche, Friedrick. *The Philosophy of Nietzsche*. New York: Modern Library Edition, 1937. (Contains selections from *Zarathustra, Beyond Good and and Evil, The Genealogy of Morals*, and *The Birth of Tragedy*.)

Ogden, C. K. *Bentham's Theory of Fictions*. New York and London, 1932.

Pascal, Blaise. "The Difference between the Mathematical and the Intuitive Mind." In *Pensées*, translated by W. S. Trotter. New York, 1941.

Poulet, George. "The Dream of Descartes." In *Studies in Human Time*, translated by Elliot Coleman. Baltimore, 1956.

Pufendorf, Samuel. *Of the Law of Nature and of Nations*. Translated by Basil Kennett. 3d ed. London, 1717.

Reichenbach, Hans. *Experience and Prediction*. Chicago, 1938.

———. *The Rise of Scientific Philosophy*. Berkeley, 1951.

Russell, Bertrand. *Analysis of Matter*. Dover, 1954.

———. *Analysis of Mind*. London, 1921.

———. *Mysticism and Logic*. London, 1932.

Schopenhauer, Arthur. *The World as Will and Idea*. Translated by R. B. Haldane. London, 1957.

Smith, A. H. *Kantian Studies*. Oxford, 1947.

Smith, Adam. *The Early Writings of Adam Smith*. New York: Kelley, 1967.

———. *The Principles which Lead and Direct Philosophical Inquiries: Illustrated by the History of Astronomy*. Reprinted in *The Early Writings of Adam Smith*, edited by A. M. Kelley. New York, 1967.

Smith, Norman Kemp. *Prolegomena to an Idealist Theory of Knowledge*. London, 1924.

Spinoza, B. *A Theological-Political Treatise*. Edited and translated by A. G. Wernham. Oxford, 1958.

Stephen, Sir Leslie. *History of English Thought in the Eighteenth Century*. New York and Burlingame, 1962.

Strawson, P. F. *The Bounds of Sense: An Essay on Kant's Critique of Pure Reason*. London, 1966.

Vaihinger, H. *The Philosophy of "As If": A System of the Theoretical, Practical and Religious Fictions of Mankind*. Translated by C. K. Ogden. New York, 1935.

Veblen, Thorstein. *The Place of Science in Modern Civilization*. New York, 1919.

Versfeld, Marthinus. *An Essay on the Metaphysics of Descartes.* London, 1940.
Whitehead, Alfred North. *The Concept of Nature.* Ann Arbor, 1957.
————. *Science and the Modern World.* New York, 1928.
Willey, Basil. *The Seventeenth-Century Background: Studies in the Thought of the Age in Relation to Poetry and Religion.* New York, 1950.

Sociological and Political Aspects of Theories

Adams, E. D. *The Power of Ideals in American History.* New Haven, 1913.
Arendt, Hannah. *The Origins of Totalitarianism.* New York, 1966.
Arnold, Thurman W. *The Folklore of Capitalism.* New Haven, 1937.
————. *The Symbols of Government.* New Haven, 1935.
Bentham, Jeremy. *Deontology: Or, The Science of Morality.* London and Edinburgh, 1834.
————. *An Introduction to the Principles of Morals and Legislation.* Edited by J. H. Burns and H. L. A. Hart. London, 1970.
Bobbio, N. "Vilfredo Pareto's Sociology in His Letters to Maffeo Pantaleoni." *Banca Nazionale del Lavoro Quarterly Review* (September 1961):301, 308–9.
Bury, J. S. *The Idea of Progress.* London, 1920.
Cassirer, Ernst. *The Myth of the State.* London and New Haven, 1946.
————. *The Philosophy of the Enlightenment.* Translated by Fritz C. A. Koellin and James P. Pettegrove. Princeton, 1951.
Coker, F. W. *Readings in Political Philosophy.* New York, 1938.
Collingwood, R. G. *The Idea of History.* Oxford, 1946.
Greene, Murray. "Schumpeter's Imperialism—A Critical Note." *Social Research, an International Quarterly of Political and Social Science* (December 1952), pp. 453–63.
Hayek, Friedrich A. *Individualism and Economic Order.* Chicago, 1948.
Hayes, Carlton J. H. *A Generation of Materialism.* New York, 1941.
Hegel, G. W. F. *Philosophy of Right.* Translated by T. M. Knox. Oxford, 1953.
Mannheim, Karl. *Essays in the Sociology of Knowledge.* London, 1952.
————. *Ideology and Utopia: An Introduction to the Sociology of Knowledge.* Translated by Edward Shils. London, 1940.
Marx, Karl. *Economic and Philosophic Manuscripts of 1844.* Edited by Dirk J. Struick and translated by Martin Milligan. New York, 1964.
————. *The Poverty of Philosophy.* New York, 1963.
————, and Engels, Friedrick. *The German Ideology.* Edited by R. Pascal. New York, 1947.
————. *The Holy Family.* Facsimile edition. New York: International Publishers, 1953.
Meyerhoff, Hans, ed. *The Philosophy of History in Our Time.* Garden City, N.Y., 1959.
Monsen, R. J., Jr. *Modern American Capitalism. Ideologies and Issues.* Boston, 1963.
Popper, Karl. *The Open Society and Its Enemies.* 2 vols. Princeton, 1950.
Robinson, Edward S. *Law and Lawyers.* New York, 1937.
Schneider, W. *Adam Smith's Moral and Political Philosophy.* New York, 1948.
Sorel, Georges. *The Illusions of Progress.* Berkeley and Los Angeles, 1969.
Sorokin, Piterim Aleksandrovich. *Facts and Foibles in Modern Sociology and Related Sciences.* Chicago, 1956.

Stark, Werner. *The Fundamental Forms of Social Thought.* New York, 1963.
————. *The Sociology of Knowledge. An Essay in Aid of a Deeper Understanding of the History of Ideas.* Glencoe, Ill., 1958.
Veblen, Thorstein. *The Higher Learning in America. A Memorandum on the Conduct of Universities by Businessmen.* New York, 1918.
————. "The Intellectual Pre-eminence of Jews in Modern Europe." *Political Science Quarterly* (March 1919), pp. 33–42.
White, Morton. *Social Thought in America: The Revolt against Formalism.* Boston, 1961.

The Methodology of Economics

Cairnes, J. E. *The Character and Logical Method of Political Economy.* London, 1888.
Chapernowne, David G. "Unemployment, Basic and Monetary: The Classical Analysis and the Keynesian." *Review of Economic Studies* (June 1936), pp. 201–16.
Friedman, Milton. *Essays in Positive Economics.* Chicago, 1953.
Galbraith, John Kenneth. *American Capitalism: The Concept of Countervailing Power.* Boston, 1952.
Gurley, John G. "The State of Political Economics." *American Economic Review* (May 1971), pp. 53–62.
Hahn, F. H. "Some Adjustment Problems." *Econometrica* (January 1970).
Hamilton, David. *Newtonian Classicism and Darwinian Institutionalism: A Study of Change in Economic Theory.* Albuquerque, N.M., 1953.
Houthakker, H. S. "Revealed Preference and the Utility Function." *Economica* (May 1950), pp. 159–74.
Hutchison, T. W. *"Positive" Economics and Policy Objectives.* Cambridge, Mass., 1964.
Johnson, Harry G. "The Keynesian Revolution and the Monetarist Counter-revolution." *American Economic Review* (May 1971), pp. 1–14.
Keynes, John Maynard. "The General Theory of Employment." *Quarterly Journal of Economics* (February 1937).
Keynes, John Neville. *The Scope and Method of Political Economy.* London, 1917.
Leontief, W. "Implicit Theorizing: A Methodological Criticism of the Neo-Cambridge School." *Quarterly Journal of Economics* (February 1937), pp. 337–51.
————. "Theoretical Assumptions and Nonobserved Facts." *American Economic Review* (March 1971).
Liebenstein, H. "Notes on Welfare Economics and the Theory of Democracy." *Economic Journal* (June 1962), pp. 299–317.
Little, I. M. D. *A Critique of Welfare Theory.* London, 1957.
Machlup, Fritz. "Theories of the Firm: Marginalist, Behavioral, Managerial." *American Economic Review* (March 1967).
Menger, Carl. *Problems in Economics and Sociology.* Translated by Francis J. Nock. Urbana, Ill., 1963.
Mill, John Stuart. *Essays on Some Unsettled Questions of Political Economy.* London: London School of Economics reprint, 1948.
von Mises, Ludwig. *Epistemological Problems in Economics.* Princeton, 1960.
————. *Ultimate Foundations of Economic Science.* New York, 1962.
Myrdal, Gunnar. *The Political Element in the Development of Economic Theory.* Translated by Paul Streeten. London, 1953.

————. *Value in Social Theory*. Edited by Paul Streeten. London, 1958.

Pigou, Arthur C. "The Classical Stationary State." *Economic Journal* (December 1943).

Robbins, Lionel. *An Essay on the Nature and Significance of Economic Science*. London, 1935.

Robinson, Joan. *Marx, Marshall, and Keynes*. Delhi, 1955.

Valavanis, S. "A Denial of Patinkin's Contradiction." *Kyklos* 8 (1935):351–66.

Viner, Jacob. "Mr. Keynes on the Causes of Unemployment." *Quarterly Journal of Economics* (November 1936).

Other Works

Ackley, Gardiner. *Macroeconomic Theory*. New York, 1961.

Babbage, Charles. *On the Economy of Machinery and Manufacture*. New York: A. M. Kelley, 1963.

Baumol, William. *Business Behavior, Value and Growth*. New York, 1959.

Blaug, M. *Economic Theory in Retrospect*. Homewood, Ill., 1962.

Bober, M. M. *Karl Marx's Interpretation of History*. 2d rev. ed. Cambridge, Mass., 1948.

Boulding, Kenneth E. *The Meaning of the Twentieth Century: The Great Transition*. New York, 1964.

Bronfenbrenner, Martin, and Mayer, Thomas. "Liquidity Functions in the American Economy." *Econometrica* (October 1960), pp. 810–34.

Clairmonte, Frederic. *Economic Liberalism and Underdevelopment: Studies in the Disintegration of an Idea*. New York, 1960.

Cole, A. H. "Puzzles of the Wealth of Nations." *Canadian Journal of Economics and Political Science* 24 (February 1958):1–8.

Croce, Benedetto. *Historical Materialism and the Economics of Karl Marx*. Translated by C. M. Meredith. New York, 1914.

Ellis, Howard S., ed. *A Survey of Contemporary Economics*. Vol. 1. Homewood, Ill., 1948.

Federn, Karl. *The Materialistic Conception of History*. London, 1959.

Flint, Robert. *Vico*. New York, 1884.

Friedman, Milton, and Schwartz, Anna Jacobson. *Monetary History of the United States: 1867–1960*. Princeton, 1963.

Fromm, Erich. *Marx's Concept of Man*. New York, 1961.

Furniss, Edgar S. *The Position of the Laborer in a System of Nationalism*. Boston and New York, 1920.

Galbraith, John Kenneth. *The Great Crash: 1929*. Boston, 1961.

Goethe. *Faust*. Translated by Albert G. Latham. London, 1908.

Gruchy, Allan G. *Modern Economic Thought: The American Contribution*. New York, 1947.

Haddon, A. C. *History of Anthropology*. Boston, 1910.

Haley, Bernard F., ed. *A Survey of Contemporary Economics*. Vol. 2. Homewood, Ill., 1952.

Harris, S. E., ed. *The New Economics, Keynes' Influence on Theory and Public Policy*. New York, 1948.

Harrod, R. F. *The Life of John Maynard Keynes*. London and New York, 1963.

Heaton, Herbert. "Heckscher on Mercantilism." *Journal of Political Economy* 45 (June 1937).

Hegel, G. W. F. *Hegel's Political Writing*. Translated by T. M. Knox. Oxford, 1964.

————. *On Christianity: Early Theological Writings.* New York, 1961.

————. *The Philosophy of History.* New York, 1956.

Hook, Sidney. *From Hegel to Marx: Studies in the Intellectual Development of Karl Marx.* New York, 1936.

————. *Towards the Understanding of Karl Marx. A Revolutionary Interpretation.* New York, 1933.

Hughes, H. Stuart. *Oswald Spengler.* New York, 1952.

Keynes, John Maynard. *The Economic Consequences of the Peace.* New York, 1920.

————. *The End of Laissez-Faire.* London, 1926.

————. *Essays in Biography.* Edited by Geoffrey Keynes. New York, 1951.

————. *The General Theory of Employment, Interest and Money.* New York, 1936.

————. "Recent Economic Events in India." *Economic Journal* (March 1909), pp. 51–67.

————. *A Treatise on Probability.* London, 1948.

Leijonhufvud, Alex. *On Keynesian Economics and the Economics of Keynes: A Study in Monetary Theory.* New York, 1968.

Letwin, William. *The Origins of Scientific Economics.* London, 1963.

Macaulay, Frederick R. *Some Theoretical Problems Suggested by the Movements of Interest Rates, Bond Yields, and Stock Prices in the United States since 1856.* New York, 1938.

Machiavelli, N. *The Prince.* Translated by Luigi Ricci. Oxford, 1960.

McKenna, Joseph P. *Aggregate Economic Analysis.* New York, 1969.

Mantoux, Paul. *The Industrial Revolution in the Eighteenth Century.* New York, 1928.

Marx, Karl. *Capital: A Critique of Political Economy.* Translated by S. Moore and F. Aveling. New York, 1967.

————. *A Contribution to the Critique of Political Economy.* Chicago, 1904.

Mazlish, Bruce. *The Riddle of History: The Great Speculators from Vico to Freud.* New York and London, 1966.

Mill, John Stuart. *Principles of Political Economy.* Edited by W. J. Ashley. New York: A. M. Kelley, 1965.

Modigliani, Franco. "Liquidity Preference and the Theory of Interest and Money." *Econometrica* (January 1944), pp. 45–88.

Montagu, M. F. Ashley, ed. *Toynbee and History: Critical Essays and Reviews.* Boston, 1956.

Morris, Lloyd. *Postscript to Yesterday.* New York, 1947.

Pigou, Arthur. *Economics of Welfare.* 3d ed. London, 1929.

de Quincey, Thomas. *The Confessions of an English Opium Eater.* New York: Illustrated Editions, 1923.

Ricardo, David. *Principles of Political Economy and Taxation.* New York: Everyman Edition, 1926.

Robbins, Lionel. *The Economic Basis of Class Conflict and Other Essays in Political Economy.* London, 1939.

————. "On the Elasticity of Demand for Income in Terms of Effort" (1930). Reprinted in the American Economic Association, *Readings in the Theory of Income Distribution*, pp. 237–44. Homewood, Ill., 1951.

————. *The Evolution of Modern Economic Theory and Other Papers on the History of Economic Thought.* London, 1970.

Robinson, Joan. *Essays on Marxian Economics.* London, 1942.

Roll, Eric. *A History of Economic Thought.* New York, 1942.

Russell, Bertrand. *The Autobiography of Bertrand Russell.* London, 1967.

Schumpeter, Joseph A. *Capitalism, Socialism, and Democracy.* New York, 1942.

———. *History of Economic Analysis.* New York, 1954.

———. *Imperialism and Social Classes.* Translated by Heinz Norden and edited by Paul Sweezy. New York, 1951.

Senior, Nassau William. *An Outline of the Science of Political Economy.* New York: A. M. Kelley, 1951.

Smith, Adam. *The Theory of Moral Sentiments.* In *Adam Smith's Moral and Political Philosophy,* edited by W. Schneider. New York, 1948.

———. *An Enquiry into the Causes of the Wealth of Nations.* New York: Cannan Edition, 1937.

Spengler, Oswald. *The Decline of the West.* Translated by Charles Francis Atkinson, New York, 1946.

Stark, Werner. *The Contained Economy: An Interpretation of Medieval Economic Thought.* London, 1956.

———. *The History of Economics in Its Relation to Social Development.* London, 1944.

Stigler, George J. *Essays in the History of Economics.* Chicago and London, 1965.

———. *Production and Distribution Theories: 1870–1895.* New York, 1941.

Sweezy, P. M. *The Theory of Capitalist Development.* New York, 1942.

Tawney, R. H. *Land and Labour in China.* New York, 1932.

Toynbee, Arnold J. *A Study of History.* London, 1939.

Tucker, Robert C. *Philosophy and Myth in Karl Marx.* Cambridge, Mass., 1961.

Turvey, Ralph. Review of *Public Finance in Theory and Practice,* by A. R. Prest. *Economic Journal* (March 1961), pp. 149–50.

Van Tassel, Roger C. *Economic Essentials: A Core Approach.* New York, 1969.

Veblen, Thorstein. *Essays in Our Changing Order.* New York, 1934.

Viner, Joseph. *The Long View and the Short: Studies in Economic Theory and Policy.* Glencoe, Ill., 1958.

———. *Studies in the Theory of International Trade.* New York, 1937.

Weisskopf, Walker A. *The Psychology of Economics.* Chicago, 1955.

Wolfe, Bertram D. *Three Who Made a Revolution.* New York, 1948.

Woolf, Leonard S. *Empire and Commerce in Africa: A Study in Economic Imperialism.* London, 1919.

Index of Subjects

Absolutist methodologists: nature of their work, 3–9; on hypostatization, 143–44

Activism: in Marx, 175–78; in Cartesianism, 284–87

Aggregate demand: and supply, 275–76

Alienation: of economists, 140–42, 148, 218; Hegel on, 165–66; Marx on, 188–90; Tucker on, 190–92; Kierkegaard on, 215

Analogical fictions. See Fictions

"As if": in social contract theories, 30–34; in Kant, 52; in Friedman, 138–39; in pragmatism, 220; Keynes and, 265–66

Bifurcation, of nature and mind: in Descartes, 16–24; in Locke, 26–27. See also Dualism

Capitalism: Marx on, 194–95; Keynes on, 233–34

Cartesian doubt, 23; Kierkegaard on, 214

Cartesianism: dualism of, 16–24, 34, 61–62; and money, 43; J. S. Mill on, 58–59; and Marxism, 62; and value, 135; and Pascal, 146–47; and social manipulation, 284–87. See also Truth

Certainty: in Descartes, 16–19, 21; in Locke, 25–28. See also Truth

Cogito: tautological nature of, 21–22; Kierkegaard on, 22, 213–14; Nietzsche on, 217; James on, 221–22

Communism: Marx on, 195–96

Consciousness: Marx on, 173–74; Schopenhauer on, 211–13; James on, 221–22. See also Cogito; Ego

Definitions: in economics, 107–8

Demonstration: in Locke, 27

Dialectic: in Hegel, 157–66

Diminishing returns, 95–96

Dualism: in Descartes, 16–18; in Locke, 26–27; in Kant, 51–54; in J. S. Mill, 101–3; in positive/normative controversy, 128–35; not in Marx, 202–4; passim. See also Smith; Ricardo; Keynesian economics

Economics: teaching of, 211

Economic theory: its esthetic and ethical value, 149–50

Ego: in Descartes, 16–23; James on, 221–22; in economic theory, 68–70, 127–36, passim; in Malthus, 96–99. See also Cogito; Consciousness; Dualism; Tautology

Egoism: in Smith, 78–79

Index of Names

Archimedes, 150
Arendt, Hannah: on Descartes, 21; on imperialism, 232
Aristotle: Bentham on, 48
Arnold, Thurman W.: on legal fictions, 49

Babbage, Charles, 95
Bacon, Francis: on hypostatization, 70
Beard, C. A.: on historiography, 226
Beethoven, 151
Bentham, Jeremy: solipsism in, 45–46; springs of action, 45–50; on fictions, 46–49; and Keynes, 249–50, 261–66; and Keynesian economics, 271–75; passim
Bergson, Henri: and rationalism, 60–61; on logic, 89; and Huxley, 117–18; on intuition, 218–19, 267; mentioned, 11, 218n
Berkeley, George: on truth, 28; on money, 39
Bober, M. M.: on Marx, 200–202
Bronfenbrenner, M., 275
Burrt, Edwin Arthur: on Descartes, 18

Cairnes, J. E.: on reason, 105
Clemenceau, Georges: Keynes on, 236

Comte, Auguste: on methodology, 1
Condillac, 33

Darwin, Charles: and Malthus, 98; and classical economics, 148
Descartes, René: his philosophic influence, 14–15; on truth, 15–23; Arendt on, 21; vs. Cartesianism, 23–25; Diderot on, 29; and Newton, 85–86; his dream, 132; and Hegel, 154–55; Kierkegaard on, 213; Nietzsche on, 217; James on, 221–22; his influence on modern economics, 284–87
Dewey, John: on logic, 226; mentioned, 12
Diderot, Denis: on Descartes' method, 29
Dostoevsky, F.: on logic, 209

Edgeworth, F. Y.: on economic theory, 113–14
Einstein, Albert: on geometry, 21–22; on the ether, 25

Fisher, Irving, 66
Flux, A. W., 113
Foxwell, H. S.: letter to J. N. Keynes, 230–31
Friedman, Milton: on positivism, 8,